The greatest thing a human soul ever does in this world
is to see something and tell what it saw in a plain way.
Hundreds of people can talk for one who can think,
but thousands can think for one who can see.
To see clearly is poetry, prophecy and religion,
all in one.

John Ruskin, *Modern Painters,* 1888

First published in the UK in 2025 by Clearview Books
99 Priory Park Road, London NW6 7UX

www.clearviewbooks.com

For permission to reproduce material by the following authors from copyright works, the author and publisher gratefully acknowledges the following:

W. H. Auden, CURTIS BROWN AND PENGUIN RANDOM HOUSE; Barbara Pym, TOM HOLT; Alfred Noyes, SOCIETY OF AUTHORS; C S Lewis, CS LEWIS COMPANY LTD; John Betjeman, HODDER AND STOUGHTON; Philip Larkin, FABER AND FABER; Joanna Kavenna, QUERCUS; Nancy Campbell, ELLIOTT & THOMPSON; Philip Pullman, SCHOLASTIC; Elizabeth Jennings, DAVID HIGHAM ASSOCIATES; Harold Nicolson, HAROLD NICOLSON ESTATE; James Lees-Milne, DAVID HIGHAM ASSOCIATES; E. M. Forster quotation from *Howard's End* by permission of PETERS FRASER & DUNLOP on behalf of The Provost and Scholars of the King's College of our Lady and Saint Nicholas, Cambridge; Vera Brittain, VERA BRITTAIN LITERARY ESTATE; Iris Murdoch CHATTO AND WINDUS and PENGUIN RANDOM HOUSE; Javier Marais, PENGUIN RANDOM HOUSE; Evelyn Waugh, PENGUIN RANDOM HOUSE; Dorothy L Sayers, HODDER AND STOUGHTON; Robert Liddell, PUSHKIN PRESS; J C Masterman, CURTIS BROWN; Penelope Fitzgerald, THE HISTORY PRESS and FLINT BOOKS; A. N. Wilson, THE SPECTATOR; Harold Macmillan, TIMES NEWSPAPERS

Every effort has been made to trace copyright holders and obtain their permission for the use of copyright material. The publisher apologises for any errors or omissions, and would be grateful if notified of any corrections that should be incorporated in future reprints or editions of this book.

ISBN: 978-1908337-757

Design: Kath Fotheringham
Editor: Ronald J Caffrey
Production: Rosanna Dickinson
Reproduction: Eric Bailey-Ladd, Pixywalls
Photography: PAINTINGS: Brian Peart and Matt Pia
ARTIST IN SITU: Darrin Roles *pg 4*; Fred Ezekiel *pg 70*; Rory Carnegie *jacket*

A CIP record of this book is available from the British Library.

PRINTED IN EUROPE

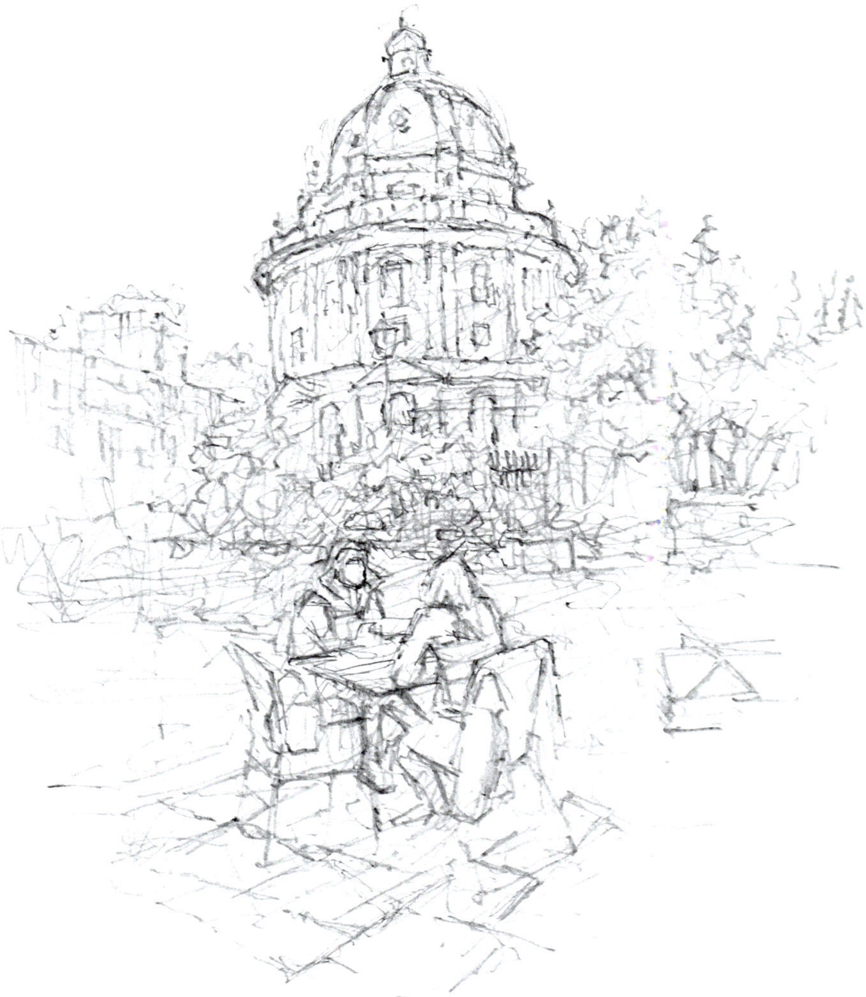

Oxford is, without a doubt, one of the cities in the World where least work gets done.

Javier Marais, All Souls, 1992

Javier Marais (1951–2022) was a prolific Spanish writer, once described as "the best English novelist writing in the Spanish language." He taught translation (an abiding interest and practice) at Oxford and, as Xavier I, was the King of Redonda (an uninhabited Caribbean island) his Nobles included Philip Pullman, John Banville, Umberto Eco and Milan Kundera.

FRANCIS HAMEL

THE OXFORD PAINTINGS

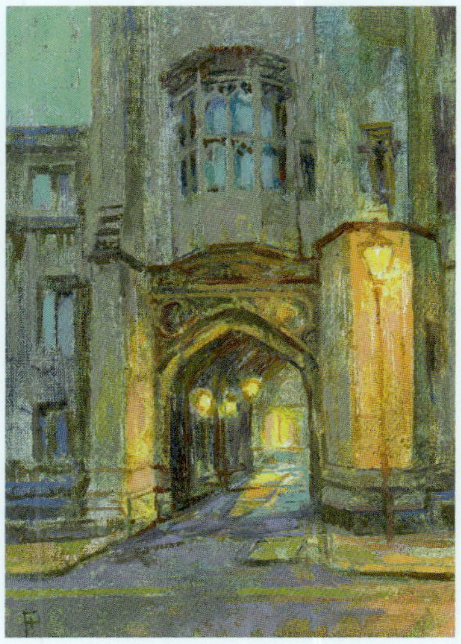

Edited and compiled by Ronald J Caffrey

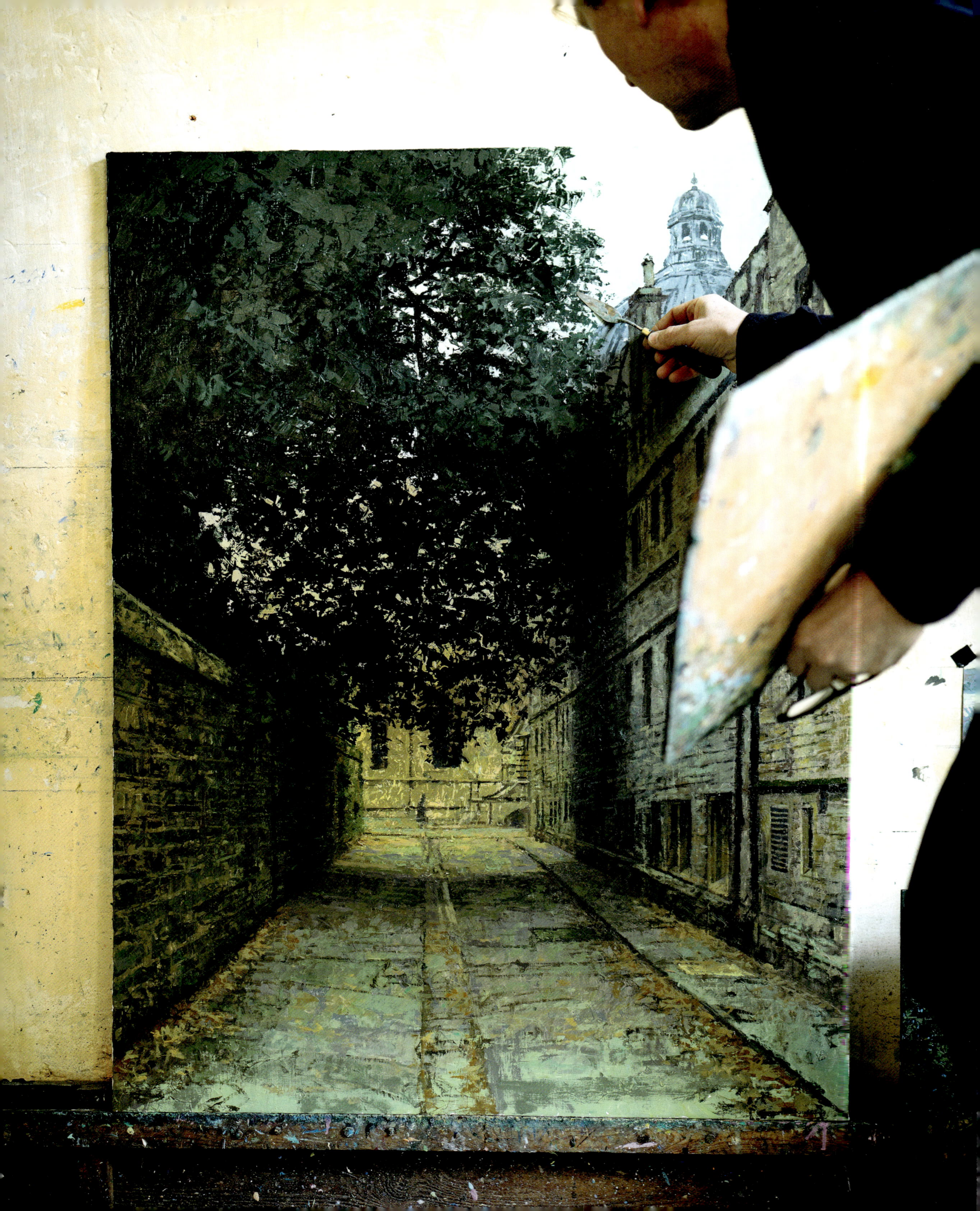

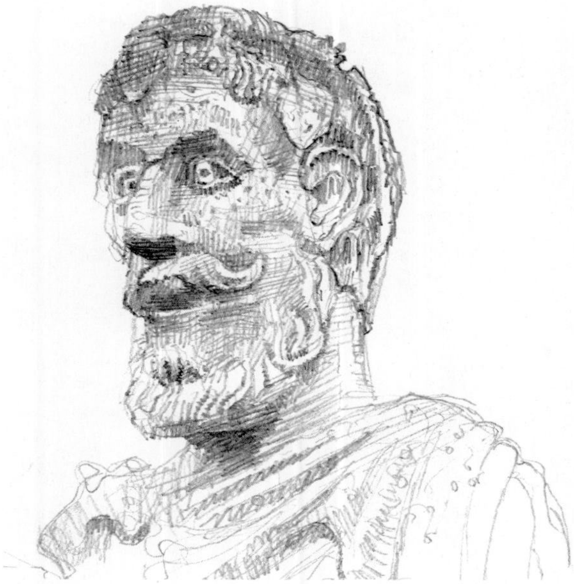

Dr Bloxam was fond of relating how, when shortly after 1848 he took Henri Montalembert into Magdalen College Hall, the Comte exclaimed, looking at the portraits of Wolsey and Pole: "What, you have cardinals in your Hall. I thought this was a Protestant college!" "Yes, we keep our cardinals, and are very proud of them," said Dr Bloxam. "Ah!" replied Montalembert, "in England you do not destroy the past!" This has been the secret (may it remain so) of English progress. It has certainly been the secret of college history, in which nothing is so noteworthy as the intermixture of old and young, of the historic and the modern."

Thomas Herbert Warren, Magdalen College, 1907

Thomas Herbert Warren (1853–1930) President of Magdalen for 43 years, is now best known as a crashing snob, largely due to James Lees-Milne's description in *Another Self*. C.S. Lewis was much more charitable and, having secured the Prince of Wales as a Magdalen undergraduate, perhaps Warren would feel he had no need to explain himself.

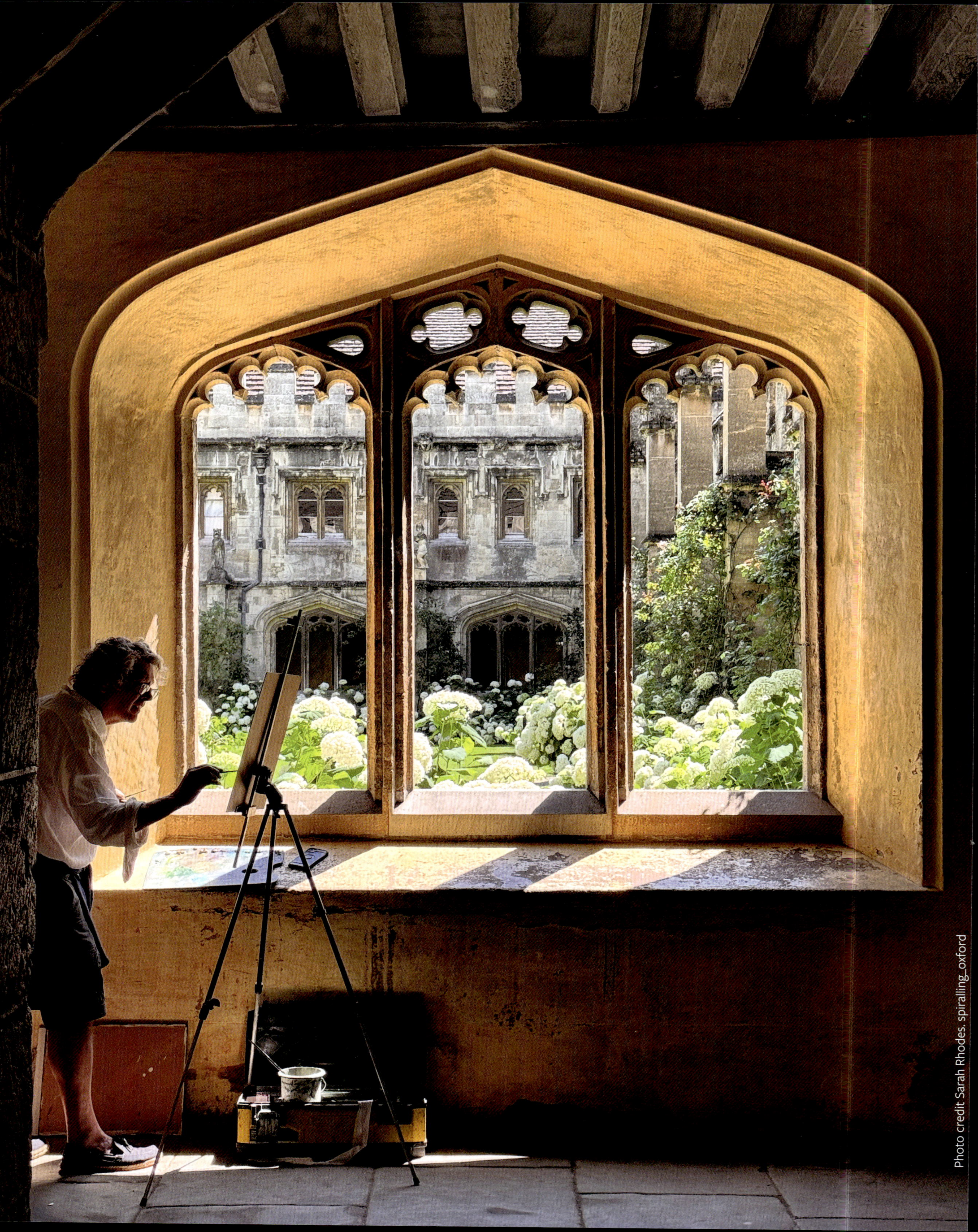

Photo credit Sarah Rhodes. spiralling_oxford

Introduction

My parents met in the President's lodgings at Magdalen in 1946, escaping from their homes in Blitz-torn Birmingham, that was where their love affair with each other as well as their love affair with Oxford began. Nearly fifty years later my father, by now a clergyman approaching retirement, married me and my wife in the college chapel. I had been a schoolboy in Oxford as well as an undergraduate at Magdalen. The chapel with its sculpted reredos and prodigious choir combines and magnifies powerful streams of intimacy, theatre and devotion.

Last year I found myself asking Dinah Rose, the current president of the college, if I could have my old studio back to use as a base for making my third collection of paintings of Oxford.

This book combines three collections of paintings from 2002, 2012, and 2024 intermingled with an ephemeral collection of writing about the city and the university. I have painted what speaks to me as I have walked or cycled around the city, many of the pictures are from different positions in the same streets in the centre of town. The pictures are mostly about weather and light, in Oxford there tends to be plenty of the former and not so much of the latter.

I usually start work at dawn, my bicycle has a trailer full of paints and canvasses, so I cycle into town from Magdalen or from my brother's houseboat on Port Meadow and start work with the bakers and the bin men before the city begins to fill with its vast itinerant population of tourists, students or members of the more permanent population.

Most of the paintings are from the street side, I have always tried to include the paraphernalia of modernity, patches in the tarmac, traffic lights and double yellow lines as well as the finials, columns and facades. Oxford is, and always has been a building site. It's often hard to find a view without scaffolding and white vans.

My friend Ron Caffrey has sought out an intriguing collection of written material to accompany my images. After a brief and unsuccessful episode in the mid 1980s running a tearoom together in Oxford High Street we have now found a more fruitful form of collaboration. More fruit less jam.

Francis Hamel
Magdalen College, 2024

The subtle but compelling beauty and charm of Magdalen College have been so widely recognised, sung, painted, described so often, that it would be a false reticence to ignore them.

The general situation and disposition of the buildings, fortunate and striking, the graceful tower seeming to guard the long, stately bridge and eastern approach to the city, in old days the first object to salute the traveller arriving from London; the long, low line of walls, roofs, and gables stretching up the street and losing themselves behind aged trees; within, the cloisters with their happy proportion, their sequestered, reposeful air, as of a "garden enclosed," peaceful yet not severe, monastic and domestic at once, the quaint figures on their pedestals standing sentinel round them; the Chapel with its "storied windows" and "dim religious light," its

"High embowéd roof,
And antique pillars massy proof,"

where day after day the listener still hears, as Milton may have done coming in from Horton or Forest Hill,

"The pealing organ blow
To the full-voiced choir below";

the Founder's Tower with its niched figures and its sumptuous yet delicate and restrained ornament; the Hall with its carven screen, its moulded and inlaid wainscot, and historic portraits; the "New Buildings," that "stately pile" to which, recently erected, the priggish genius of Gibbon brought his "stock of erudition that might have puzzled a doctor, and of ignorance of which a schoolboy would have been ashamed"; the "learned Grove" where the dappled deer flicker in and out amid the towering elms that make its vistas of sombre umbrage and sunny sward; the little river a natural and delightful moat to the College, to which here it seems wholly to belong; the bosky "Water-walks" where the memory of Addison yet haunts the favourite spot in which he strolled and discoursed poetry with Harry Sacheverell: all form a harmonious whole, yet a very little consideration shows it to be composed of very different and disparate parts.

Thomas Herbert Warren, Magdalen College, 1907

"The most absolute building in Oxford"

Charles I describing the tower
of Magdalen College, 1620

Magdalen Tower from the Bridge
30 x 25 cm, oil on linen, 2024

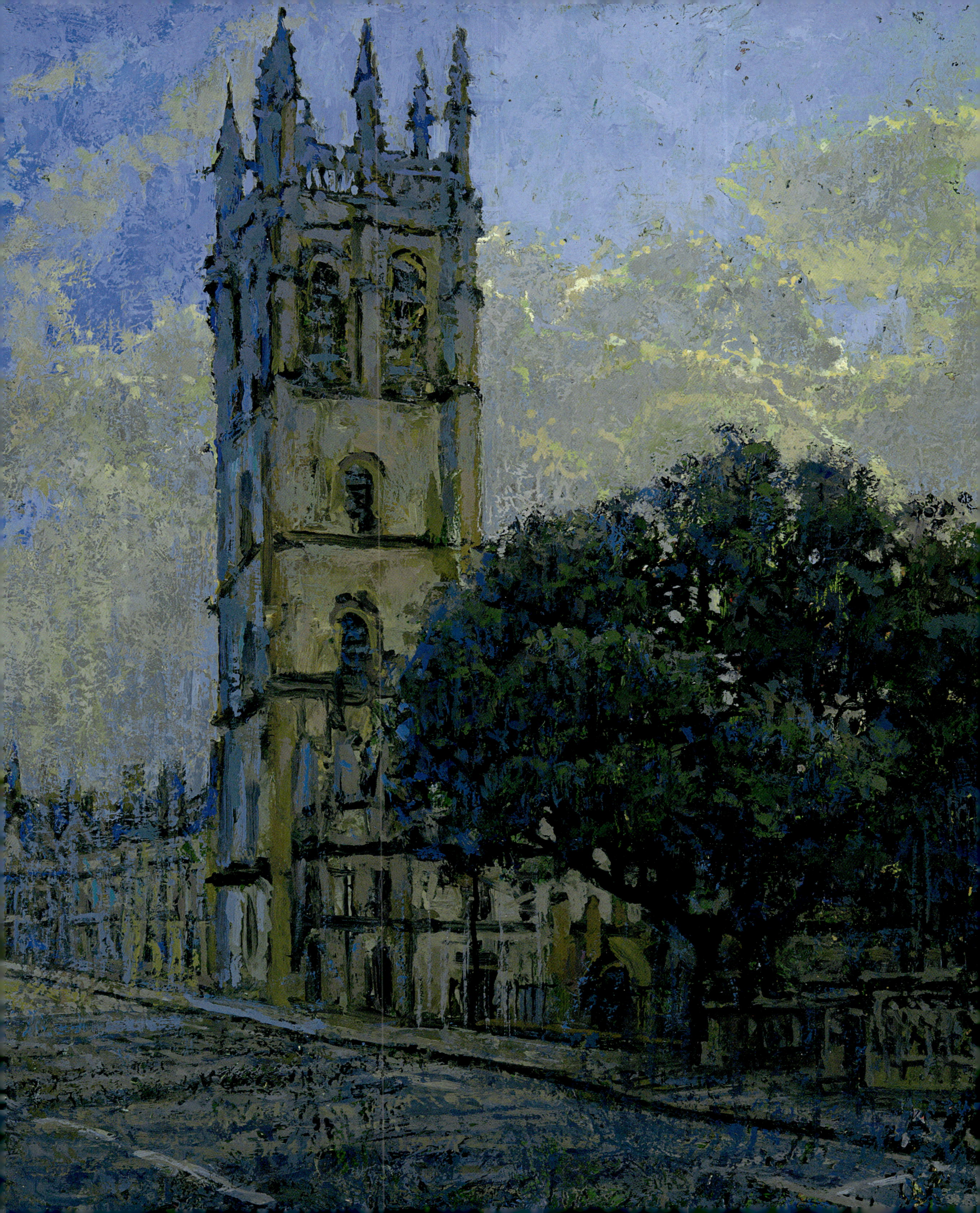

It was a wet Sunday in North Oxford at the beginning of October. The laurel bushes which bordered the path leading to Leamington Lodge, Banbury Road, were dripping with rain. A few sodden chrysanthemums, dahlias and zinnias drooped in the flowerbeds on the lawn. The house had been built in the sixties of the last century, of yellowish brick, with a gabled roof and narrow Gothic windows set in frames of ornamental stonework. A long red and blue stained-glass window looked onto a landing halfway up the pitch-pine staircase, and there were panels of the same glass let into the front door, giving an ecclesiastical effect, so that, except for a glimpse of unlikely lace curtains, the house might have been a theological college.

Barbara Pym, *Crampton Hodnet*, 1940

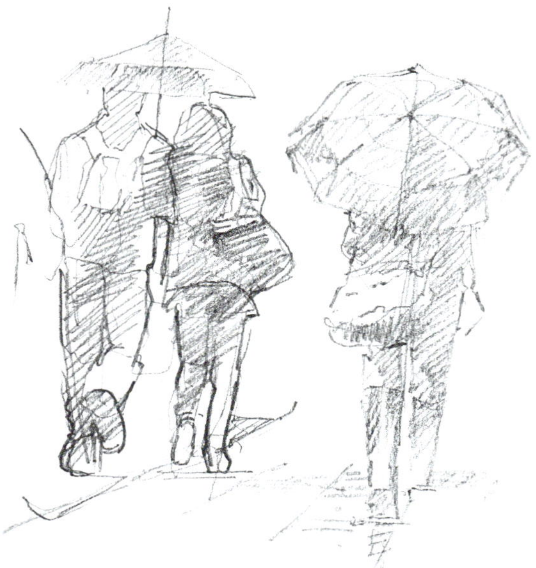

Barbara Pym (1913–1980) an alumna of St Hilda's, was a novelist whose career came in two parts. First, an initial burst of published novels between 1950 and the early 1960s which, despite positive reviews, were marked by declining sales until her publisher declined to publish any more. Secondly, a rediscovery after Philip Larkin and Lord David Cecil both recommended Pym as the most underrated writer of the last 75 years in a survey by the *Times Literary Supplement*.

St Giles' in the Rain
49 x 37 cm, oil on panel, 2003

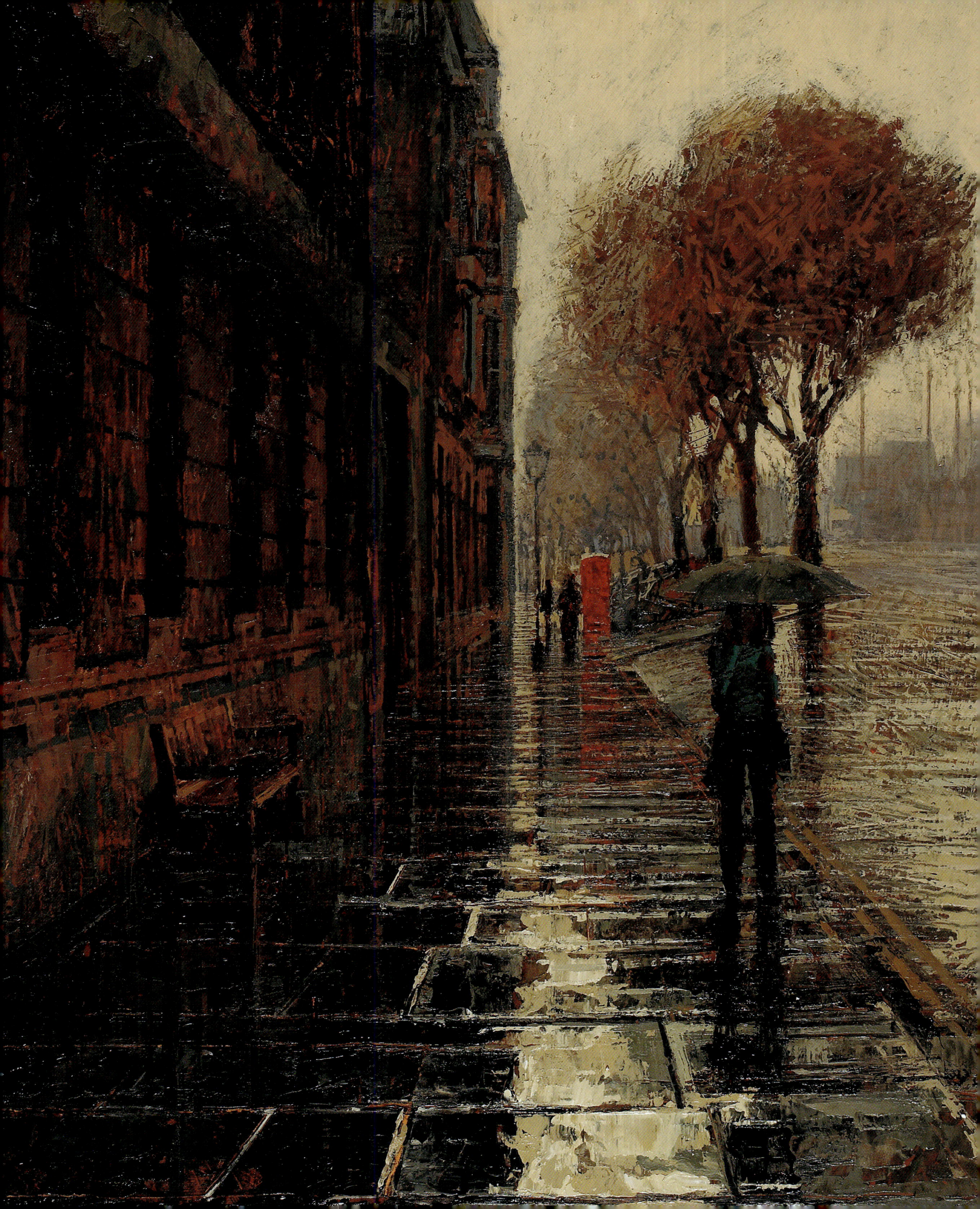

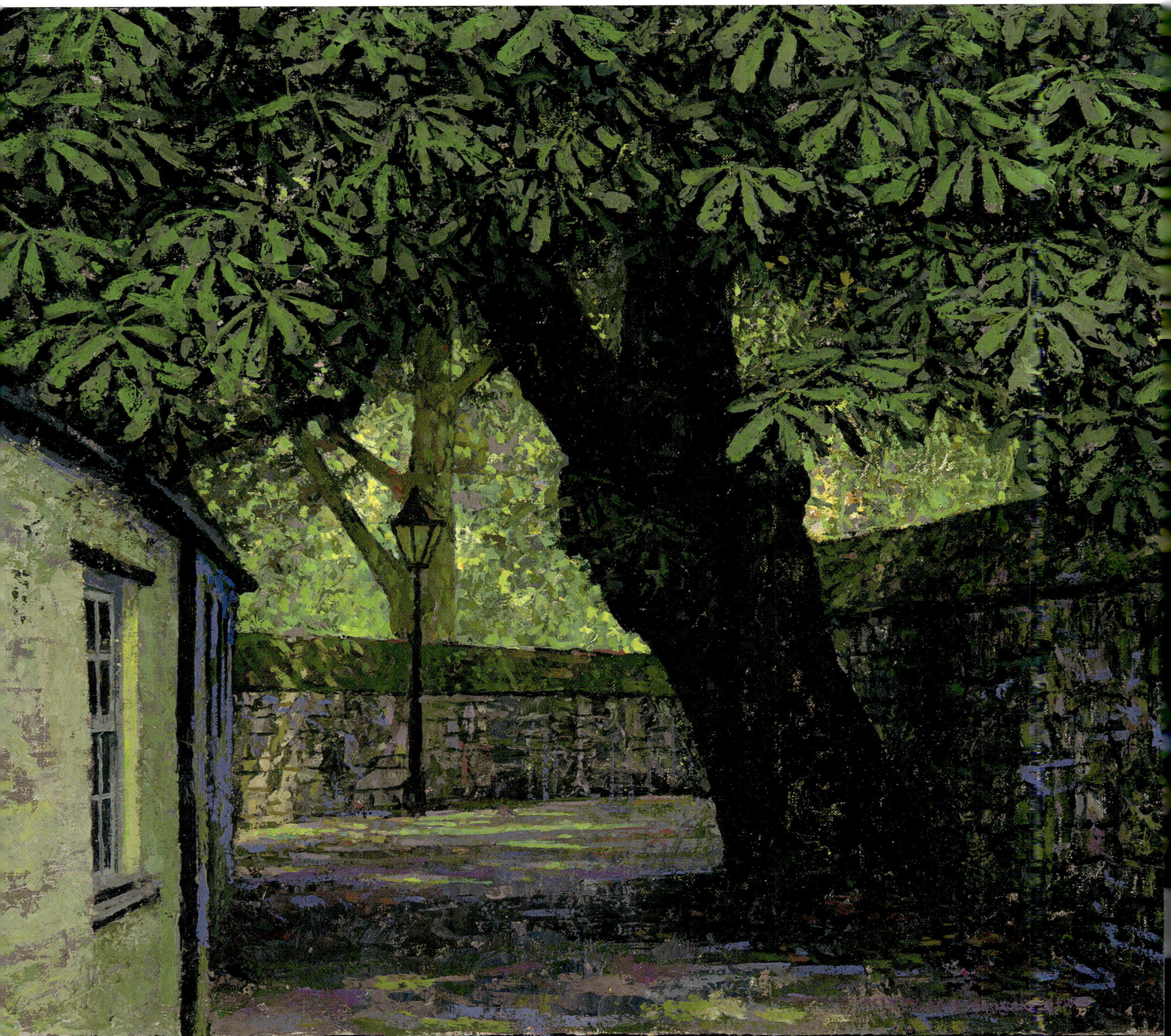

At home, as in no other city, here summer
holds her breath in a dark street
the trees nocturnally scented, lovers like moths
go by silently on the footpaths
and spirits of the young wait
cannot be expelled, multiply each year.

In the meadows, walks, over the walls
the sunlight, far-travelled, tired and content,
warms the recollections of old men, touching
the hand of the scholar on his book, marching
through quadrangles and arches, at last spent
it leans through the stained windows and falls.

This then is the city of young men, of beginning,
ideas, trials, pardonable follies,
the lightness, seriousness and sorrow of youth.
And the city of the old, looking for truth,
browsing for years, the mind's seven bellies
filled, become legendary figures, seeming

stones of the city, her venerable towers;
dignified, clothed by erudition and time.
For them it is not a city but an existence;
outside which everything is a pretence:
within, the leisurely immortals dream,
venerated and spared by the ominous hours.

Keith Douglas, *Oxford, Collected Poems*, 1951

Keith Castellain Douglas (1920–1944) is perhaps the best-known of the British War Poets of the Second World War – not a high bar compared to the fame of the War Poets of the First World War. This was written in 1941. He studied at Merton College, where he was tutored by Edmund Blunden another War Poet. He fought in the Western Desert and Normandy and was dead within three days of D-Day at the age of 24.

The Chestnut Tree in Lamb and Flag Passage
30.5 x 35.5 cm, oil on linen, 2024

Brasenose and the University Church
45 x 35 cm, oil on linen, 2024

Yesterday, at two Clock in the Afternoon, a young man, who had been a good while a seaman, flew the rope from the Battlements of St Marie's Steeple in Oxford, down to High Street, the Rope being tied or fastened at Bottom on the south side of the way at a House above St Mary Lane. He performed to the great admiration and satisfaction of all the Spectators. He first with great agility climed up to the top of the Battlement to wch the Rope was fastened, then flew down, his Arms extended, in about half a minute of an hour, then he climed up the Rope again, wch was more strange, quite to the top of the Battlement, hung by his legs upon the Rope, when he was about half way up, pulled off his clothes (nay his very shirt) as he hung upon it, put them on again, undone his breeches & tucked his shirt in, &c. done them up again as he hung, then (when he got to the top of the Pinnacle) he flew down again, and in his descent had a pint of ale (the pint being tied to a Packthread in his hand) drawn up to him, wch he drank upon the Rope. And 'tis withall remarkable that he flew down the second time with two Pistolls in his hands, both wch he let off as he came or flew down...

Thomas Hearne, Journal, 26 October 1728

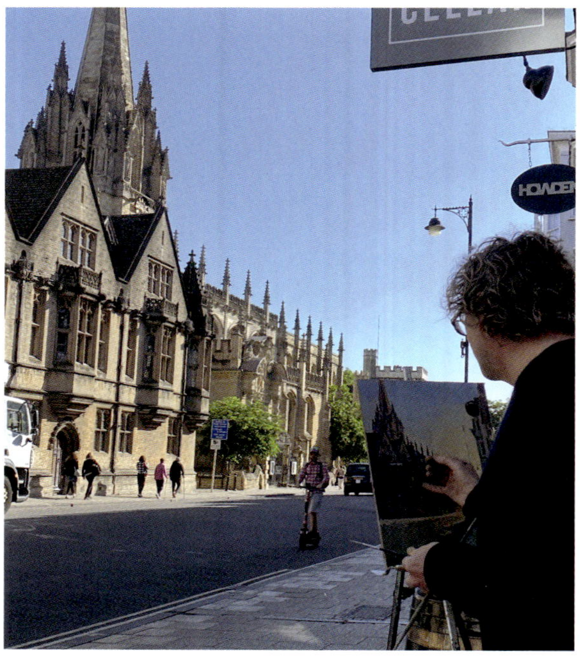

Thomas Hearne (1678–1735), alumnus of St Edmund Hall, was employed as Assistant Keeper at the Bodleian until his refusal to take an oath in 1716, in support of the new Hanoverian Dynasty led to his being "locked out of the library" for good. His scholarly work is now forgotten but his voluminous diaries give a rich portrait of the university and the city.

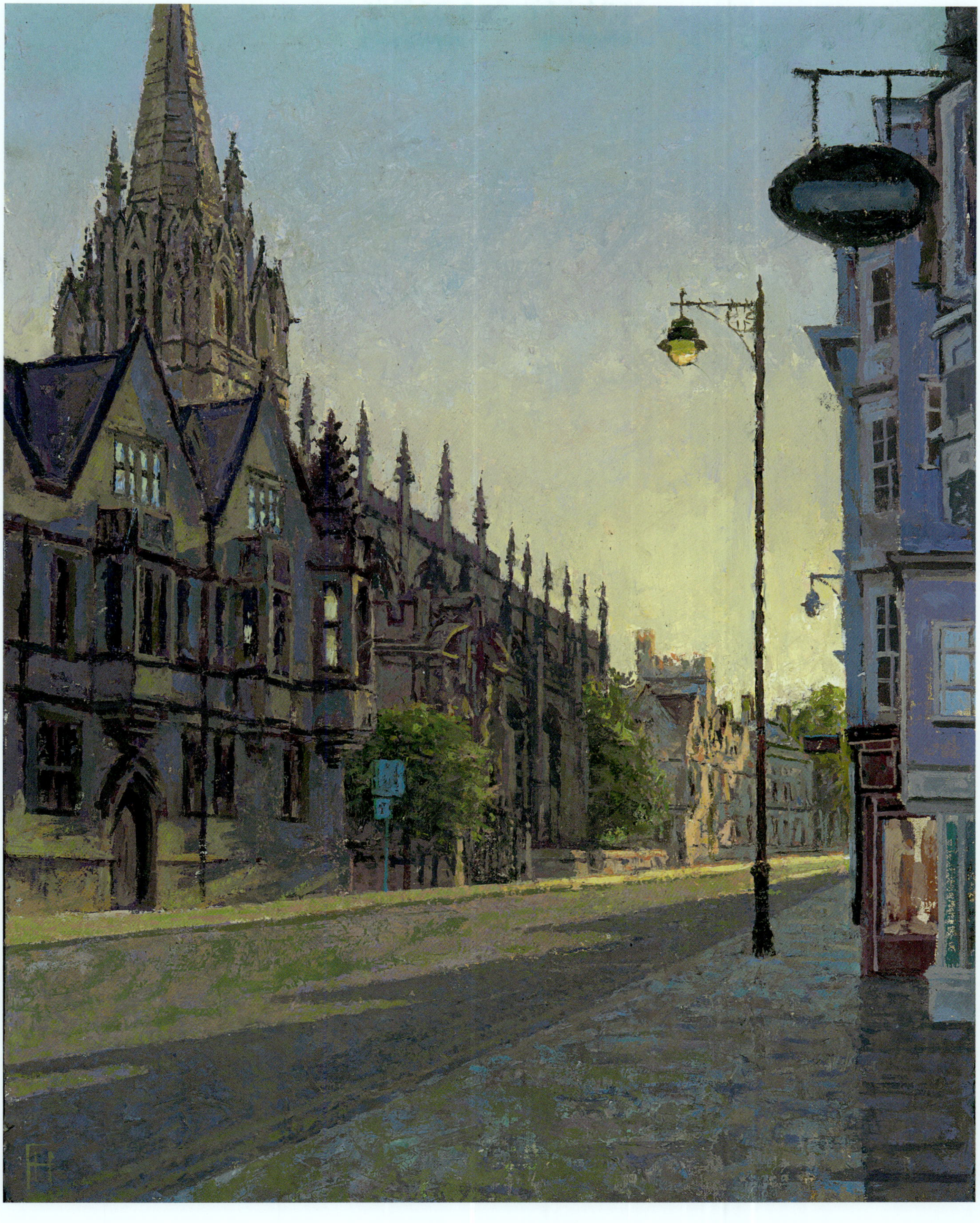

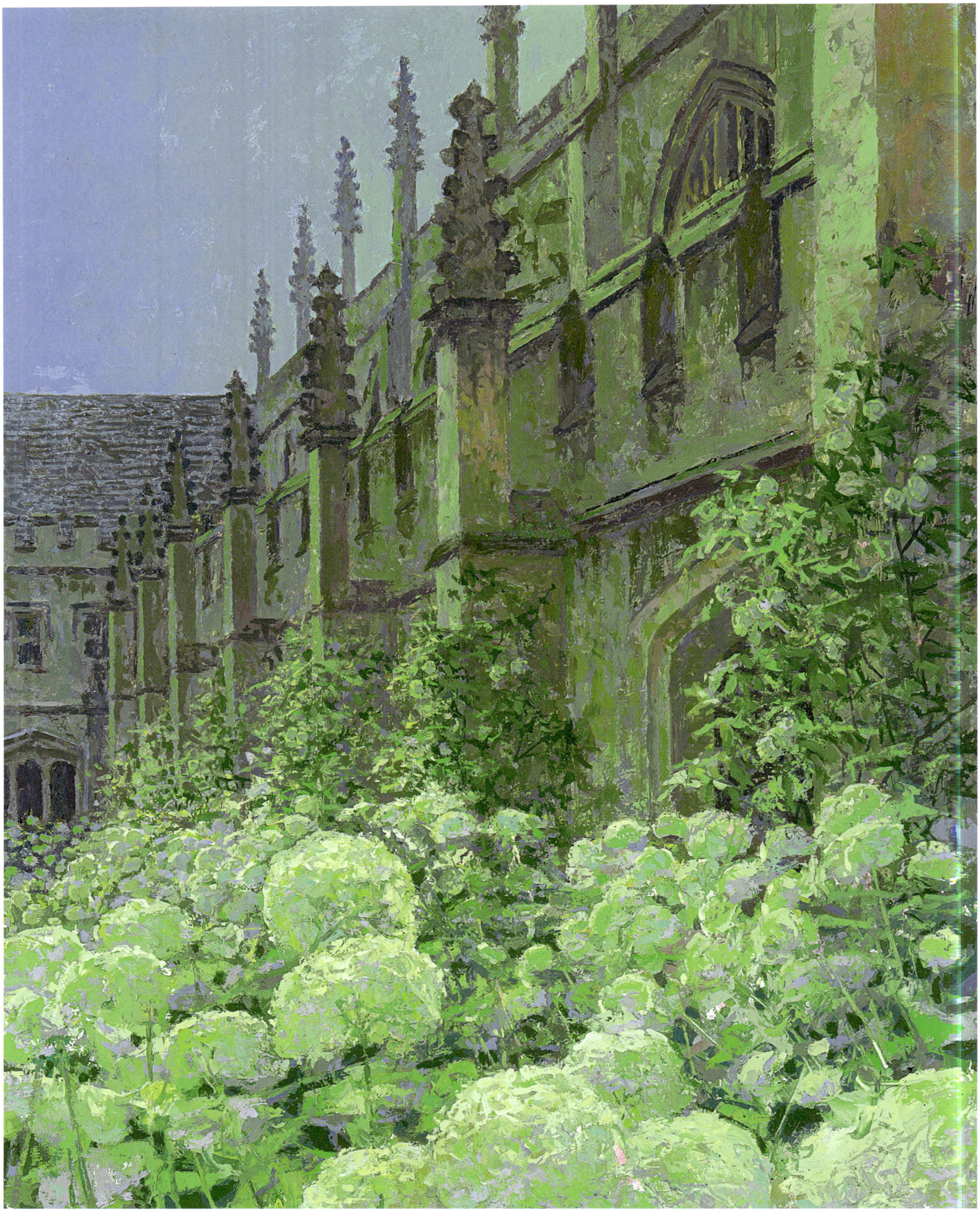

My own introduction to the university of Oxford forms a new era in my life; and at the distance of forty years I still remember my first emotions of surprise and satisfaction. In my fifteenth year I felt myself suddenly raised from a boy to a man: the persons, whom I respected as my superiors in age and academical rank, entertained me with every mark of attention and civility; and my vanity was flattered by the velvet cap and silk gown, which distinguish a gentleman commoner from a plebeian student. A decent allowance, more money than a school-boy had ever seen, was at my own disposal; and I might command, among the tradesmen of Oxford, an indefinite and dangerous latitude of credit. A key was delivered into my hands, which gave me the free use of a numerous and learned library; my apartment consisted of three elegant and well-furnished rooms in the new building, a stately pile, of Magdalen College; and the adjacent walks, had they been frequented by Plato's disciples, might have been compared to the Attic shade on the banks of the Ilissus. Such was the fair prospect of my entrance (April 3, 1752) into the university of Oxford.

I spent fourteen months at Magdalen College; they proved the fourteen months the most idle and unprofitable of my whole life...

The fellows of my time were decent easy men, who supinely enjoyed the gifts of the founder; their days were filled by a series of uniform employments; the chapel and the hall, the coffee house and the common room, till they retired, weary and well satisfied, to a long slumber. From the toll of reading, or thinking, or writing, they had absolved their conscience; and the first shoots of learning and ingenuity withered on the ground, without yielding any fruits to the owners of the public... the tutor and pupil lived in the same college as strangers to each other.

Edward Gibbon, *Memoirs of My Life*, 1792

Edward Gibbon (1737–1794) was famously critical of his education at Magdalen College, and has claims to be one of the greatest historians produced by the University let alone the College. *The History of the Decline and Fall of the Roman Empire* remains an astounding work of both scholarship and literary style even though many now doubt if the Roman Empire either declined or fell in the way Gibbon described.

Magdalen Cloisters with Hydrangeas
45 x 35 cm, oil on linen, 2024

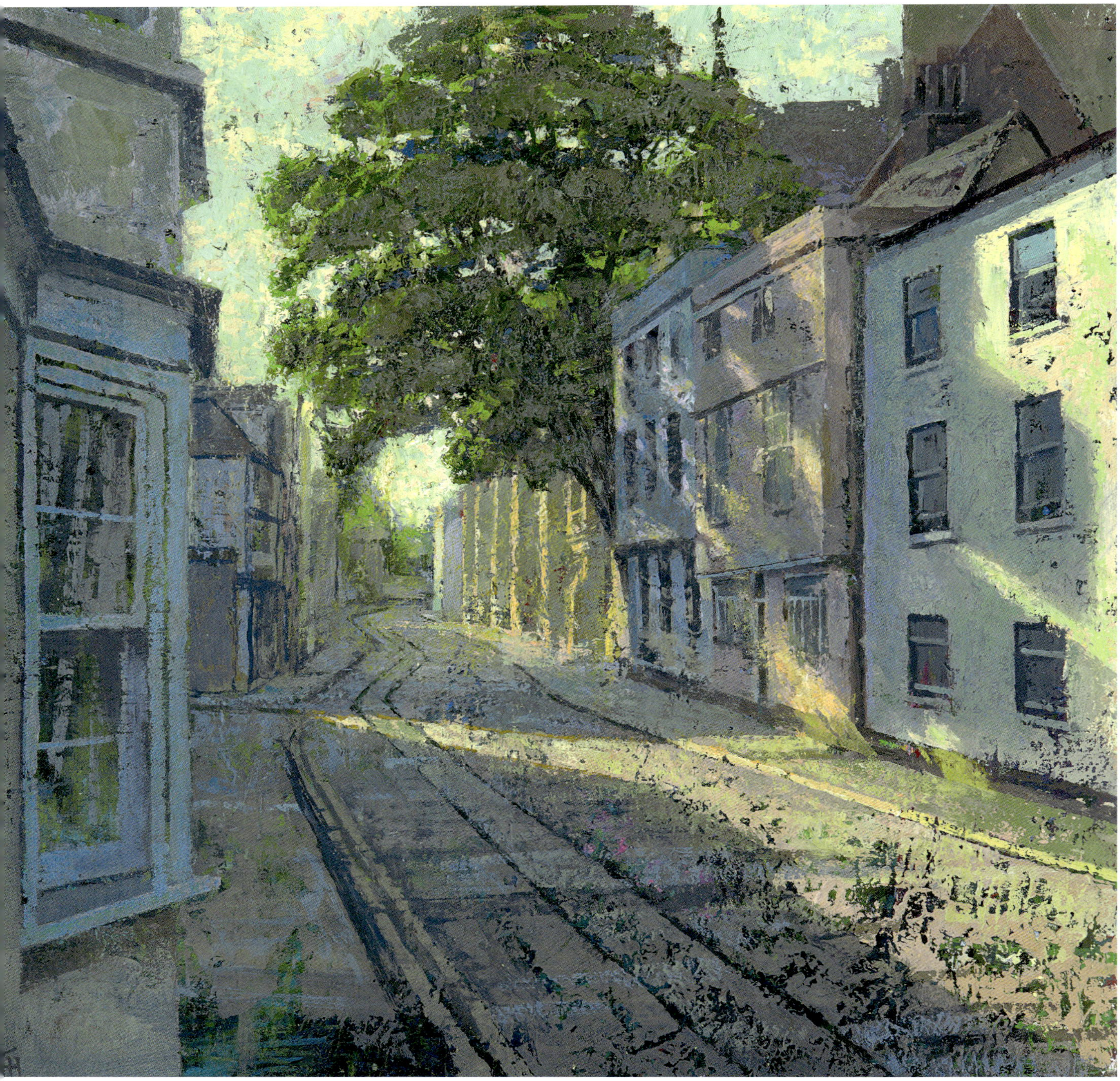

Holywell Street in the Early Morning
41 x 41 cm, oil on linen, 2024

Wednesday, 20 May 1874

Went to Oxford to stay with the kind hospitable Charles Symondses in Holywell, Mrs. Robert Dallin's father and mother. Murray Symonds met me at the station with a waggonette. He and his pretty charming wife are staying at his father's. An early dinner and we went to evensong at New College Chapel at 5 o'clock. The afternoon sun streamed glorious through the great west window of the Ante Chapel. The bells stopped chiming and suddenly the chapel seemed filled with a flood of bright-robed angels.

At 7 o'clock we went down the new walk from Christ Church to the Barges to see the boat races from the Queen's Barge. There was the old scene bright and busy which has been going on ever since I left Oxford. The river alive and moving with all sorts of boats, skiffs and canoes. The great crowd moving down the towing path and the meadows on the Oxfordshire side, the barges crowded with University men and ladies, the first gun at Iffley, the puff of white smoke far down the river succeeded after some seconds by the dull report, the 2nd and 3rd guns and soon afterwards the distant roar, growing nearer and louder, of the crowd running with the boats and pouring over the long Bridges, then the sharp nose of the first boat and the white jerseys of the straining crew gliding swiftly round the corner of the bank, the intense excitement, the shouting, the uproar as boat after boat dashed past.

Thursday, 21 May 1874

Rose early, missed the New College Matins at 7.30 by being a minute too late. Walked round the gardens in the green light of the great lime cloister and wandered round to Wadham gardens. All was as usual, the copper beech still spread a purple gloom in the corner, the three glorious limes swept their luxuriant foliage flat upon the sward, the great poplars towered like a steeple, the laburnum showered its golden rain by the quiet cloisters and the Wisteria still hung its blue flower clusters upon the garden wall. The fabric of the college was unchanged, the grey chapel walls still rose fair and peaceful from the green turf. But all else was altered, a change had come over the spirit of the dream. The familiar friendly faces had all vanished, some were dead and some were out in the world and all had gone away. Strange faces and cold eyes came out of the doorways and passed and repassed the porter's lodge. One or two of the College servants remembered my face still, almost all had forgotten my name. 'The place thereof shall know it no more.' I felt like a spirit revisiting the scenes of its earthly existence and finding itself strange, unfamiliar, unwanted.

At ten o'clock Murray Symonds and I went down to the Choral Service at Magdalen Chapel. Afterwards I went to the house of my old scout George Hawks in Holywell and borrowed a cap and gown to go to the Museum in. George Hawks was my Father's scout at Oriel 40 years ago, and he was my scout at Wadham and he is scout at Wadham still. Generation after generation. One generation passeth away and another cometh in its stead.

In the afternoon we went to see the improvements in the Cathedral. At 7 o'clock we went again to see the last night of the boat races. An exciting and splendid race between Brazennose and University left University head of the river. Then we walked up to St. John's gardens and sat under the quiet elms listening to the latest singing of the birds...

Francis Kilvert, Diary, 1960

Robert Francis Kilvert (1840–1879) was a Wadham alumnus, born into a clerical family and continued the tradition largely around Hereford and Hay. His journals were published in 1938 and have been popular ever since, depicting the life of a country curate interested in the cure of souls, the natural world and the rhythms of agricultural life. Other journals existed but were destroyed by Kilvert's niece during a clear-out before moving to residential care. William Plomer – who edited the published journals – "could have strangled her with his bare hands".

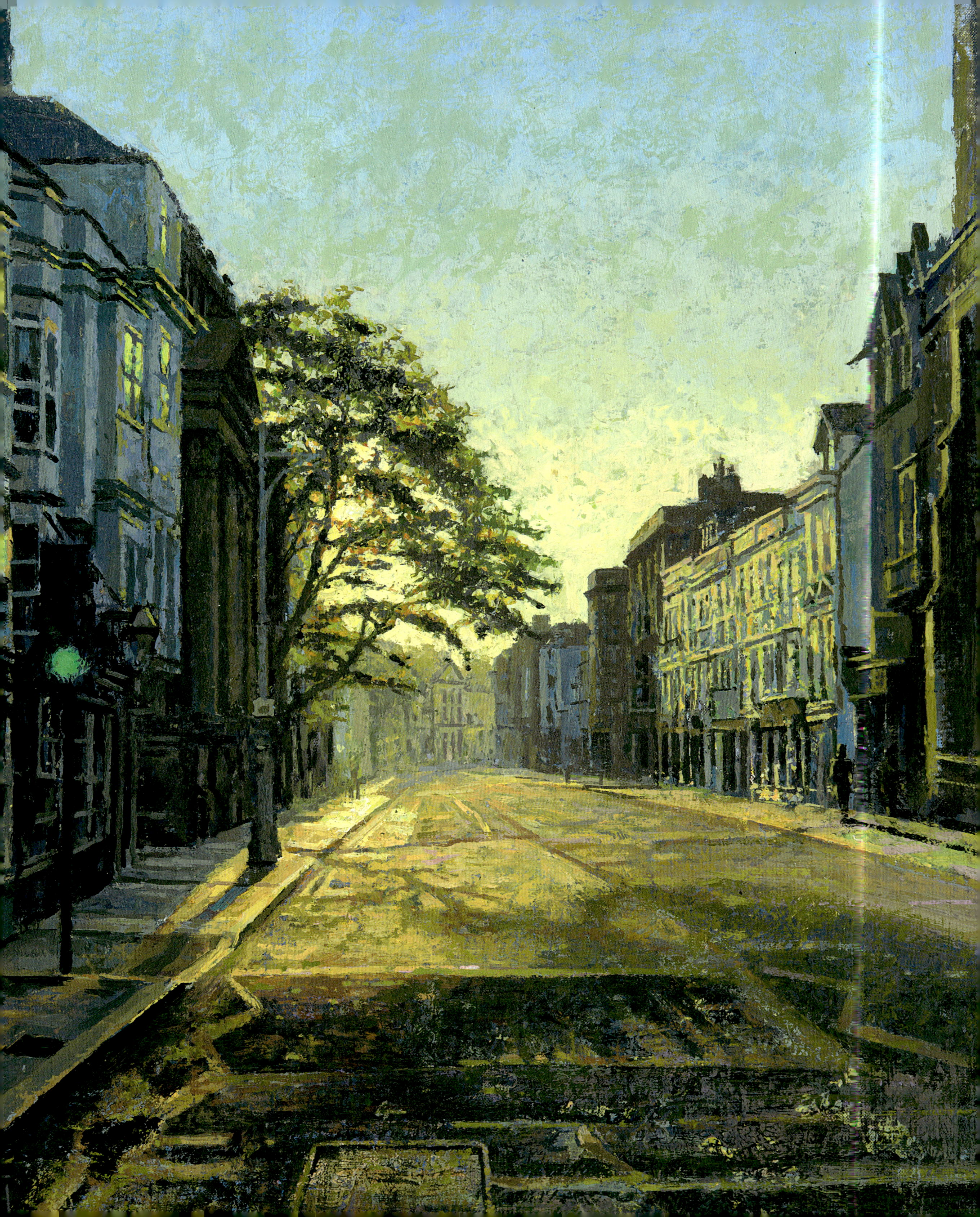

The walls of Oxford are tufted with ivy-leaved toadflax, wallflower, and the sunny plant which botanists call "inelegant ragwort." They form a trail from the villages, upon wall after wall, into Ship Street and Queen's Lane, by which the country may be traced. In the same way, the city may be said to steal out into the fields. Not only do we read the epitaph of a forgotten fellow in a quiet church, and mark a resemblance to Merton or Lincoln in the windows of an old house in North Hinksey Street, but the beauty of the windy Shotover plateau, with its slopes of hyacinth and furze, and the elmy hills of Cumnor and Radbrook, are haunted and peopled by visions of the distant spires. They give that mild, well-sculptured country a soul. Even when the city is out of sight, its neighbourhood is not to be put by. Everywhere it is a suspected presence, a hidden melodist. Whether in memory or anticipation, it is, on all our walks, like some grave thought threading a mighty dream.

Edward Thomas, *Oxford*, 1903

It is sweet to enter that peacefullest and homeliest of churchyards, St Peter's in the East, overlooked by St Edmund Hall and Queen's College and the old city wall. There is a peace which only the thrush and blackbird break, and even their singing is at length merely the most easily distinguishable part of the great melody of the place. Most of the graves are so old or so forgo'en that it is easy and in Spring it is difficult not to perceive a kind of dim reviving life among the stones, where, as in some old, quiet books, the names live again a purged and untroubled existence.

Edward Thomas, *Oxford*, 1903

The High at Dawn
45 x 35 cm, oil on linen, 2024

Philip Edward Thomas (1878–1917) was a literary critic, travel and nature writer and poet, he read Modern History at Lincoln College. Thomas married while at Oxford and found himself having to produce large numbers of book reviews – followed by travel books and anything else a publisher thought might sell – to support his growing family. His first poems were written only in 1914 at the behest of his friend Robert Frost (*The Road Not Taken* Frost). By 1917 he was dead at the Battle of Arras.

A Downe-right Scholler is one that has much learning in the Ore, unwrought and untryde, which time and experience fashions and reines. The time has got a veine of making him ridiculous, and men laugh at him by tradition; but his fault is onely this, that his mind is somewhat too much taken up with his minde, and his thoughts not loaden with any carriage besides. The hermitage of his study makes him somewhat uncouth in the world, and men make him worse by staring on him. But practise him a li'le in men, and brush him over with good company, and he shall outbalance those glisterers as much as a solid substance does a feather, or gold gold lace.

A Pretender to Learning is a kind of Scholler-Mountebank. You find him in his Slippers, and a Pen in his eare, in which formality he was asleep. His Table is spred wide with some Classick Folio, which is as constant to it as the carpet, and hath lain open in the same Page this halfe yeere. He walks much alone in the posture of Meditation, and has a Book still before his face in the fields. He is a great Nomenclator of Authors, which hee has read in generall in the Catalogue, and in particular in the Title, and goes seldome so farre as the Dedication. Hee never talkes of any thing but learning, and learnes all from talking.

A Young Gentleman of the University is one that comes there to weare a gown, and to say hereafter, he has beene at the University. His Father sent him thither, because he heard there were the best Fencing and Dancing schooles. His main loytering is at the Library, where he studies Armes and Bookes of Honour, and turnes a Gentleman Critick in Pedigrees. Of all things hee endures not to bee mistaken for a Scholler, and hates a black suit though it bee of Satin.

John Earle, *Microcosmography*, 1630

John Earle (1601–1665) was a Church of England clergyman and attended both Christ Church and Merton. Appointed Chaplain to the future Charles II in the run up to the English Civil War, he went abroad with Charles until the Restoration, becoming Bishop of Worcester and then Salisbury. *Microcosmography*, or a *Piece of the World Discovered*, in *Essayes and Characters* was a best-seller getting through ten editions in Earle's lifetime.

Carfax in the Rain
46 x 36 cm, oil on linen, 2024

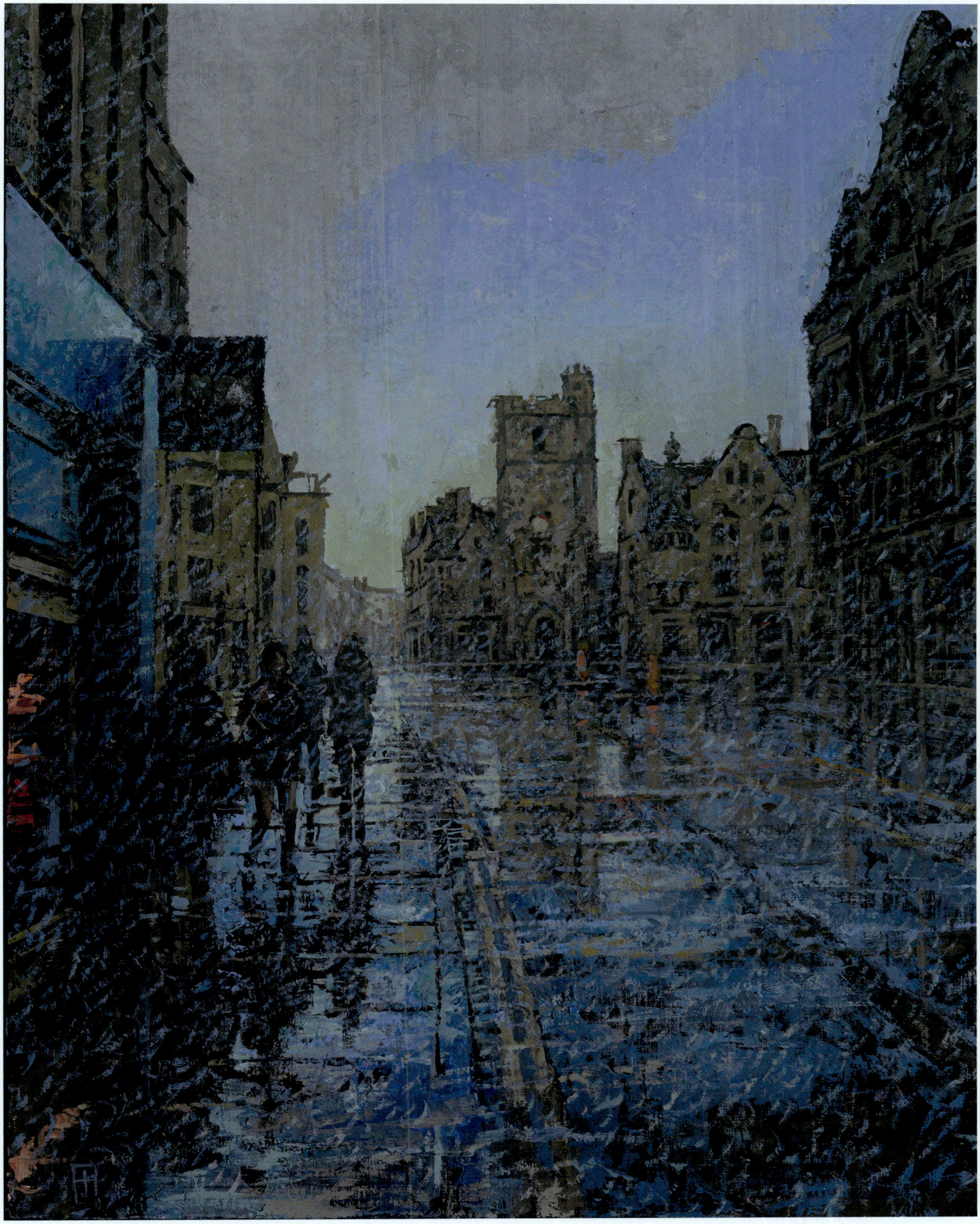

...for the common purposes of academic life, the Colleges are the University. Each College is, in fact, a microcosm of the University itself. Freedom and continuity are the hall-marks of the University; freedom and continuity are the hall-marks of the Colleges. A College is autonomous, governed by its own statutes, and responsible to no one but its corporators and its Visitor for its internal administration and policy. Each College has its own Head and Fellows, its own revenues, its own kitchen and Hall and Chapel, its own teaching and bursary staff. It is, in fact, a self-governing community, of which the Head and Fellows form the governing body. Most important of all, a College has an unfettered choice in the selection of its own members – a man may pass Responsions or its equivalent and then become eligible to enter the University, but he cannot actually matriculate until he has found a College to present him.

There were two old dons, who, by reference to the University Calendar, could be found to be eighty-five and eighty-two years old respectively. One night they fell into an altercation, and I remember the fascination of listening to remarks which, I had thought, occurred only in books and never in real life. 'I give you the lie, Sir.' 'And I, Sir, give you the lie', and so forth (I think that in those days men used the word 'Sir' more and more the angrier they became). At length they became really offended and eighty-two, rising from the table, bellowed out, 'In any other place than this, Sir, I should horsewhip you'. Eighty-five, however, had the last word. 'That,' he said, 'was a most improper observation'; then after a pause he added, 'especially from a junior man.'

J C Masterman, *To Teach the Senators Wisdom*, 1952

John Cecil Masterman (1891–1977) was born into a naval family and sent to Osborne and Dartmouth before opting for Modern History at Worcester College; he spent World War I in a German prison camp having been at Freiburg University when war broke out. Returning to Oxford he took up a fellowship at Christ Church; invented the Oxford Detective Story with *An Oxford Tragedy*; played hockey for his country and reached the quarter finals of the men's doubles two years running at Wimbledon. World War II saw him join MI5 chairing the XX Committee (think double cross), overseeing Operation Mincemeat (making the Germans believe the invasion of Sicily was headed for Greece and Sardinia) and turning 120 German Agents deceiving the Germans into believing the main thrust of the Allied invasion was headed for the *Pas de Calais* – not Normandy. Returning to Oxford he became Provost of Worcester and then Vice-Chancellor of the University.

Ship Street with Exeter College
45 x 35 cm, oil on linen, 2024

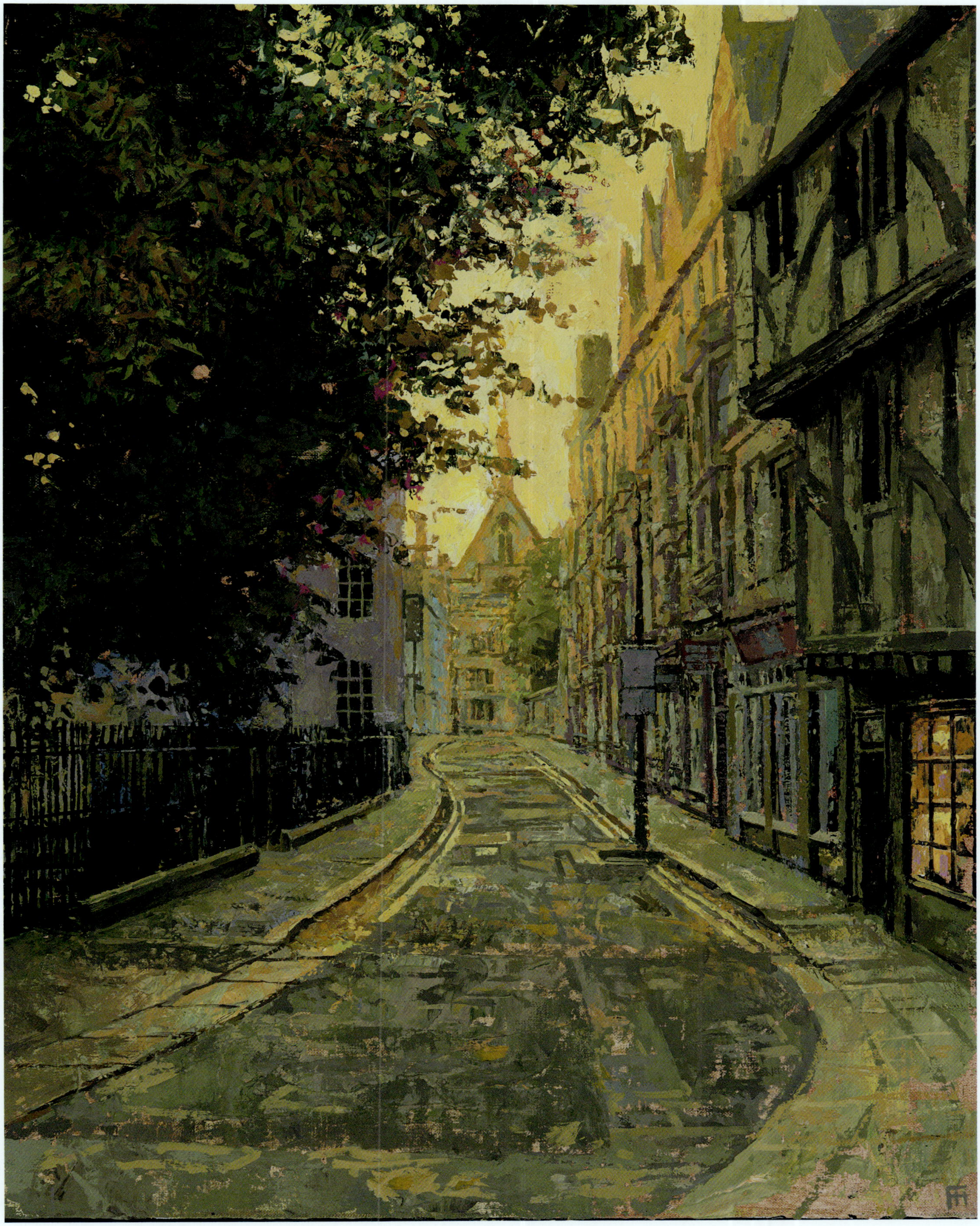

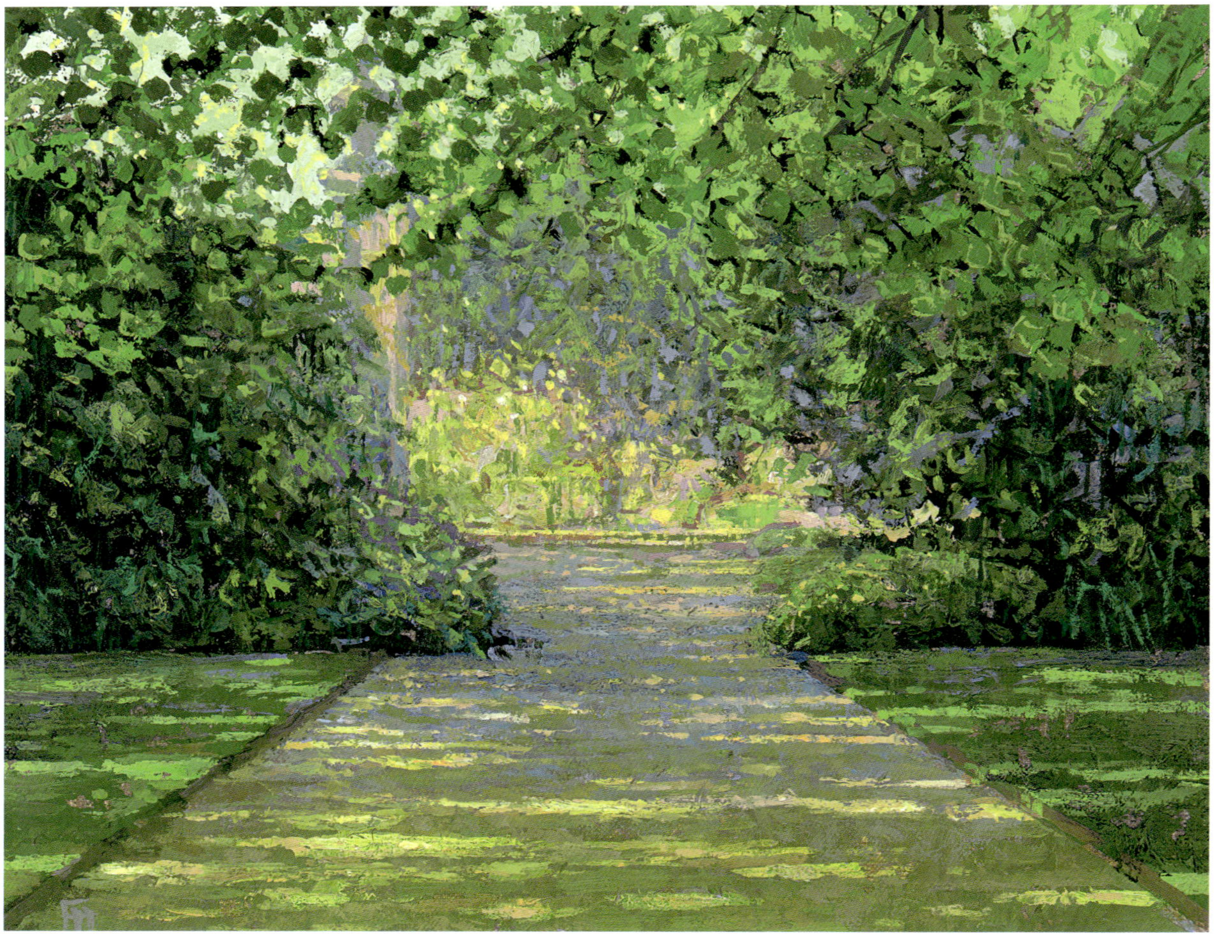

Botanical Gardens, Sunlit Path
20 x 25 cm, oil on linen, 2024

Lancelot Ridley Phelps (1853–1936) was elected to a fellowship in 1877 and was Provost from 1914 to 1929. Tall, bald, bearded, the Phelper is one of Oxford's legends. He's the one who reminded the nonconformist Master of Mansfield College that the port was with him. 'I'd rather commit adultery,' said the shocked teetotaller. 'So should we all dear man', was Phelps's reply as he reached for the decanter. It is good to find in this volume a repetition of that other old Oxford chestnut: Phelps's daily cold bath, before which his scout would hear him saying, 'Be a man, Phelps, be a man.'

When the Phelper died, his successor, Provost Ross, said, 'Phelps was the completest epitome of all that the College stands for.' My favourite anecdote about him was when he was a young fellow and Newman, who had not been to Oxford for years, returned, as a cardinal. The sight of the old Common Room which had played such a part in his life reduced the frail old churchman to sobs and the fellows who were standing round to greet him felt extremes of embarrassment. The Phelper saved the day by approaching the cardinal, shaking him heartily by the hand with the words, 'Well done, Newman, well done!'

A.N. Wilson review for *The Spectator* of *Oriel College: A History* by Jeremy Catto

Andrew Norman Wilson (born 1950) abandoned his study for the priesthood at St Stephen's House, switching to New College for English. A novelist, journalist and popular historian – he is pretty much a modern day man of letters – with a broad range of interests admirably displayed in his works.

Oxford, in those days, was still a city of aquatint. In her spacious and quiet streets men walked and spoke as they had done in Newman's day; her autumnal mists, her grey springtime, and the rare glory of her summer days – such as that day – when the chestnut was in flower and the bells rang out high and clear over her gables and cupolas, exhaled the soft airs of centuries of youth. It was this cloistral hush which gave our laughter its resonance, and carried it still, joyously, over the intervening clamour. Here, discordantly, in Eights Week, came a rabble of womankind, some hundreds strong, twittering and fluttering over the cobbles and up the steps, sight-seeing and pleasure-seeking, drinking claret cup, eating cucumber sandwiches; pushed in punts about the river, herded in droves to the college barges; greeted in the Isis and in the Union by a sudden display of peculiar, facetious, wholly distressing Gilbert-and-Sullivan badinage, and by peculiar choral effects in the College chapels. Echoes of the intruders penetrated every corner, and in my own College was no echo, but an original fount of the grossest disturbance. We were giving a ball. The front quad, where I lived, was floored and tented; palms and azaleas were banked round the porter's lodge; worst of all, the don who lived above me, a mouse of a man connected with the Natural Sciences, had lent his rooms for a Ladies' Cloakroom, and a printed notice proclaiming this outrage hung not six inches from my oak.

No one felt more strongly about it than my scout.

Evelyn Waugh, *Brideshead Revisited*, 1945

Arthur Evelyn St John Waugh (1903–1966) read Modern History at Hertford College. Novelist, conservative and Catholic. Notoriously rude to the great and the good but would go almost anywhere to give a talk to anyone who asked, as long it was for a Catholic parish or religious group. When drinking champagne with Queen Elizabeth, the Queen Mother her opening gambit was "Champagne, what a treat Mr Waugh?" His response? "Really, Ma'am?".

Magdalen Bridge with Punts
46 x 36 cm, oil on linen, 2024

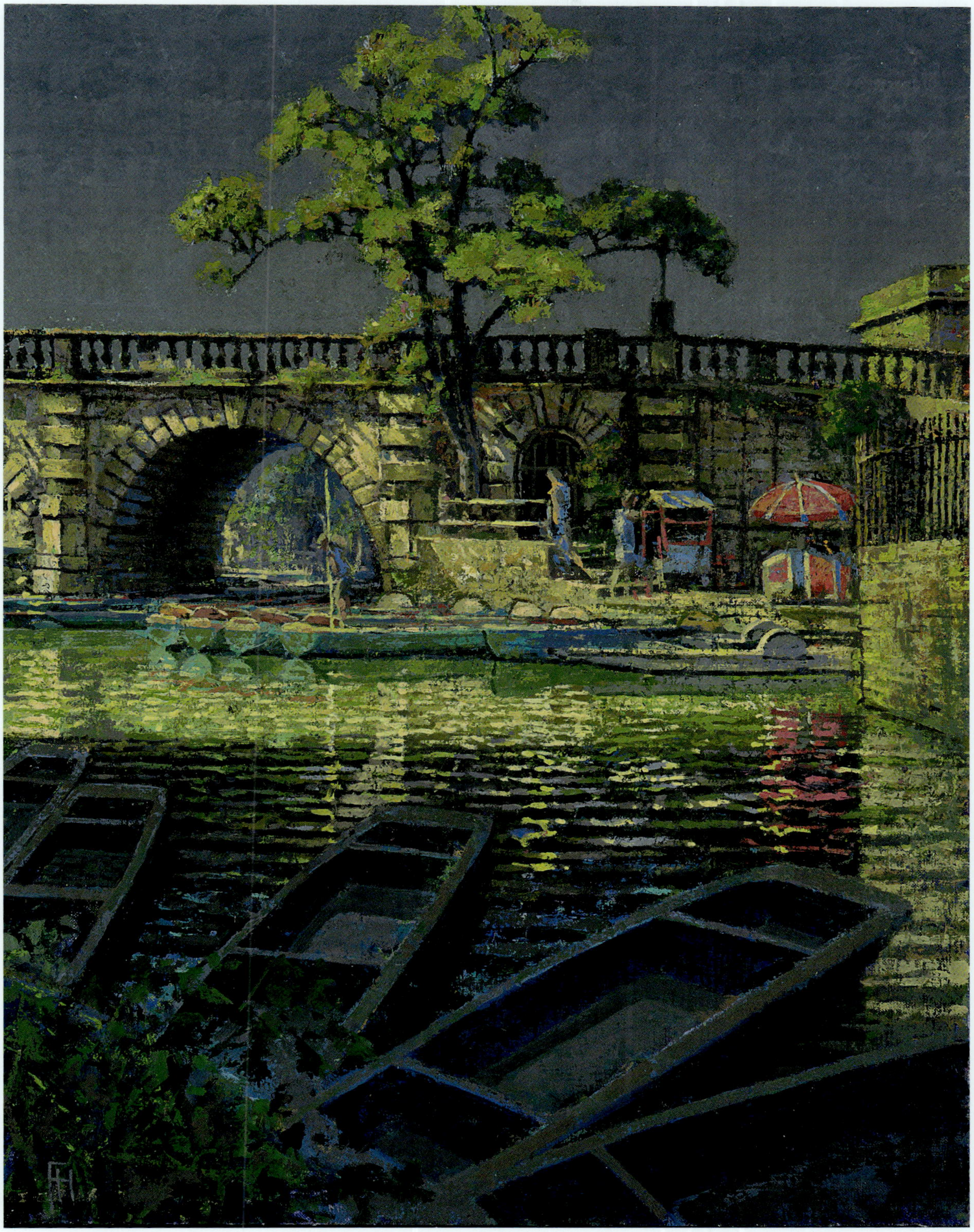

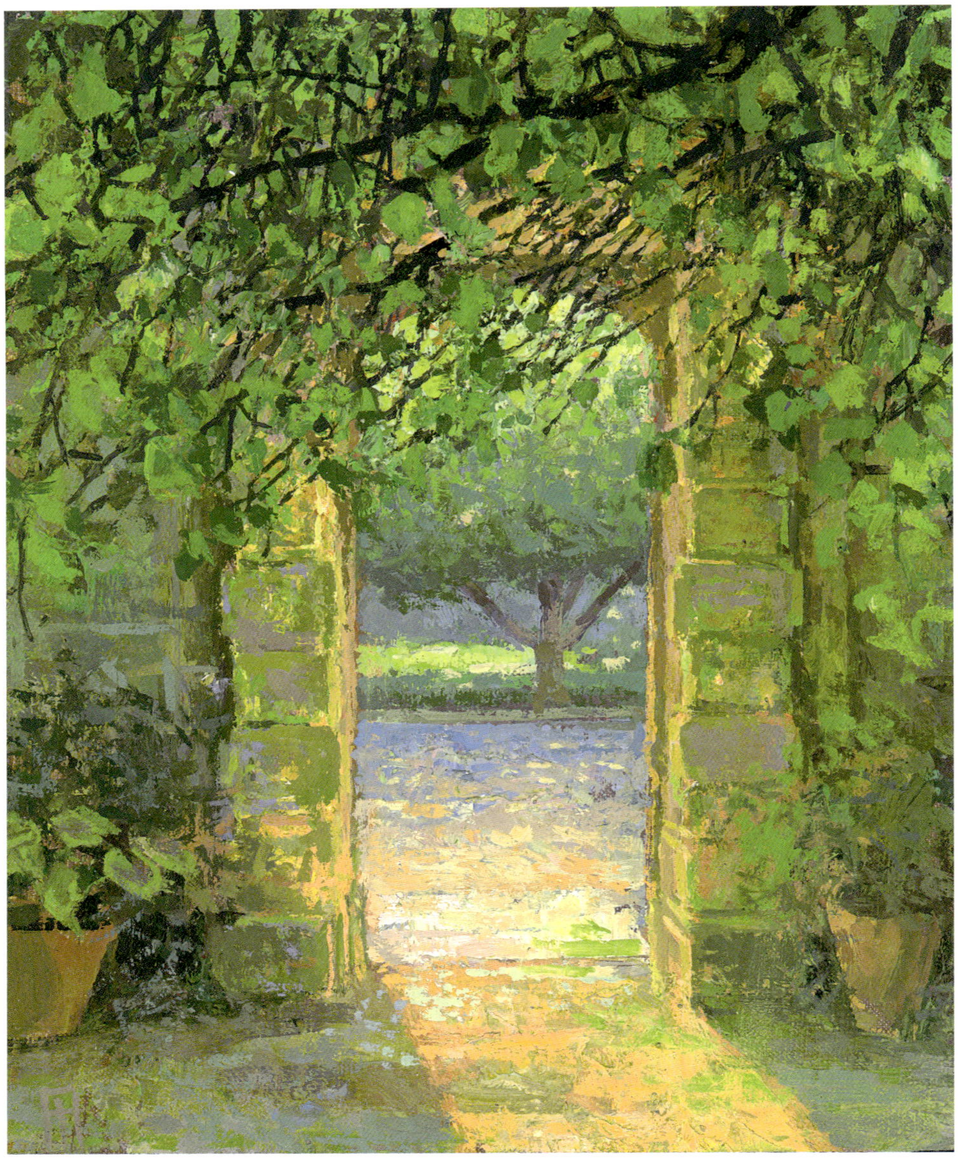

Botanical Gardens, Sunlit Doorway
25 x 20 cm, oil on linen, 2024

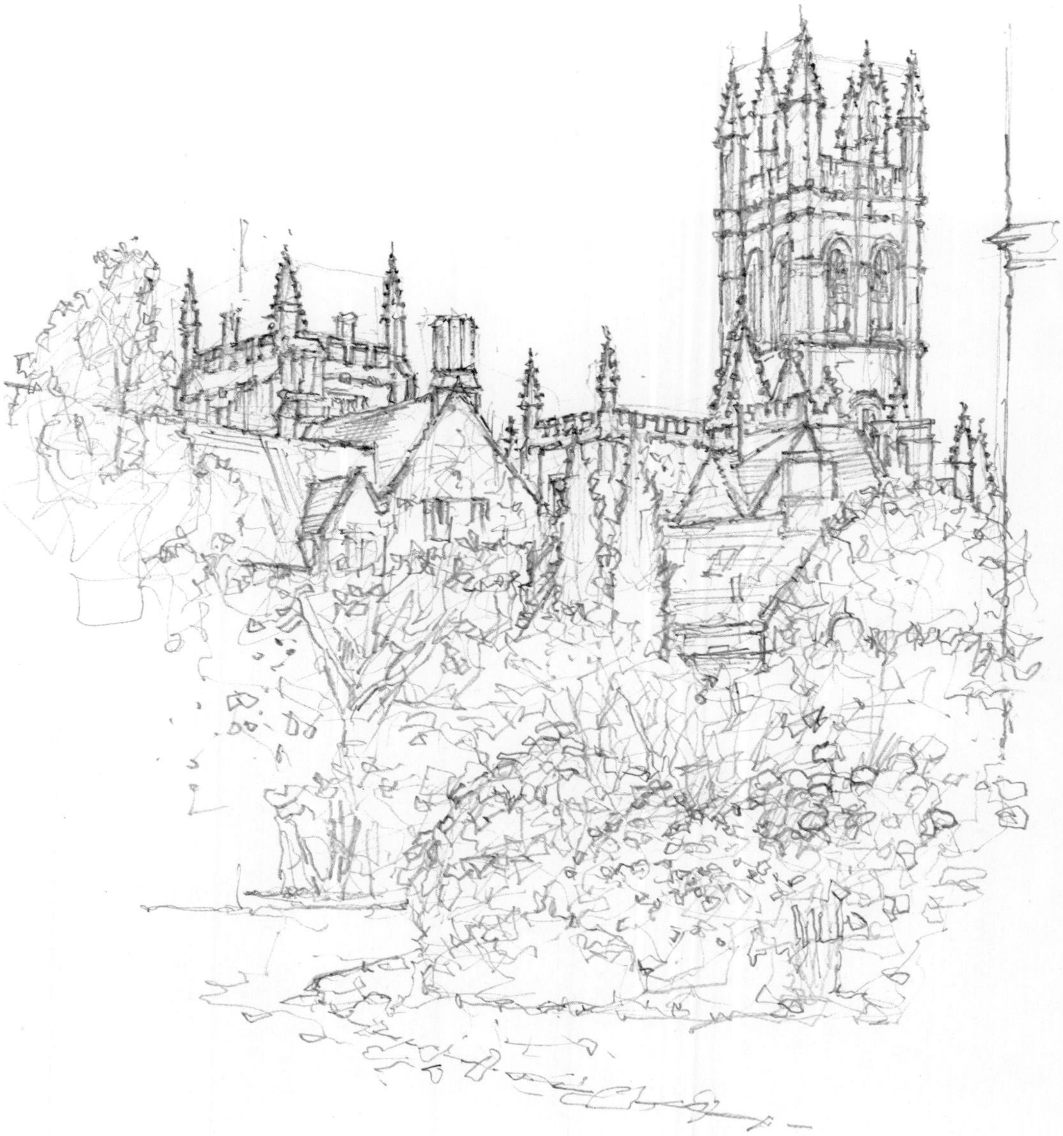

The others left soon after him. I rose to go with them, but Sebastian said: 'Have some more *Cointreau*', so I stayed and later he said, 'I must go to the Botanical Gardens.'

"Why?'

"To see the ivy.'

It seemed a good enough reason and I went with him.

He took my arm as we walked under the walls of Merton.

'I've never been to the Botanical Gardens,' I said.

'Oh, Charles, what a lot you have to learn! There's a beautiful arch there and more different kinds of ivy than I knew existed. I don't know where I should be without the Botanical Gardens.'

Evelyn Waugh, *Brideshead Revisited*, 1945

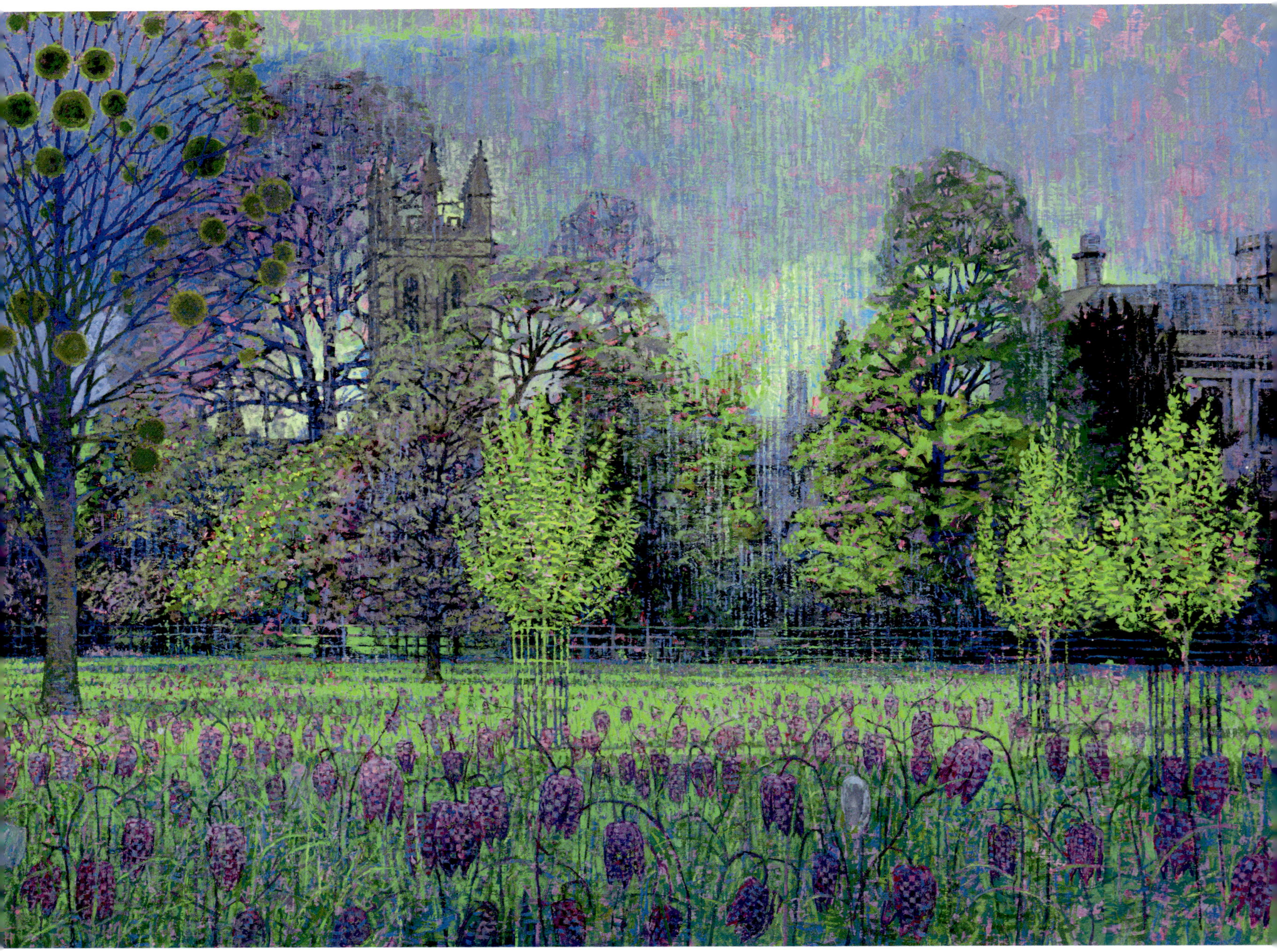

Magdalen Fritillaries

91 x 122 cm, oil on linen, 2024

Green natural cloister of our Academe,
What ghost is this that greets us as we pace

Beneath your boughs, the genius of the place,
With soft accost that fits our musing dream?
Scholar, divine, or statesman, would beseem
That reverend air, that pensive-brilliant face,
And lofty wit, and speech of Attic grace,
Rich in grave ornament and noble theme:

'Tis he who played unspoiled a worldly part,
Taught the town truth, and in a formal age,
Lured fop and toast to heed a note sublime;
Who here had early learned the crowning art,
To walk the world like Plato's monarch-sage,
'Spectator of all being and all time.'

Thomas Herbert Warren, Addison's Walk,
***The Spectator*, 1892**

I was greatly shocked by the hideous features and generally villainous appearance of this good and honest man. His wife, a filthy old hag, was with him, and although she may be the ugliest of her sex he is certainly the more repulsive of the two. An unusually pointed and very long nose, little eyes set deep in the head, a twisted mouth almost without upper lips, great deep scar in one cheek and the whole face and hands as black and coarse as those of the poorest gardener or farm-labourer. His clothing and especially his hat were also very bad. Such is the aspect of the Professor, who would most naturally be taken for the gardener.

Z.C. von Uffenbach, Oxford in 1710, 1928

Uffenbach's meeting recalled my own first meeting with a Don: revealing a world-leading scholar of Ancient Greek who was unable to shave without covering his starched, white – but heavily-worn – collar with blood.

Zacharias Conrad von Uffenbach (1683–1734) German scholar, bibliophile, traveller and palaeographer, he is best known today for his gloriously dour travelogues normally proclaiming his disappointment in all that he saw – particularly Oxford.

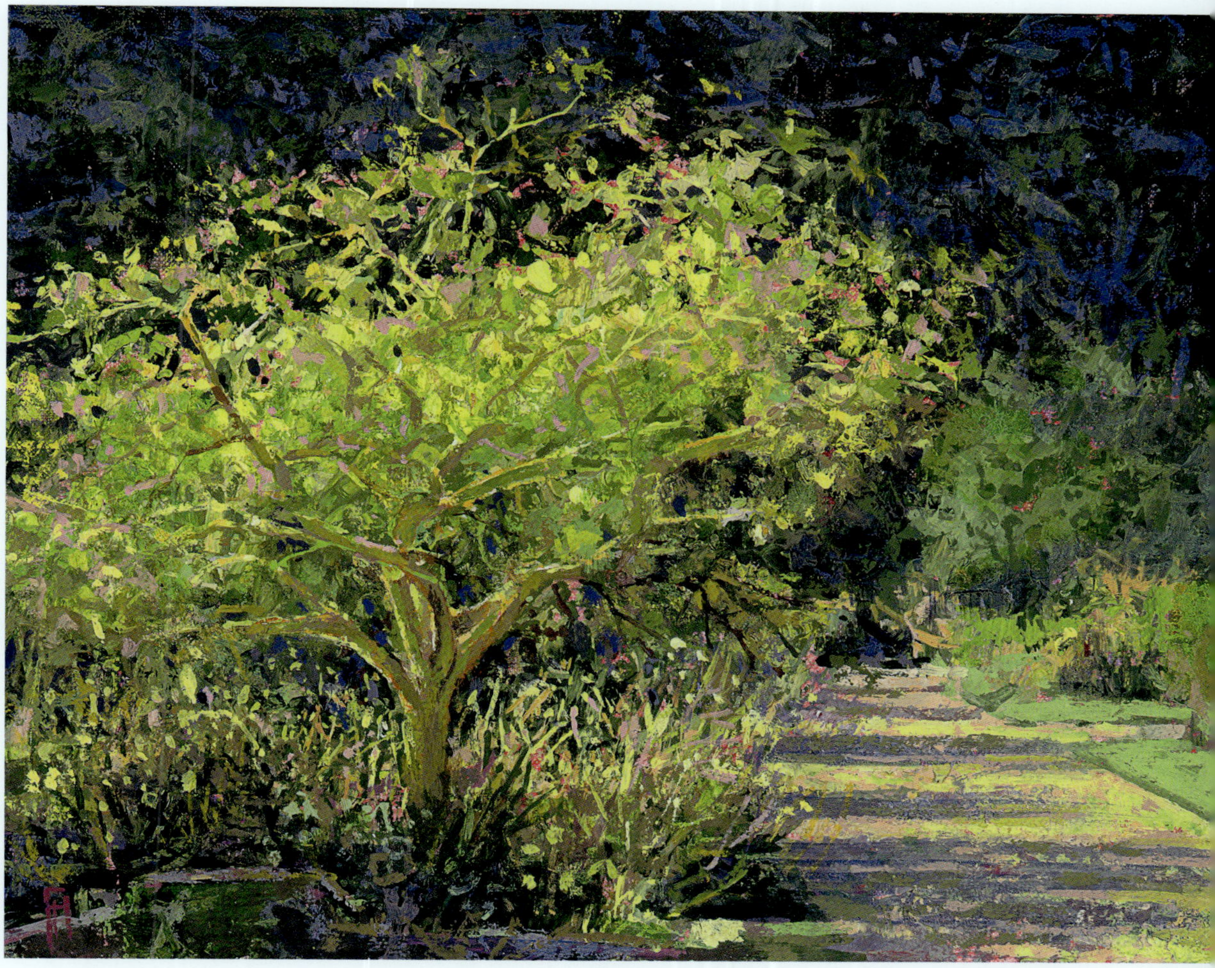

Botanical Gardens, Sunlit Tree
20 x 25 cm, oil on linen, 2024

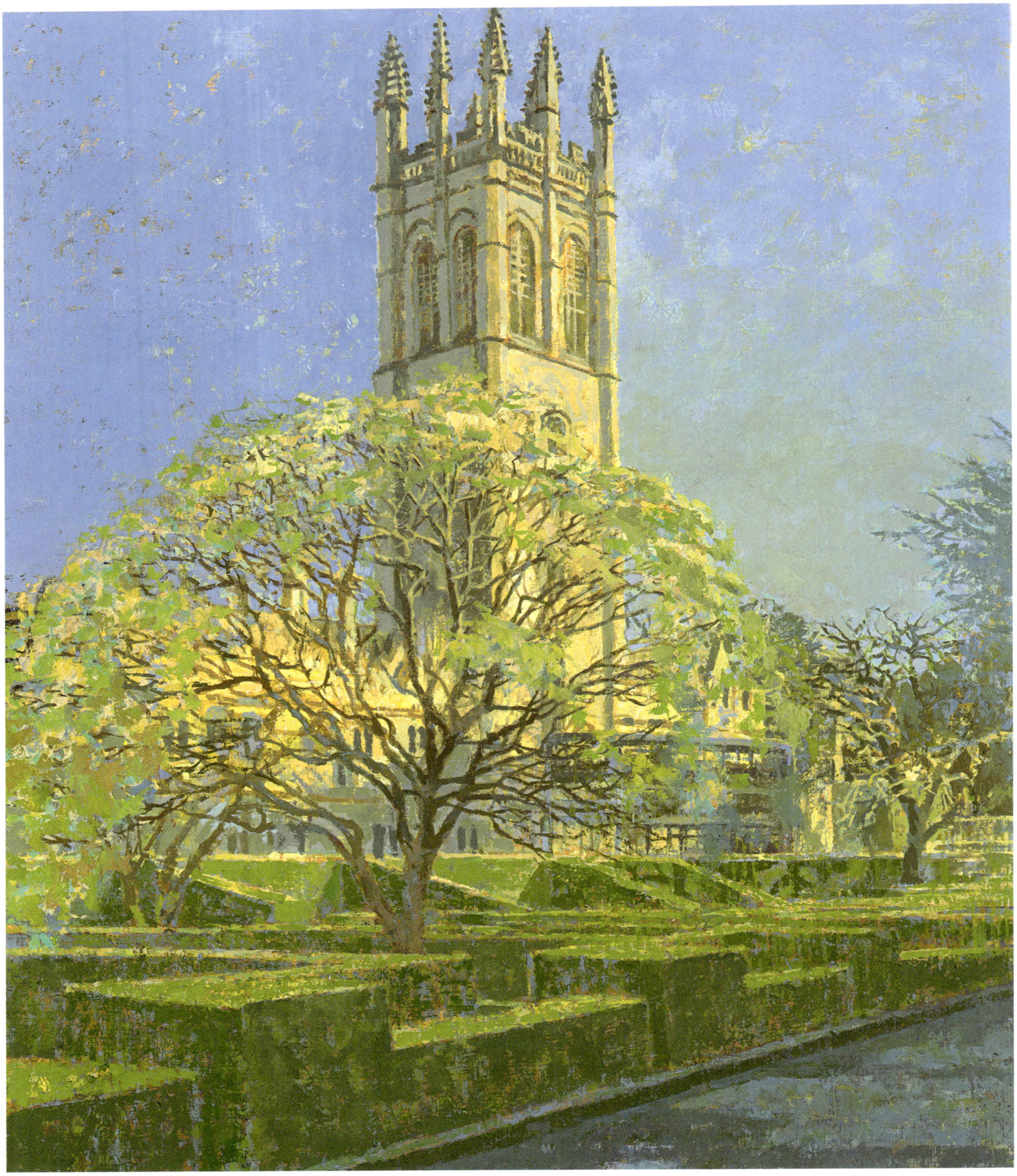

Ah! the brown bird has ceased: one exquisite trill
About the sombre woodland seems to cling
Dying in music, else the air is still,
So still that one might hear the bat's small wing
Wander and wheel above the pines, or tell
Each tiny dew-drop dripping from the bluebell's brimming cell.

And far away across the lengthening wold,
Across the willowy flats and thickets brown,
Magdalen's tall tower tipped with tremulous gold
Marks the long High Street of the little town,
And warns me to return: I must not wait.
Hark! 'tis the curfew booming from the bell in Christ Church gate.

Oscar Wilde, *The Burden of Itys, Poems by Oscar Wilde,* 1881

"While lying in bed on Tuesday morning with Swinburne (a copy of) was woken up by the Clerk of the Schools to know why I did not come up. I thought I was not in till Thursday. About one o'clock I nipped up and was ploughed* immediately in Divinity and then got a delightful viva voce, first in the Odyssey, where we discussed epic poetry in general, dogs, and women. Then in Aeschylus where we talked of Shakespeare, Walt Whitman and the Poetics. He had a long discussion about my essay on Poetry in the Aristotle paper and altogether was delightful. Of course I knew I had got a First, so swaggered horribly."

*Ploughed – failed

Oscar Wilde, Letter, July 1876

Magdalen from the Daubeny Building
61 x 51 cm, oil on linen, 2024

Oscar Fingal O'Fflahertie Wills Wilde (1854–1900) an Anglo-Irish playwright, poet, novelist and essayist, studied at Trinity College, Dublin and then Magdalen College, where he came into contact with John Ruskin and Walter Pater. Destroyed by the events stemming from his attempt to sue the Marquess of Queensberry, the father of his lover Lord Alfred Douglas, the result was two years of hard labour followed by exile and an early death. Now something of a secular saint, even the park outside Reading Gaol is named in honour of Wilde.

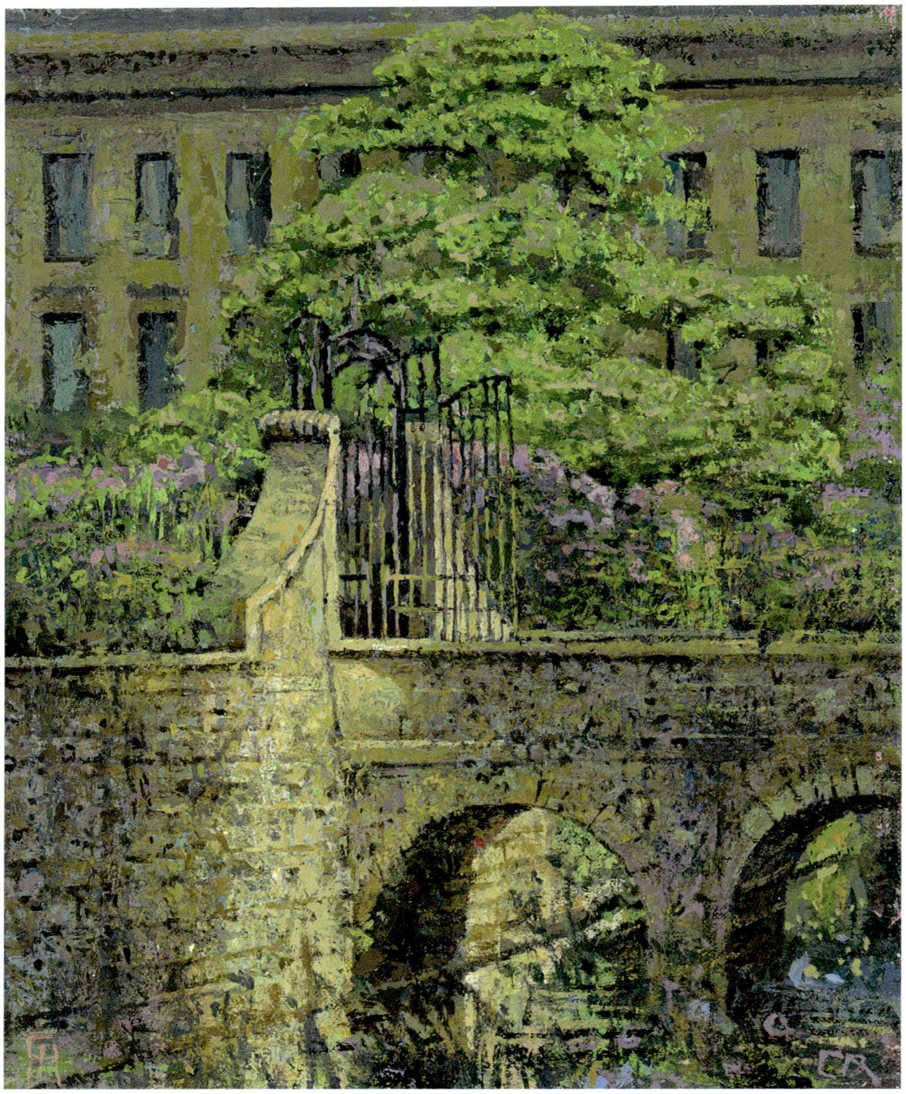

Magdalen, The New Buildings
25 x 20 cm, oil on linen, 2024

Changed and estranged, like a ghost, I pass the familiar portals,
Echoing now like a tomb, they accept me no more as of old;
Yet I go wistfully onward, a shade thro' a kingdom of mortals
Wanting a face to greet me, a hand to grasp and to hold.

Hardly I know as I go if the beautiful City is only
Mocking me under the moon, with its streams and its willows agleam,
Whether the City or friends or I that am friendless and lonely,
Whether the boys that go by or the time-worn towers be the dream;

Whether the walls that I know, or the unknown fugitive faces,
Faces like those that I loved, faces that haunt and waylay,
Faces so like and unlike, in the dim unforgettable places,
Startling the heart into sickness that aches with the sweet of the May,—

Whether all these or the world with its wars be the wandering shadows!
Ah, sweet over green-gloomed waters the may hangs, crimson and white;
And quiet canoes creep down by the warm gold dusk of the meadows,
Lapping with little splashes and ripples of silvery light.

Others as I have returned: I shall see the old faces to-morrow,
Down by the gay-coloured barges, alert for the throb of the oars,
Wanting to row once again, or tenderly jesting with sorrow
Up the old stairways and noting the strange new names on the doors.

Is it a dream? And I know not nor care if there be an awaking
Ever at all any more, for the years that have torn us apart,
Few, so few as they are, will ever be rending and breaking:
Sooner by far than I knew have they wrought this change for my heart!

Well; I grow used to it now! Could the dream but remain and for ever,
With the flowers round the grey quadrangle laughing as time grows old!
For the waters go down to the sea, but the sky still gleams on the river!
We plucked them—but there shall be lilies, ivory lilies and gold.

And still, in the beautiful City, the river of life is no duller,
Only a little strange as the eighth hour dreamily chimes,
In the City of friends and echoes, ribbons and music and colour,
Lilac and blossoming chestnut, willows and whispering limes.

Over the Radcliffe Dome the moon as the ghost of a flower
Weary and white awakes in the phantom fields of the sky:
The trustful shepherded clouds are asleep over steeple and tower,
Dark under Magdalen walls the Cher like a dream goes by.

Back, we come wandering back, poor ghosts, to the home that one misses
Out in the shelterless world, the world that was heaven to us then,
Back from the coil and the vastness, the stars and the boundless abysses,
Like monks from a pilgrimage stealing in bliss to their cloisters again.

City of dreams that we lost, accept now the gift we inherit—
Love, such a love as we knew not of old in the blaze of our noon,
We that have found thee at last, half City, half heavenly Spirit,
While over a mist of spires the sunset mellows the moon.

Alfred Noyes, *Oxford Revisited*, 1907

Alfred Noyes (1880–1958) a prolific poet, novelist, playwright and all round *belle lettrest*, his work is largely forgotten today save for his poem *The Highwayman* which has been committed to heart by many while at school. He was at Exeter College but failed to obtain a degree as he prioritised meeting his publisher about his first book over being in Schools taking his finals. He married an American and spent a large part of his life in the US teaching at Princeton University where his students included F. Scott Fitzgerald and Edmund Wilson. Elgar was the most famous of the composers who set Noyes's work to music. Despite working for British propaganda during World War I and producing patriotic poems in both World Wars, Noyes was an influential pacifist and, following his conversion to Catholicism, a noted writer of apologetics.

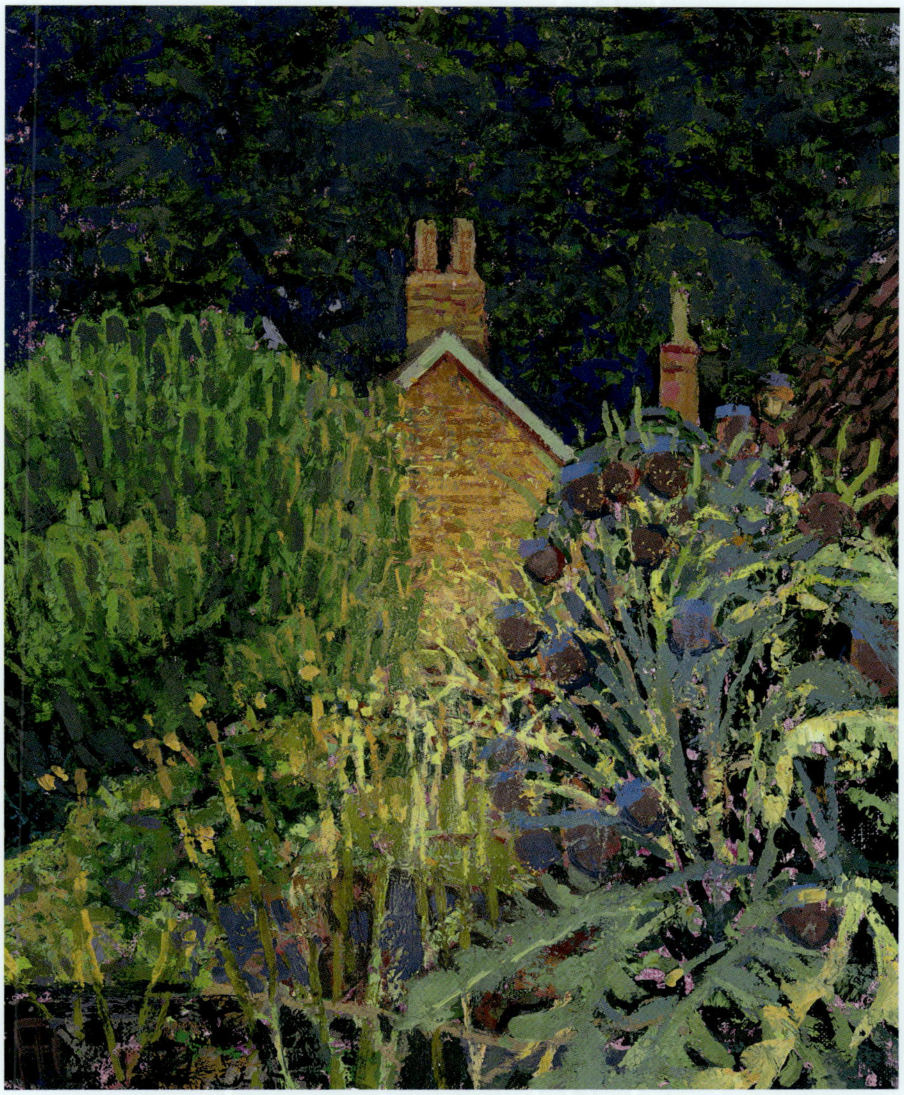

The Botanical Gardens, Keeper's Cottage
25 x 20 cm, oil on linen, 2024

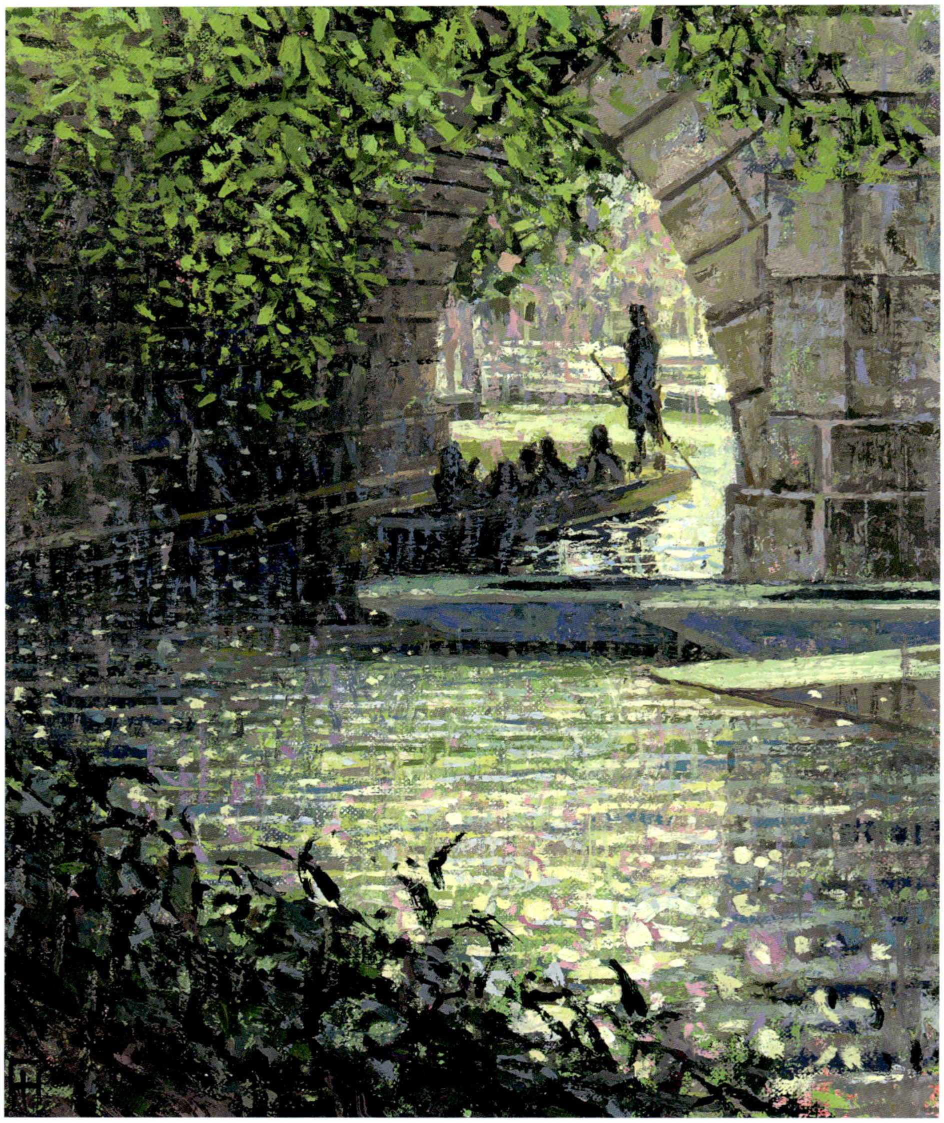

Punting Under the Bridge
25 x 20 cm, oil on linen, 2024

Later, they took the boy for a walk, she and he, and as she stood watching the yellow of an autumn leaf so sharp against the darkness of the trees behind it, he said to her, it has always haunted me that I may have been the last person to see your uncle alive, I was driving him to the station, you see, and as we crossed Magdalen Bridge, he suddenly asked to be set down there, he said he had just remembered a few errands that he might as well run while he was there, of course I obliged and turning the car around, I saw him disappear down in the direction of the river, which I thought was odd, but nothing more than just odd, until that evening when the dreadful news came that he had drowned.

They never found his body, she said.

He was doing up the laces on one of his son's shoes but he looked up quickly and said without hesitation, do you think he might not have drowned?

It is one of my favourite fantasies, she admitted.

And mine, he said dreamily, I sometimes imagine that if I wait long enough beside the bridge, he will walk up the stone path again and pick up where he left off a dozen years ago.

She wondered what he did for a living that did not consume all his energy and imagination so he still had some left over to spill upon the memory of one of his father's students who had found a watery grave in the Cherwell so many years ago. And suddenly in this day of unreal people and unreal events, he seemed unbearably real to her, this man, her acquaintance of a few hours, the last person to have seen her uncle alive.

Sunetra Gupta, *A Sin of Colour*, 1999

Sunetra Gupta (born 1965) is a professor of Theoretical Epidemiology in the Department of Zoology at the University of Oxford, She was one of the primary authors of the Great Barrington Declaration in 2020.

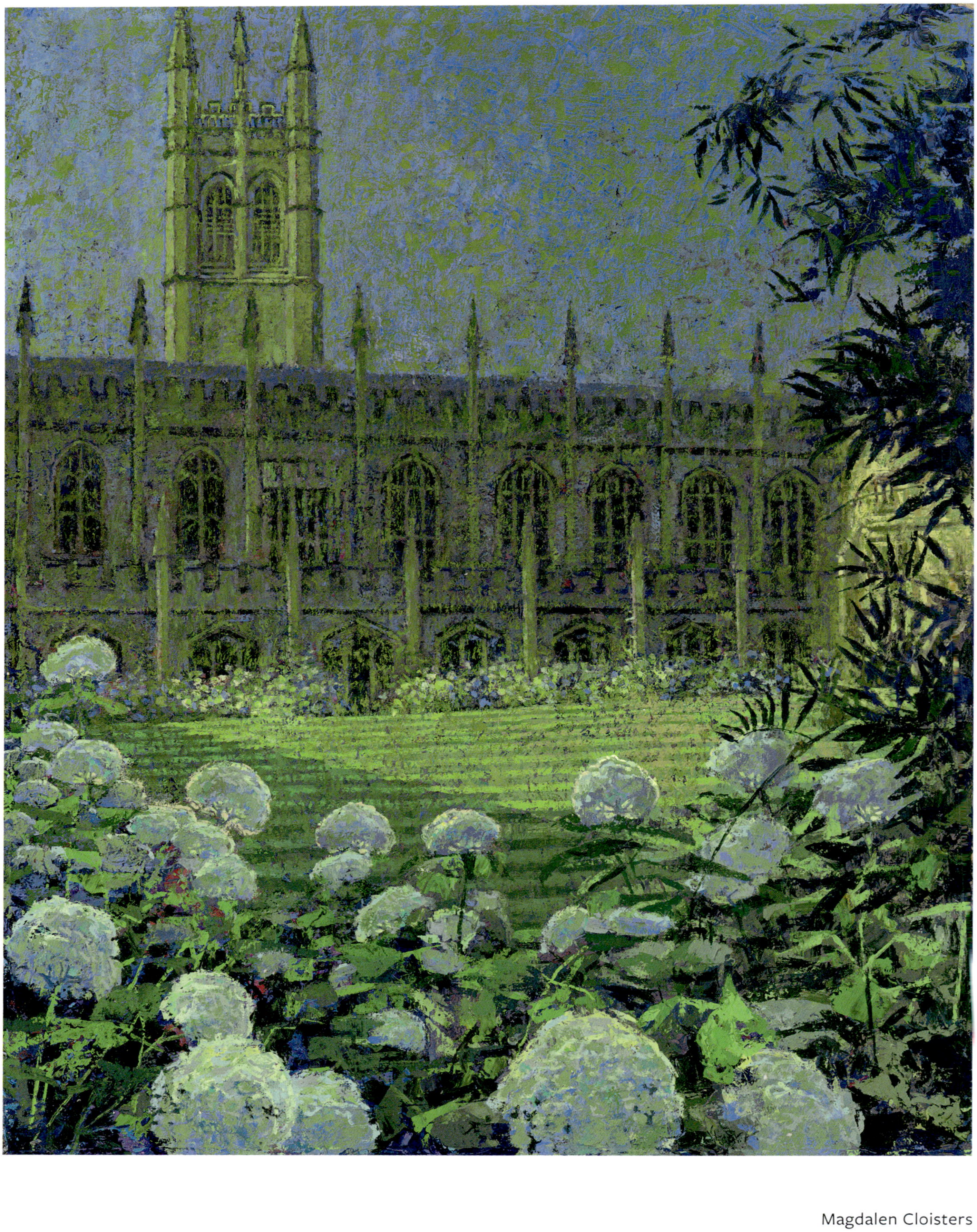

Magdalen Cloisters
56 x 46 cm, oil on linen, 2024

I spend all my mornings in the Bodleian... If only one could smoke and if only there were upholstered chairs, this would be one of the most delightful places in the world. I sit in 'Duke Humphrey's Library', the oldest part, a Fifteenth Century building with a very beautiful wooden painted ceiling above me and a little mullioned window on my left hand through which I look down on the garden of Exeter, where these mornings I see the sudden squalls of wind and rain driving the first blossoms off the fruit trees and snowing the lawn with them. At the bottom of the room the gilt bust of Charles I, presented by Laud, faces the gilt bust of Strafford – poor Strafford. The library itself, I mean the books, is mostly in a labyrinth of cellars under the neighbouring squares. This room however is full of books which stand in little cases at right angles to the wall, so that between each pair there is a kind of little 'box', in the public-house sense of the word, and in these boxes one sits and reads. By a merciful provision, however many books you send for, they will be left on your chosen table at night for you to resume work next morning; so that one gradually accumulates a pile as comfortably as in one's own room. There is not, as in modern libraries, a forbidding framed notice to shriek 'Silence'; on the contrary the more moderate request, 'Talk little and treat lightly'. There is indeed always a faint murmur going on of semi-whispered conversations in the neighbouring boxes. It disturbs no one. I rather like to hear the hum of the hive.

As you may imagine, one sees many oddities amongst one's fellow readers – people whom I have never met elsewhere and who look as if they were shut up with the other properties every night. Positively the only drawback is that beauty, antiquity and overheating weave a spell very much more suited to dreaming than to working. But I trust in time to become inoculated. (The practice of opening the window in one's box is not, I need hardly say, encouraged.)

Letter to his Father, 31st March 1928

... the best thing that has happened to me lately is to have assisted at such a scene in the Magdalen smoking room as rarely falls one's way. That perfectly ape-faced man whom I have probably pointed out to you was seated on the padded fender with his back to the fire, bending down to read a paper, and thus leaving a tunnel-shaped aperture between his collar and the nape of his neck. A few yards in front of him stood M. Let M. now light a cigarette and wave the match to and fro in the air to extinguish it. And let the match be either not wholly extinguished or so recently extinguished that no fall in the temperature of the wood has occurred. Let M. then fling the match towards the fire in such a way that it enters the aperture between ape-face's neck and his collar with the most unerring accuracy. For a space of time which must have been infinitesimal but which seemed long to us as we watched in the perfect silence which this very interesting experiment so naturally demanded, ape-face, alone ignorant of his fate, continued absorbed in the football results. His body then rose in a vertical line from the fender, without apparent muscular effort, as though propelled by a powerful spring under his bottom. Re-alighting on his feet, he betook himself to a rapid movement of the hands with the apparent intention of applying them to every part of his back and buttocks in the quickest possible succession; accompanying the exercise with a distention of the cheeks and a blowing noise. After which exclaiming (to me) in a heightened voice, 'It isn't so bloody funny', he darted from the room. The learned Dr. Hope.... who alone had watched the experiment with perfect gravity, at this stage remarked placidly to the company in general, 'Well well, the match will have gone out by now', and returned to his periodical... But the luck of it! How many shots would a man have taken before he succeeded in throwing a match into that tiny aperture if he had been trying?

C S Lewis, letter to his brother, 20 March 1932, *Letters of C S Lewis,* 1966

Clive Staples Lewis (1898–1963). His studies at University College were interrupted by war service and on returning to Oxford he took a triple first in Honour Moderations, Greats and in English. Elected to a fellowship at Magdalen College, he stayed for almost 30 years until in 1954 he assumed the Professorship of Medieval and Renaissance Literature at Cambridge University. Lewis's academic work focused on Courtly Love and the late Middle Ages. His Narnia books have enchanted children and grownups ever since they were published and are of course Christian allegories as are his science fiction novels. Lewis is a powerful writer of apologetics and is one of the few modern writers to be revered and loved by Anglicans, Evangelicals and Catholics alike.

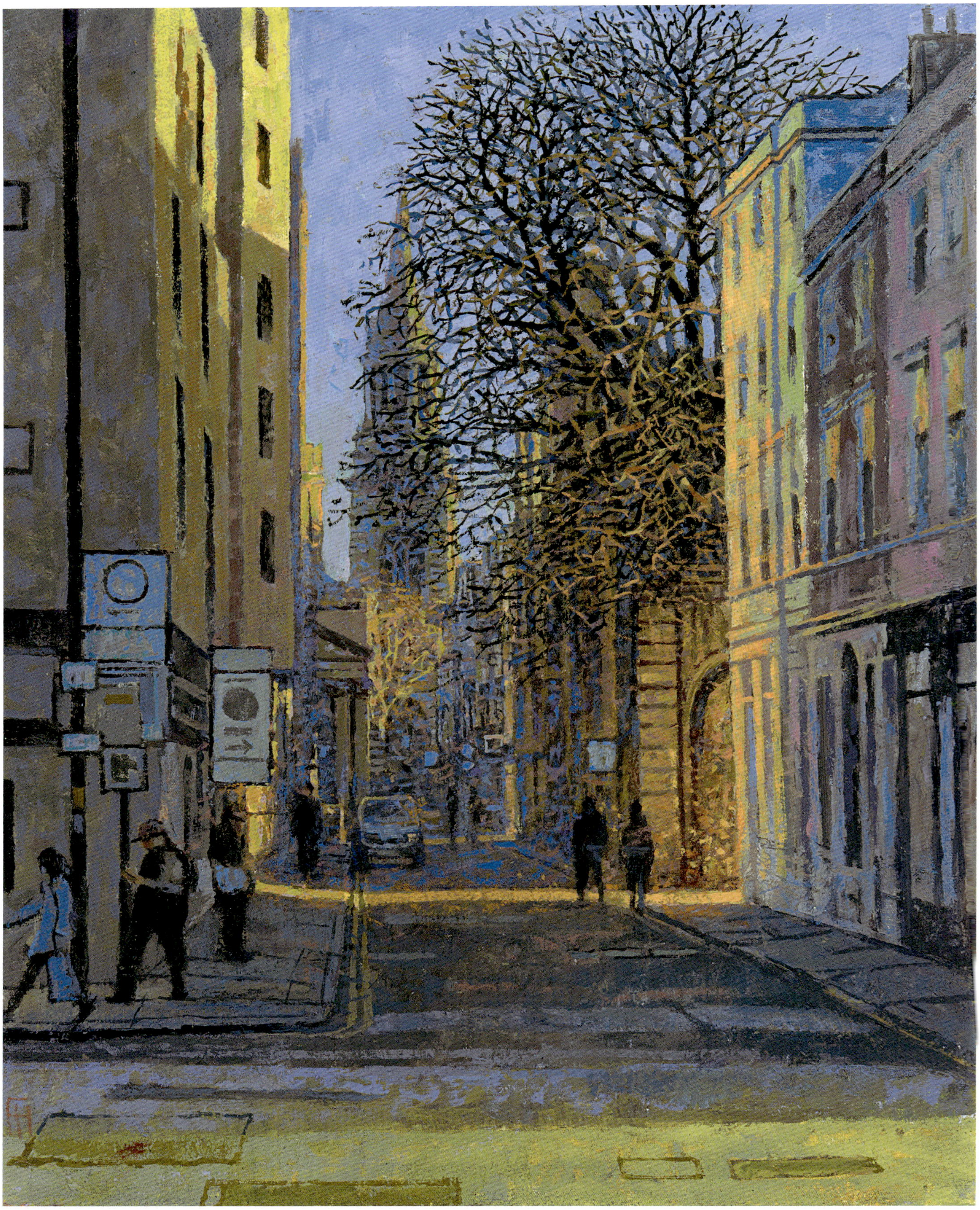

Failed in Divinity! Oh count the hours
Spent on my knees in Cowley, Pusey House,
St. Barnabas', St. Mary Mag's, St. Paul's,
Revering chasubles and copes and albs!
Consider what I knew of 'High' and 'Low'
Failed in Divinity! O, towers and spires!
Could no one help? Was nothing to be done?
No. No one. Nothing. Mercilessly calm,
The Cherwell carried under Magdalen Bridge
Its leisured puntfuls of the fortunate
Who next term and the next would still come back.
Could no one help? I'd seen myself a don,
Reading old poets in the library
Attending chapel in an M.A. gown
And sipping vintage port by candlelight.
I sought my tutor in his arid room,
Who told me, "You'd have only got a Third."
I wandered into Blackwell's, where my bill
Was so enormous that it wasn't paid
Till ten years later, from the small estate
My father left. Not even dusty shelves
Of folios of architectural plates
Could comfort me. Outside, the sunny Broad,
The mouldering busts round the Sheldonian,
The hard Victorian front of Exeter,
The little colleges that front the Turl,
The lean acacia tree in Trinity,
Stood strong and confident, outlasting me.

John Betjeman, *Summonèd by Bells,* 1960

John Betjeman (1906–1984) read English at Magdalen College under C S Lewis and was famously sent down, but for failing in Welsh not Divinity (which heroically he passed on his third attempt). Poet, writer (particularly on architecture), broadcaster, TV personality, and Poet Laureate. "Not enough sex" was his answer when asked what he most regretted as he approached death.

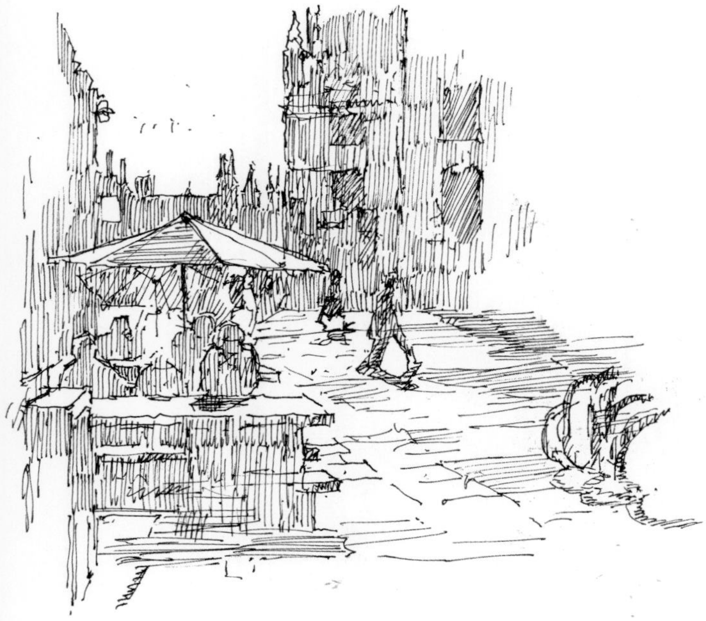

The Turl in Winter Sun
46 x 36 cm, oil on linen, 2024

A clerk ther was of Oxenford also,
That unto logyk hadde long ygo.
As lene was his hors as is a rake,
And he was nat right fat, I undertake,
But loked holwe, and therto soberly.
Ful thredbar was his overeste courtepy;
For he hadde geten him yet no benefice,
Ne was so worldly for to have office.
For hym was levere have at his beddes heed
Twenty bookes, clad in blak or reed,
Of Aristotle and his philosophie,
Than robes riche, or fithele, or gay sautrie.
But al be that he was a philosophre,
Yet hadde he but litel gold in cofre;
But al that he myghte of his freendes hente,
On bookes and on lernynge he it spente,
And bisily gan for the soules preye
Of hem that yaf hym wherwith to scoleye.
Of studie took he moost cure and moost heede.
Noght o word spak he moore than was neede,
And that was seyd in forme and reverence,
And short and quyk, and ful of hy sentence;
Sownynge in moral vertu was his speche,
And gladly wolde he lerne, and gladly teche.

Geoffrey Chaucer, *Canterbury Tales,* c.1400

Geoffrey Chaucer (1343–1400) an all round man of the world, was widely travelled, he was a civil servant, diplomat, courtier and Member of Parliament as well as being the Father of English Literature. His decision to write in English rather than French or Latin was akin to Virgil's decision to give Latin a chance. No Oxford connections as far as one can tell but Oxford-educated Terry Jones made perhaps the most original recent contribution to Chaucer scholarship with his work on the Knight in Canterbury Tales – finding him less the embodiment of Chivalry and more a vicious, murderous mercenary.

The University Church from Merton Street
61 x 51 cm, oil on linen, 2024

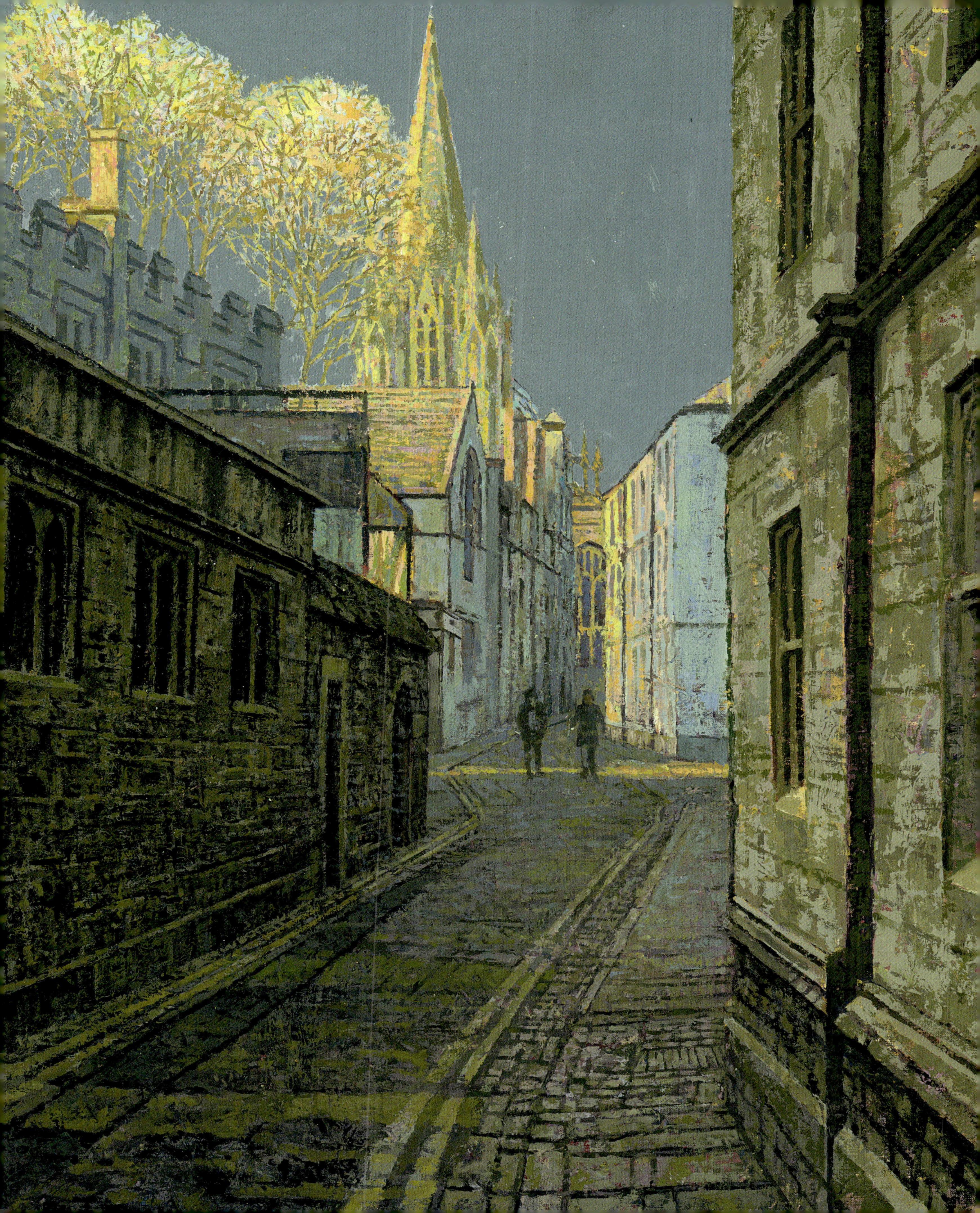

The more he lived among us, the more he caught the humour of the place. Never would he venture into college, save on the day in Summer term when the college was photographed. Then he strode in, settled himself on a table in the midst of the group, and faced the camera with placid courage. He knew every member of the college, and would go with an Oriel man anywhere, but to all others he turned a deaf ear. His attendance at college matches, whether cricket or football, was unfailing, and thereby hangs a tale. He had been with the eleven to the Keble ground, the day was hot, and his energy exhausted by encouraging applause. Seeing a hansom just starting for the town, he jumped in and was driven home.

Provost Phelps, *Oriel Bill*

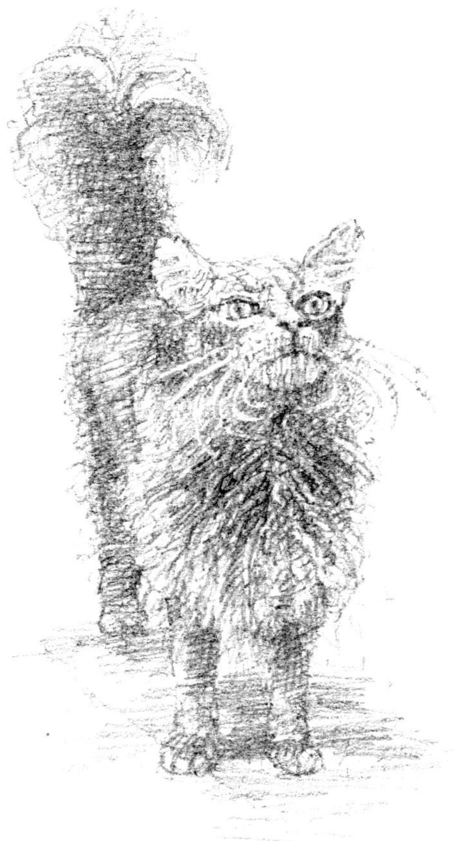

Lancelot Ridley Phelps (1853–1936), affectionately referred to as "The Phelper", is one of those figures who bestride Oxford through the force of their personality. Provost of Oriel from 1914 to 1936, he was noted for his habit of taking cold baths – "Be a Man, Phelps, be a Man" was his battle-cry as he steeled himself for entry into the bath.

Oriel Street
40 x 30 cm, oil on linen, 2024

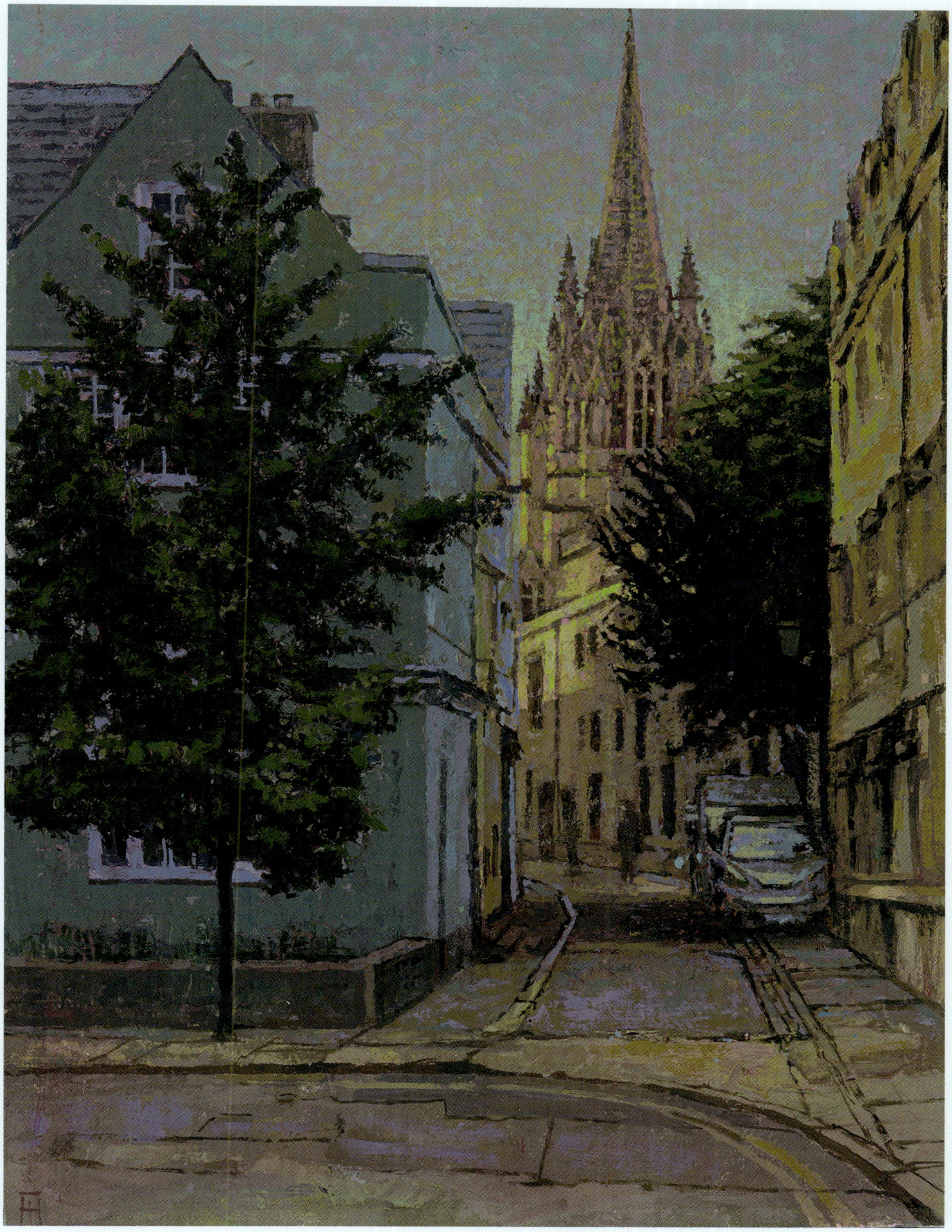

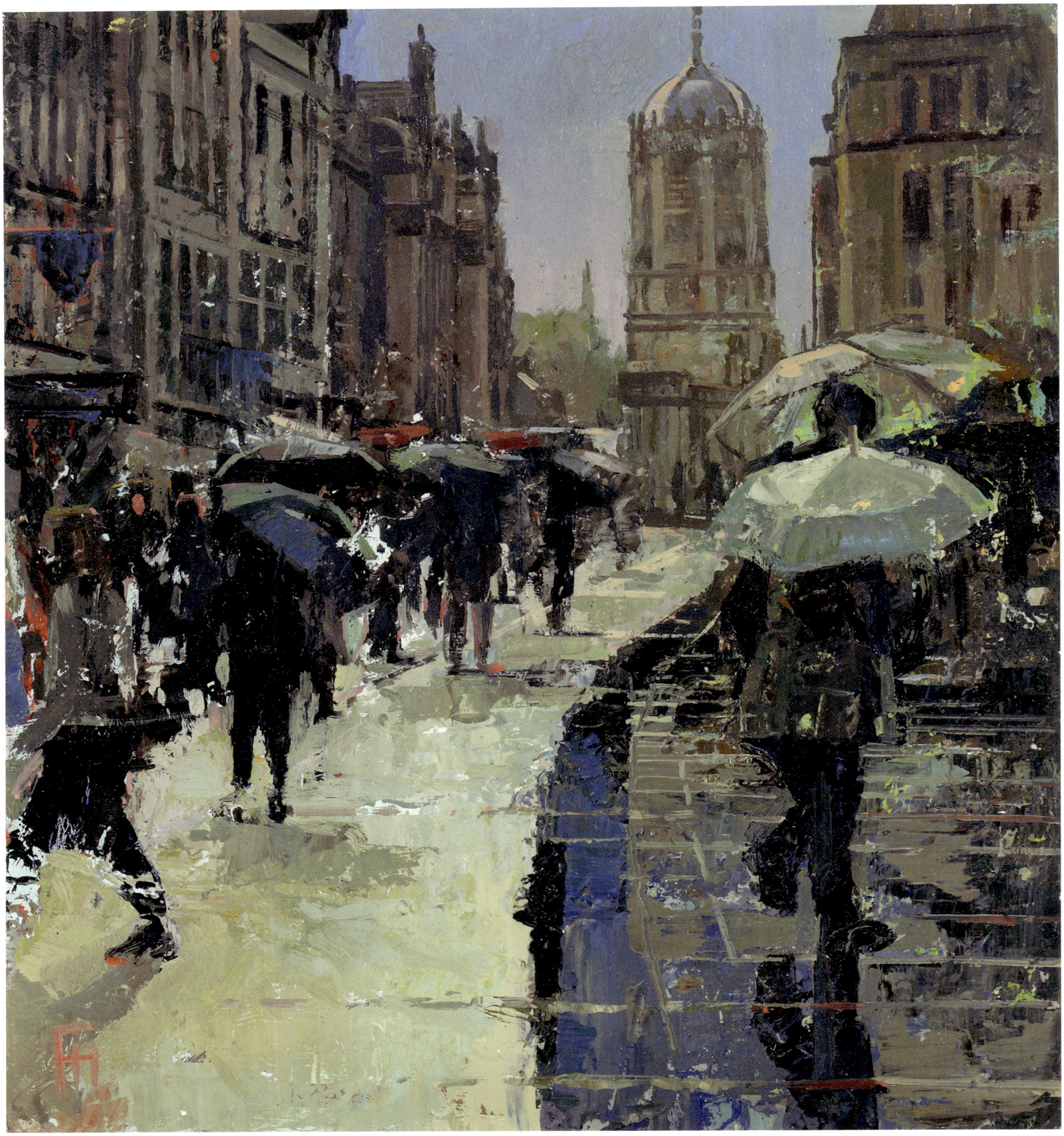

In the afternoon, we went to the Bodleian Library, where we were instructed to take the oath; but the Proctor (as he is called), really *Procurator Academiae*, who was to receive it was not there for an Englishman owing to a general lack of courtesy is seldom up to time.

Afterwards Mr Crab led us up to the so-called gallery and showed us a poor little room on the right which he called 'the study'. It would perhaps serve as a museum for the Librarian or old Fellows in winter. In here hung some pictures, amongst which were several embroidered in silk. Mr Crab made a great fuss over them, although I have seen many more beautiful, and even have better ones worked by my own grandmother. After this a great armchair was pointed out to us, as something very special, because it is said to have been made out of the ship in which Captain Drake sailed round the world; also several Chinese staves, bows and arrows, and again a cylinder with some vile figures.

In Christ Church Cathedral are various epitaphs which, like the monuments throughout England, are neither very valuable nor well-sculptured, and indeed nowhere, either in London or elsewhere, did we see a memorial approaching in interest those in Lubeck or other places. One cannot but wonder at this, as in most things, the English are so wasteful and expensive.

We saw Christ Church hall or dining-room, which is fearfully large and high but otherwise poor and ugly in appearance; it also reeks so strongly of bread and meat that one cannot remain in it, and I should find it impossible to dine and live there. The disgust was increased (for the table was already set), when we looked at the coarse and dirty and loathsome table cloths, square wooden plates and the wooden bowls into which the bones are thrown; this odious custom obtains in all the colleges. The *socii collegiorum* as well as the students or scholars must dine here; but the most important have their meals brought to their rooms at incredibly high cost. In the centre of Christ Church quadrangle is a fountain with a Mercury, which does not play. At 7 o'clock in the evening the Grassys conducted us to the usual *collegium musicum* held every Wednesday. On this occasion the music was very weak and poor.

The present Professor of Chemistry, Richard Frewyn, troubles himself very little about (the chemistry laboratory). The operator, Mr White (who is said to be very debauched) still less. The result is that the furnaces look entirely uncared for and not only are the finest instruments, crucibles and other things belonging to the place almost all of them lying in pieces, but everything is covered in filth. Who could imagine that so fine and costly an undertaking should receive so little attention? Indeed who would believe such a thing of England, which we foreigners hold so much in awe that we believe all subjects, and chemistry in particular, to be passing through a golden age? Herr von Uffenbach could be pithier:

The Physic Garden: wild and overgrown.

New College gardens: very mediocre.

Exeter College: tolerable-looking building in front, at the back old and poor.

Pembroke College: very indifferent and confused building.

Merton College: consists of several ugly old buildings.

Magdalen College: very old and badly built.

Ashmolean Museum: *Herr Burgermeister Reimer* in Luneburg has twice as many specimens.

Z.C. von Uffenbach, Oxford in 1710, 1928

Umbrellas in the Cornmarket
31 x 28 cm, oil on panel, 2012

Rome has been called the 'Sacred City', might not our Oxford be called so too? There is an air about it, resonant of joy and hope: it speaks with a thousand tongues to the heart: it weaves its mighty shadow over the imagination: it stands in lowly sublimity, on the hill of ages, and points with prophetic fingers to the sky: it greets the eager gaze from afar, with glistening spires and pinnacles adorned, that shine with an eternal light as with the lustre of setting suns; and a dream and a glory hover round its head, as the spirits of former times, a throng of intellectual shapes, are seen retreating or advancing to the eye of memory: its streets are paved with the names of learning that can never wear out: its green quadrangles breathe the silence of thought, conscious of the weight of yearnings innumerable after the past, of loftiest aspirations for the future: Isis babbles of the Muse, its waters are from the springs of Helicon, its Christ Church meadows, classic, Elysian fields! We could pass our lives in Oxford without having or wanting any other idea, that of the place is enough. We imbibe the air of thought; we stand in the presence of learning. We are admitted into the Temple of Fame, we feel that we are in the Sanctuary, on holy ground, and 'hold high converse with the mighty dead.' The enlightened and the ignorant are on a level, if they have but faith in the tutelary genius of the place. We may be wise by proxy, and studious by prescription. Time has taken upon himself the labour of thinking; and accumulated libraries leave us leisure to be dull. There is no occasion to examine the buildings, the churches, the colleges, by the rules of architecture, to reckon up the streets to compare it with Cambridge (Cambridge lies out of the way, on one side of the world) but woe to him who does not feel in passing through Oxford that he is in 'no mean city,' that he is surrounded with the monuments and lordly mansions of the mind of man, outvying in pomp and splendour the courts and palaces of princes, rising like an exhalation in the night of ignorance, and triumphing over barbaric foes, saying, 'All eyes shall see me, and all knees shall bow to me!' as the shrine where successive ages came to pay their pious vows, and slake the sacred thirst of knowledge, where youthful hopes (an endless flight) soared to truth and good, and where the retired and lonely student brooded over the historic, or over fancy's page, imposing high tasks for himself, framing high destinies for the race of man, the lamp, the mine, the well-head whence the spark of learning was kindled, its stream flowed, its treasures were spread out through the remotest corners of the land and to distant nations. Let him who is fond of indulging a dream-like existence go to Oxford, and stay there; let him study this magnificent spectacle, the same under all aspects, with the mental twilight tempering the glare of noon, or mellowing the silver moonlight; let him not catch the din of scholars or teachers, or dine or sup with them, or speak a word to any of its privileged inhabitants; for if he does, the spell will be broken, the poetry and the religion gone, and the palace of enchantment will melt from his embrace into thin air!

William Hazlitt, 'Pictures at Oxford and Blenheim',
The Works of William Hazlitt, 1823

William Hazlitt (1778–1830) an essayist, drama and literary critic, painter and philosopher, was from a dissenting background. He sympathised with the French Revolution and the idea of Liberty, this informs his writings. He became friends with Coleridge and Wordsworth at a time when 'to be young was very heaven'. Later friends included Charles Lamb, Benjamin Haydon and John Keats.

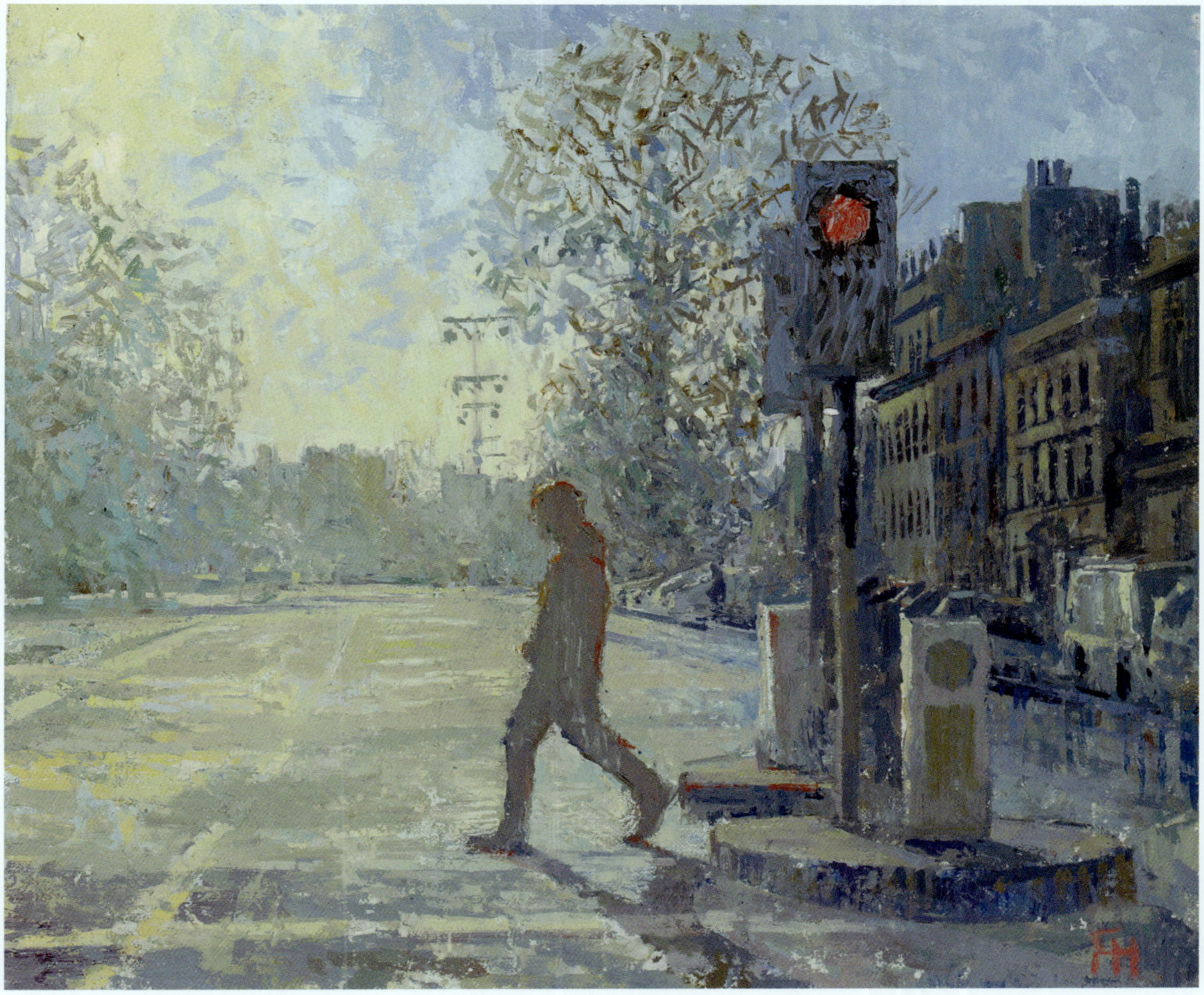

St Giles' Winter Morning
25 x 29 cm, oil on panel, 2012

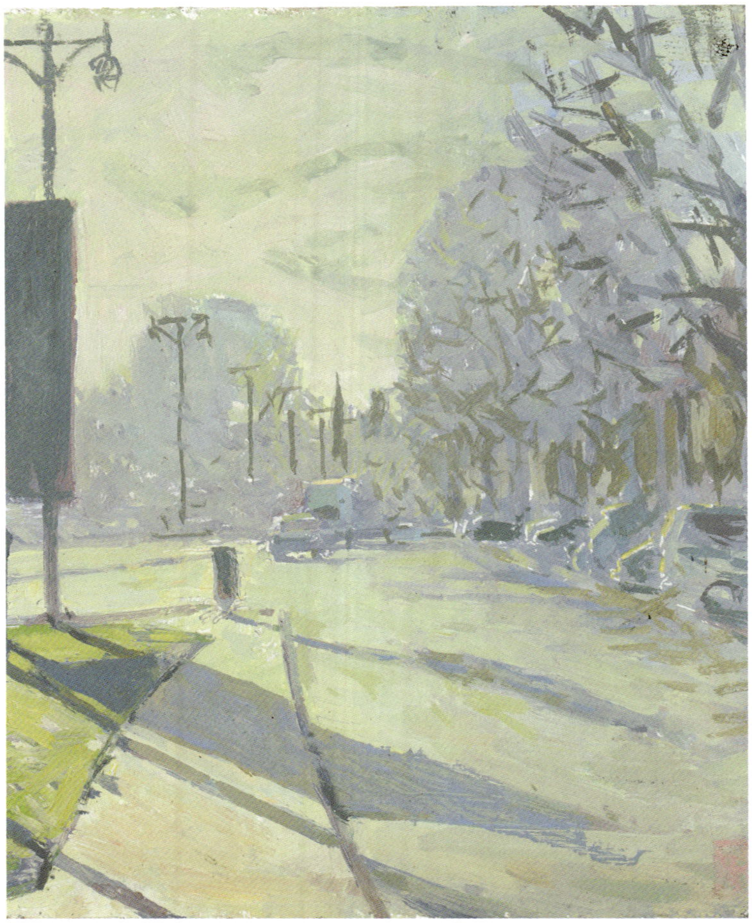

What he could see did not look very remarkable; there were hoardings advertising beans and the ATS, people pushing towards a red bus, a glazed-brick public-house. A pony and cart creaked down the road, the man holding the slack reins, a bowed figure in the faint dusk. John looked about for colleges and old buildings, but could only see distantly a spire or two, and watched a woman buying some sprouts at a greengrocer's fifty yards away. His bag stood beside him on the curb.

Philip Larkin, *Jill,* 1946

Philip Larkin (1922–1985), poet, novelist and librarian read English at St John's College, where he made lifelong friendships with Kingsley Amis and Robert Conquest. He was an innovative librarian – most notably at Hull University. As well as his poetry which sold fantastically compared to his peers, he was a jazz fanatic writing a weekly column for *The Telegraph* and editing *The Oxford Book of Twentieth Century English Verse*.

St Giles' March Morning
25 x 29 cm, oil on panel, 2012

Bicycles in St Giles'
61 x 51 cm, oil on linen, 2024

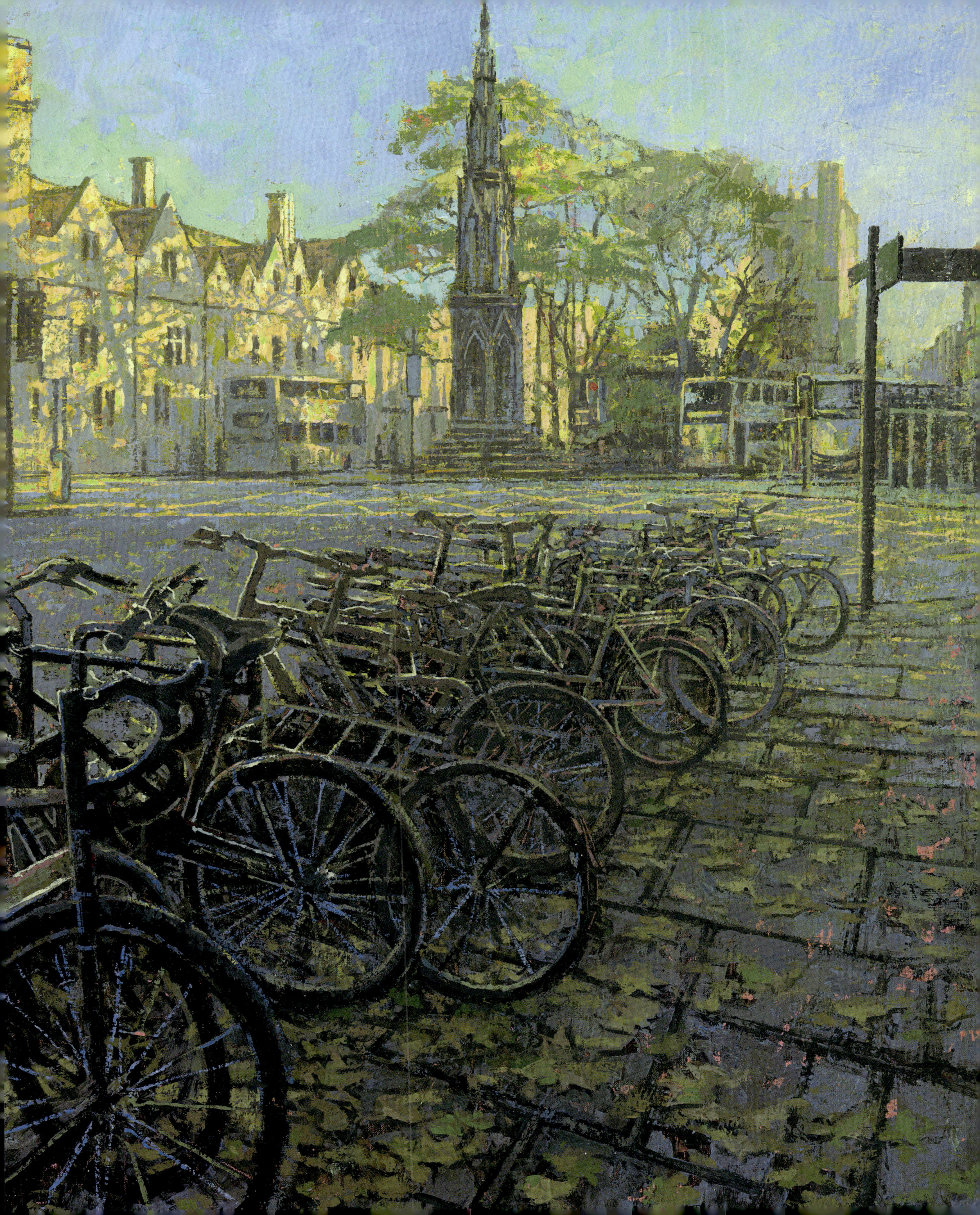

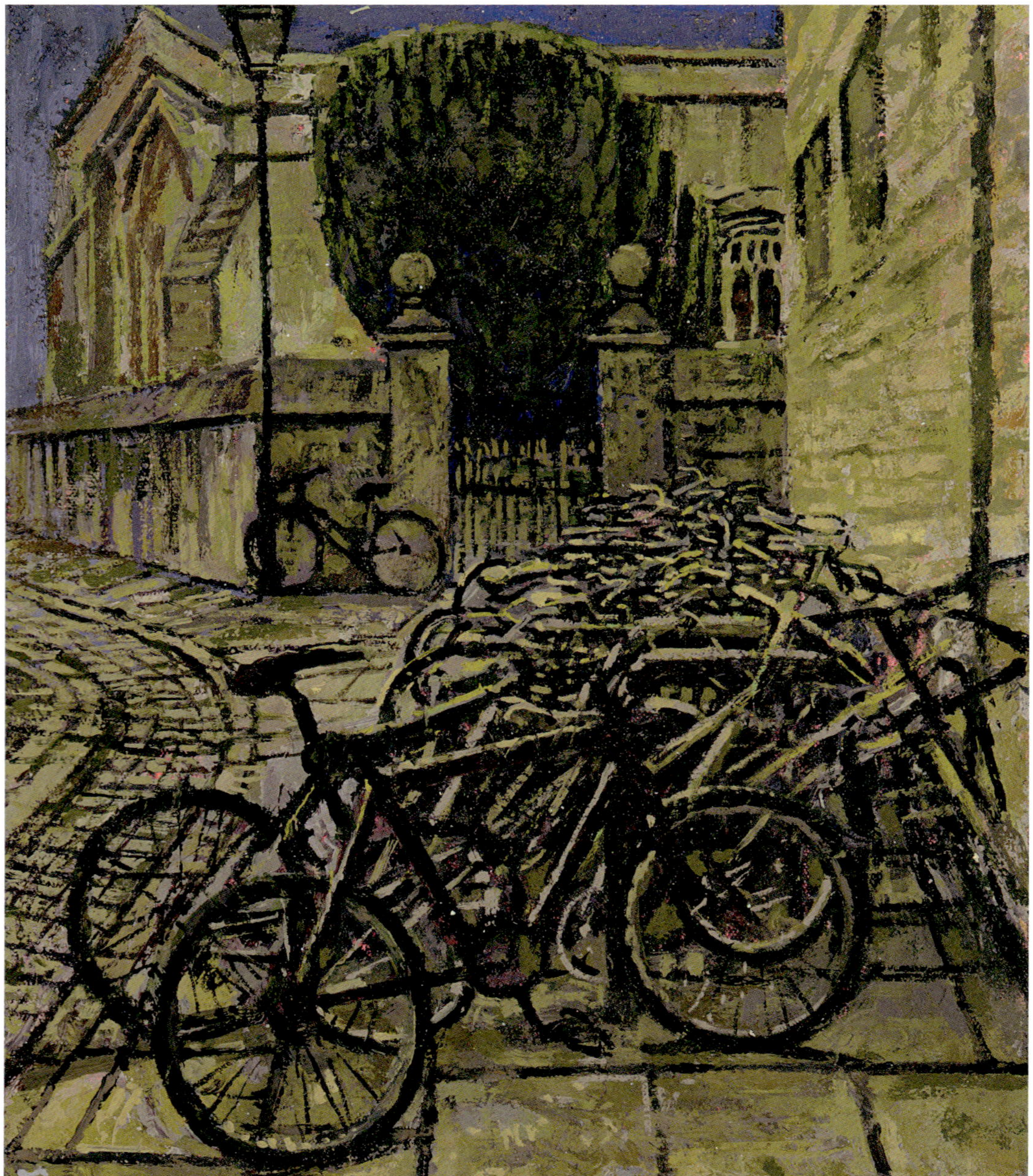

Nature invades: old rooks in each college garden
Still talk, like agile babies, the language of feeling;
By towers a river still runs coastward and will run,
  Stones in these towers are utterly
  Satisfied still with their weight.

Mineral and creature, so deeply in love with themselves
Their sin of accidie excludes all others,
Challenge our high-strung students with a careless beauty,
  Setting a single error
  Against their countless faults.

Outside, some factories, then a whole green country
Where a cigarette comforts the evil, a hymn the weak;
Where thousands fidget and poke and spend their money:
  Eros Paidagogos
  Weeps on his virginal bed.

And over the talkative city like any other
Weep the non-attached angels. Here too the knowledge of death
Is a consuming love, and the natural heart refuses
  The low unflattering voice
  That sleeps not till it find a hearing.

W. H. Auden, *Oxford*, 1937

Wystan Hugh Auden (1907–1973) read English at Christ Church, where he met Stephen Spender, Cecil Day Lewis and Louis MacNeice. Considered a major poet almost from his first book, this group of friends went on to be the "Oxford Group" or even the "Auden Generation." The Group was left-oriented, anti-fascist and interested in Freudian ideas. All found other concerns as they grew older – Auden becoming a Christian humanist sage.

St Peter-in-the-East with Bicycles
25 x 20 cm, oil on linen, 2024

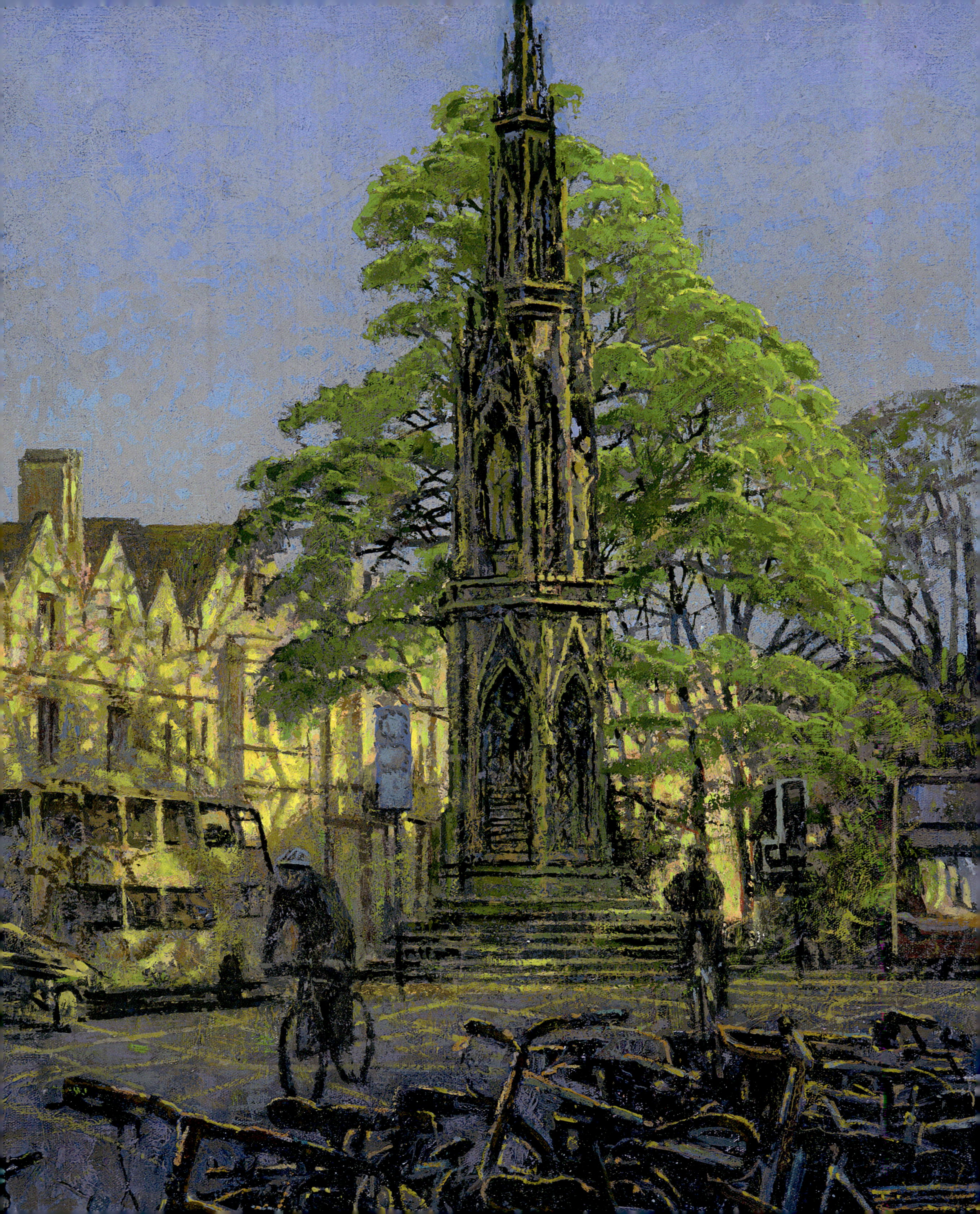

Life in thirteenth-century Oxford is hard and dangerous. The homicide rate exceeds modern-day Bogota. Each year for every hundred monks attending the university (all students must be in religious orders), three are murdered, fifteen die of dysentery, and twenty-six run away to London.

The gates of the town close at dusk.

Walter Raleigh has not yet visited the New World and there are no potatoes or tobacco. The staple foods are bread, porridge and gruel. Meat is expensive and only the rich are assured of a reliable supply. Because of the Eucharist, bread is endowed with particular status and is consumed regularly, incessantly –

With deleterious physical effects and perhaps to the general despond of all:

Menu Prix Fixe

Starter: Bread

Main: Parsimonious cuts of meat with Ample Bread

Dessert: Bread Pudding

The sallow streets of medieval Oxford are riddled with people in varying states of acute and even chronic indigestion, trying to walk off the latest incursion of

Bread

As the first Chancellor of the university, Robert Grosseteste presides over a series of monastic Halls –

Worm Hall

Cat Hall

Bull Hall

Hare Hall Unicorn Hall Woodcock Hall Nightingale Hall Eagle Hall Sparrow Hall Hawk Hall

Ape Hall Beefe Hall Perilous Hall

Kepeharm Hall Aristotle Hall Nun's Hall

Pie Hall

Grosseteste is also known as Grossteste, Grostest, Grostet, Grosthead, Grouthead, Grostede, Greatheade, Grosteheved, Greateheved, Grosehede, Grokede, and Goschede. In this era, spellings are not fixed and the creative possibilities are endless. Yet Grosseteste of the mutable and at times suggestive name has more pressing matters to deal with. He is transfixed by mysteries. *How do we see what we see? How do we know that what we see is real? Is Light a material substance?*

Grosseteste presents an epistemology of light, a metaphysics of light, an etiology of light, and a theology of light. He describes the birth of the universe in an explosion, and a further crystallisation of matter.
All creation emerges from an expanding –
and contracting – sphere of light.

And the Lord said, 'Let there be Light!'

Joanna Kavenna, *A Field Guide to Reality*, 2016

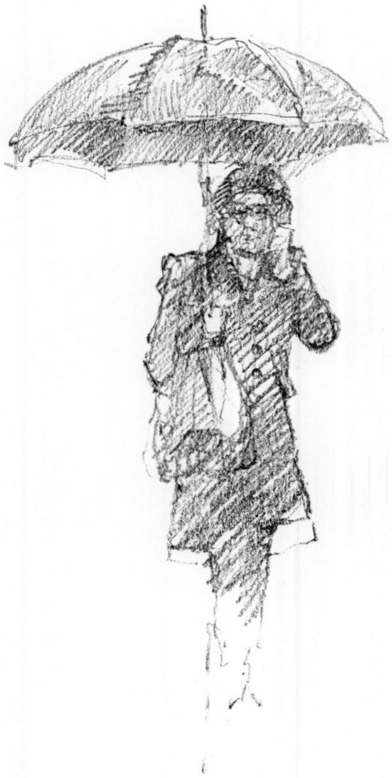

Joanna Kavenna (born 1974), novelist, essayist and travel writer, studied at Linacre College. She was included on Granta's 2013 list of 20 Best Young Writers and has published six books most recently her satirical novel *ZED* about a powerful global media company.

The Martyrs' Memorial
40 x 30 cm, oil on linen, 2024

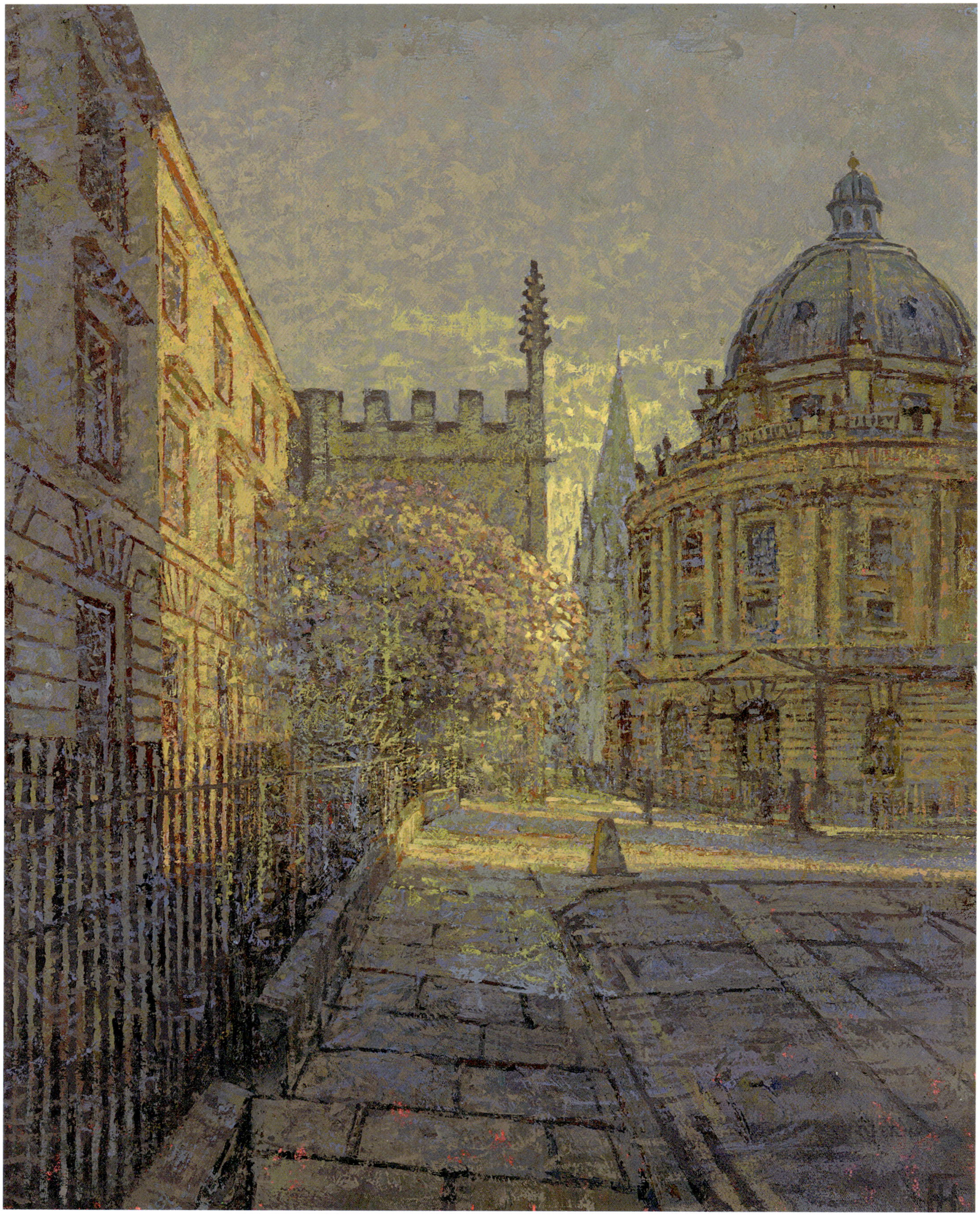

Radcliffe Square

46 x 36 cm, oil on linen, 2024

I heard of a Brasenose Don who wanted to return to College having dined rather too well at All Souls. He reached the Camera – which in those days had no railings – and placed his hand on it for support. He was on his third or fourth revolution before a friend found him in this sorry state and got him home.

Ronald J Caffrey, 2024

As we approach the Bodleian from Catte Street there is nothing to be seen but its noble cube. Advancing we see first the Rotunda, then the spire of St Mary's, then the dome of the Radcliffe coming into view. As this vast circular bulk separates from the Bodleian, the tower of St Mary's also emerges. Despite the fact that each of these three buildings is in its own way as sophisticated a piece of architecture as there is, the experience is elemental beyond the power of words or photographs to describe. Cube, cylinder and cone are suddenly juxtaposed, or rather suddenly deploy, the one from the other with a result that is architecturally speaking sensational.

Thomas Sharp, *Oxford Replanned*, 1948

Ronald J Caffrey (born 1961) read Modern History and Economics at Magdalen College, sometime in the last century. He has had a varied career in investment banking, corporates and education. He presently lives with his wife in Oundle where she teaches Classics and he sells secondhand books.

Thomas Sharp (1901–1978) was an Influential town planner and polemicist whose 1940 work *Town Planning* for Penguin helped shape the discussion for post-war urban planning. His *Oxford Replanned* (commissioned by Oxford Council) was something of a curate's egg and not implemented – mercifully so in the case of the proposed bypass through Christ Church Meadow, an idea which wasn't killed off until the 1970s.

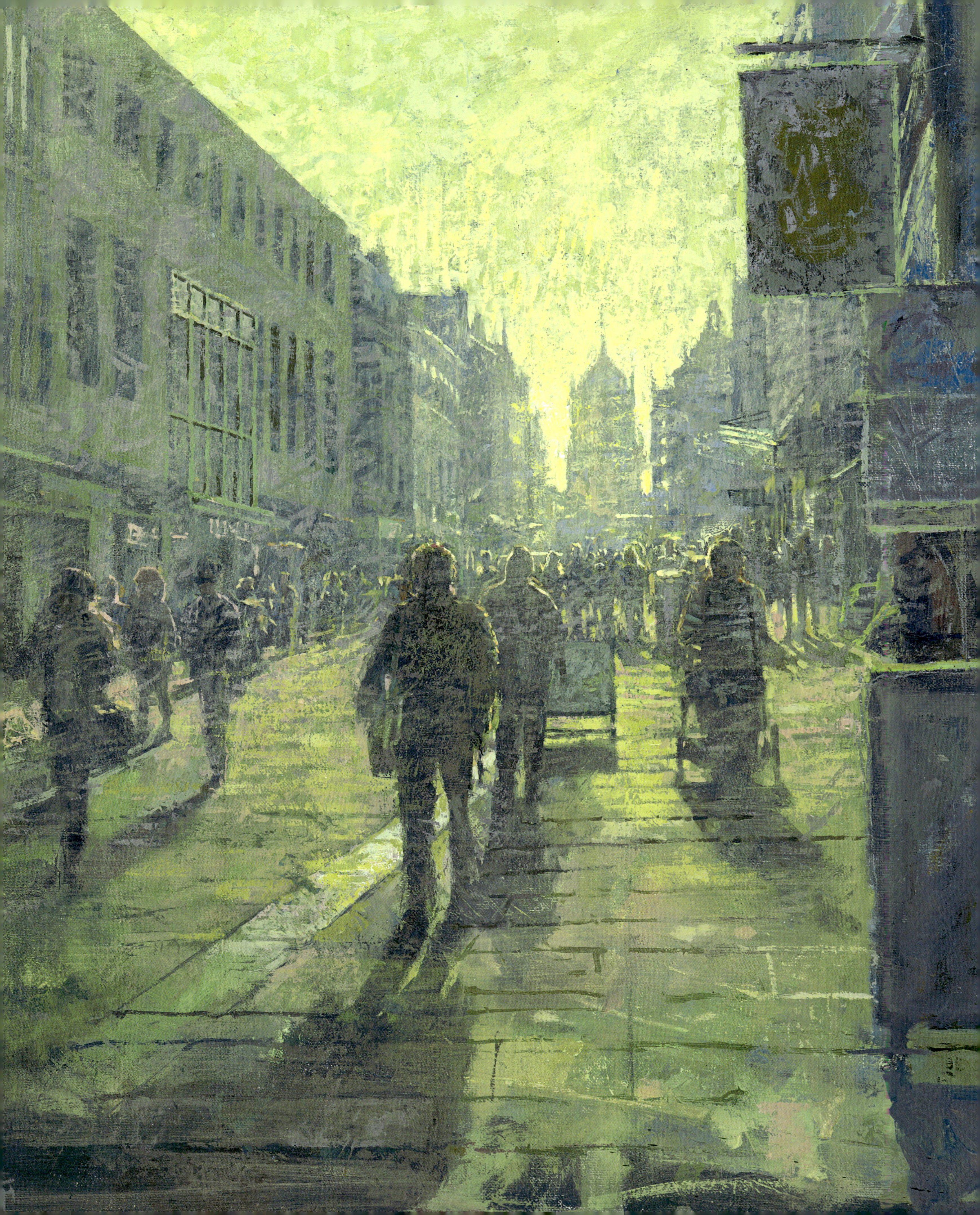

Many shops have closed and from their gutted interiors
Covid testing centres have sprung. I take my phone to
Javed at Only Connect on the Cornmarket for repair.
He also deals in vape supplies and tourist merchandise.
Rows of plastic Elvises rotate their hips gently, a shelf of
Queen Elizabeth IIs sway and wave their white-gloved
hands. While Javed melts the back off my phone, I
browse the vape flavours: mint, strawberry, pure.
A tourist from Birmingham drifts in:
'Do you have any tea towels?'
Javed waves dismissively to the Harry and Meghan
Wedding Commemorative items beside the till.
'Is that all?' she says.
'Yes,' he says 'No one buys tea towels now'.

Nancy Campbell, *Thunderstone,* 2022

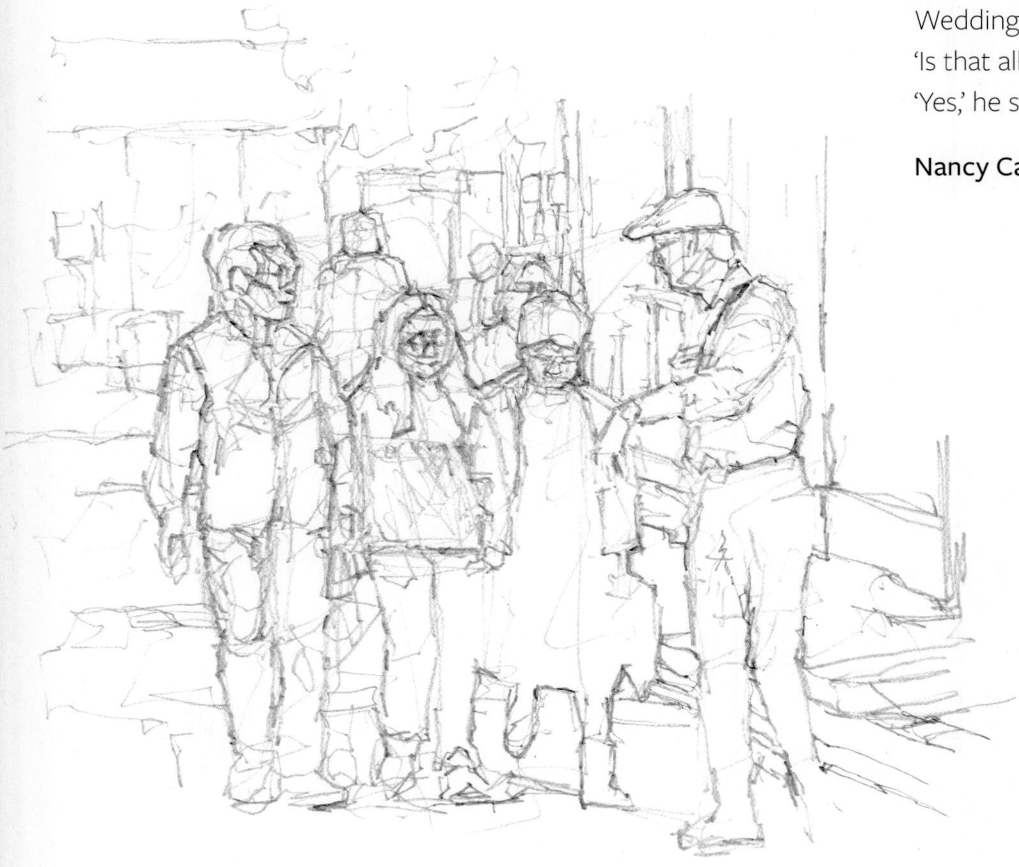

Cornmarket Street
56 x 46 cm, oil on linen, 2024

Nancy Campbell (born 1978) read English at Lady Margaret Hall. Poet, non-fiction writer and maker of fine press books.

Harriet Vane sat at her writing-table and stared out into Mecklenburg Square. The late tulips made a brave show in the square garden, and a quartet of early tennis-players were energetically calling the score of a rather erratic and unpractised game. But Harriet saw neither tulips nor tennis-players. A letter lay open on the blotting-pad before her, but its image had faded from her mind to make way for another picture. She saw a stone quadrangle, built by a modern architect in a style neither new nor old, but stretching out reconciling hands to past and present. Folded within its walls lay a trim grass plot, with flower-beds splashed at the angles, and surrounded by a wide stone plinth. Behind the level roofs of Cotswold slate rose the brick chimneys of an older and less formal pile of buildings – a quadrangle also of a kind, but still keeping a domestic remembrance of the original Victorian dwelling-houses that had sheltered the first shy students of Shrewsbury College. In front were the trees of Jowett Walk and, beyond them, a jumble of ancient gables and the tower of New College, with its jackdaws wheeling against a windy sky.

Memory peopled the quad with moving figures. Students sauntering in pairs. Students dashing to lectures, their gowns hitched hurriedly over light summer frocks, the wind jerking their flat caps into the absurd likeness of so many jesters' cockscombs. Bicycles stacked in the porter's lodge, their carriers piled with books and gowns twisted about their handlebars. A grizzled woman don crossing the turf with vague eyes, her thoughts riveted upon aspects of sixteenth-century philosophy, her sleeves floating, her shoulders cocked to the academic angle that automatically compensated the backward drag of the pleated poplin. Two male commoners in search of a coach, bareheaded, hands in their trousers-pockets, talking loudly about boats. The Warden – grey and stately – and the Dean – stocky, brisk, bird-like, a Lesser Redpoll – in animated conference under the archway leading to the Old Quadrangle. Tall spikes of delphinium against the grey, quiveringly blue-like flames, if flame were ever so blue. The college cat, preoccupied and remote, stalking with tail erect in the direction of the buttery.

It was all so long ago; so closely encompassed and complete; so cut off as by swords from the bitter years that lay between. Could one face it now?

Dorothy L. Sayers, *Gaudy Night*, 1935

Dorothy Leigh Sayers (1893–1957) read Modern Foreign Languages at Somerville College. She was a novelist, playwright, translator, advertising creative and critic. One of the four "Queens of the Detective Novel", the Lord Peter Wimsey and Harriet Vane relationship featured in her Wimsey novels are decidedly modern. Her play about Jesus for the BBC provoked great controversy with Sayers being blamed for the Fall of Singapore. Her translations of Dante's *Divine Comedy* and the *Chanson de Roland* remain in print as Penguin Classics. She was in the first batch of women to take their degrees in 1920 when the University admitted women.

Magdalen in Winter
46 x 36 cm, oil on linen, 2024

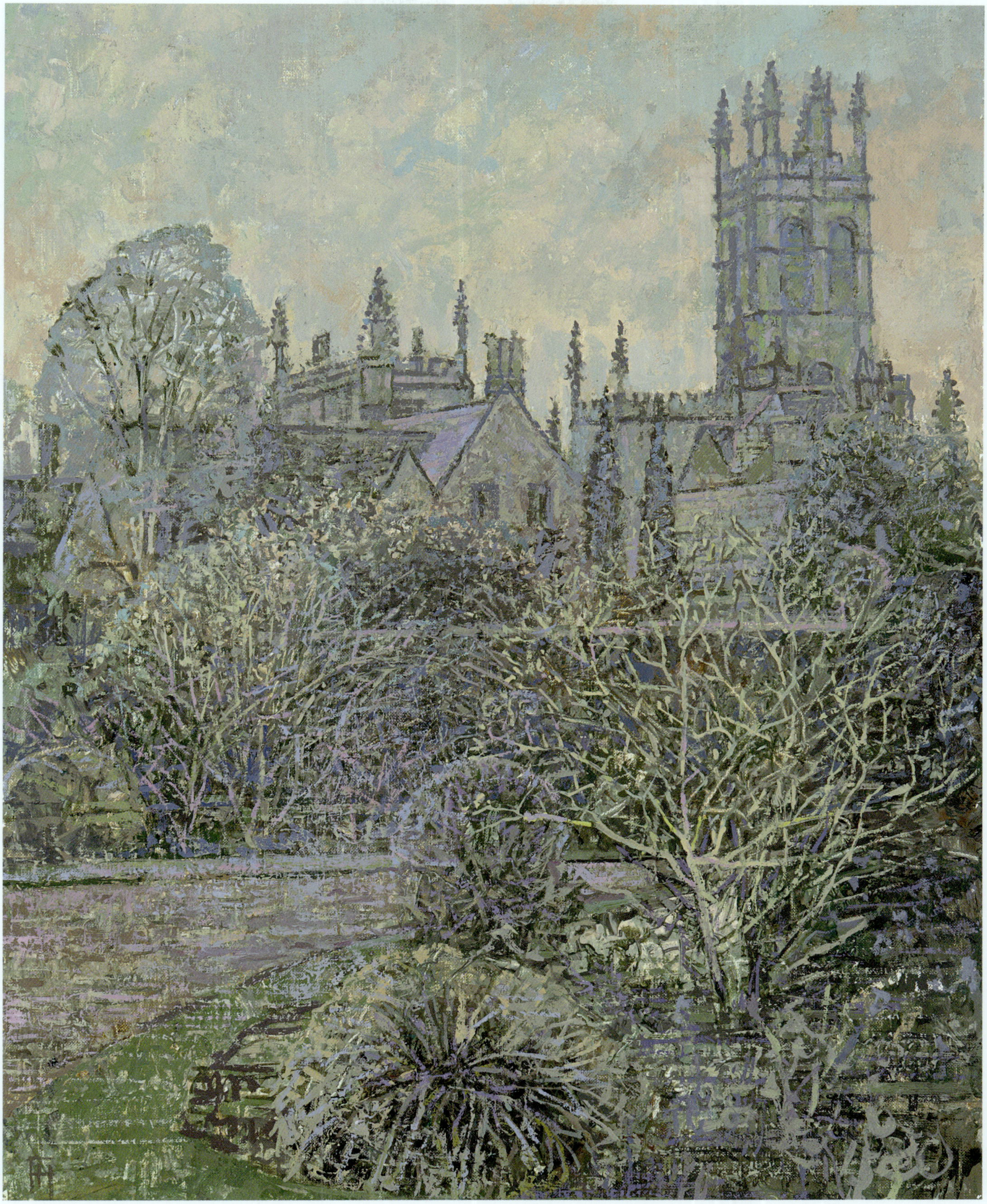

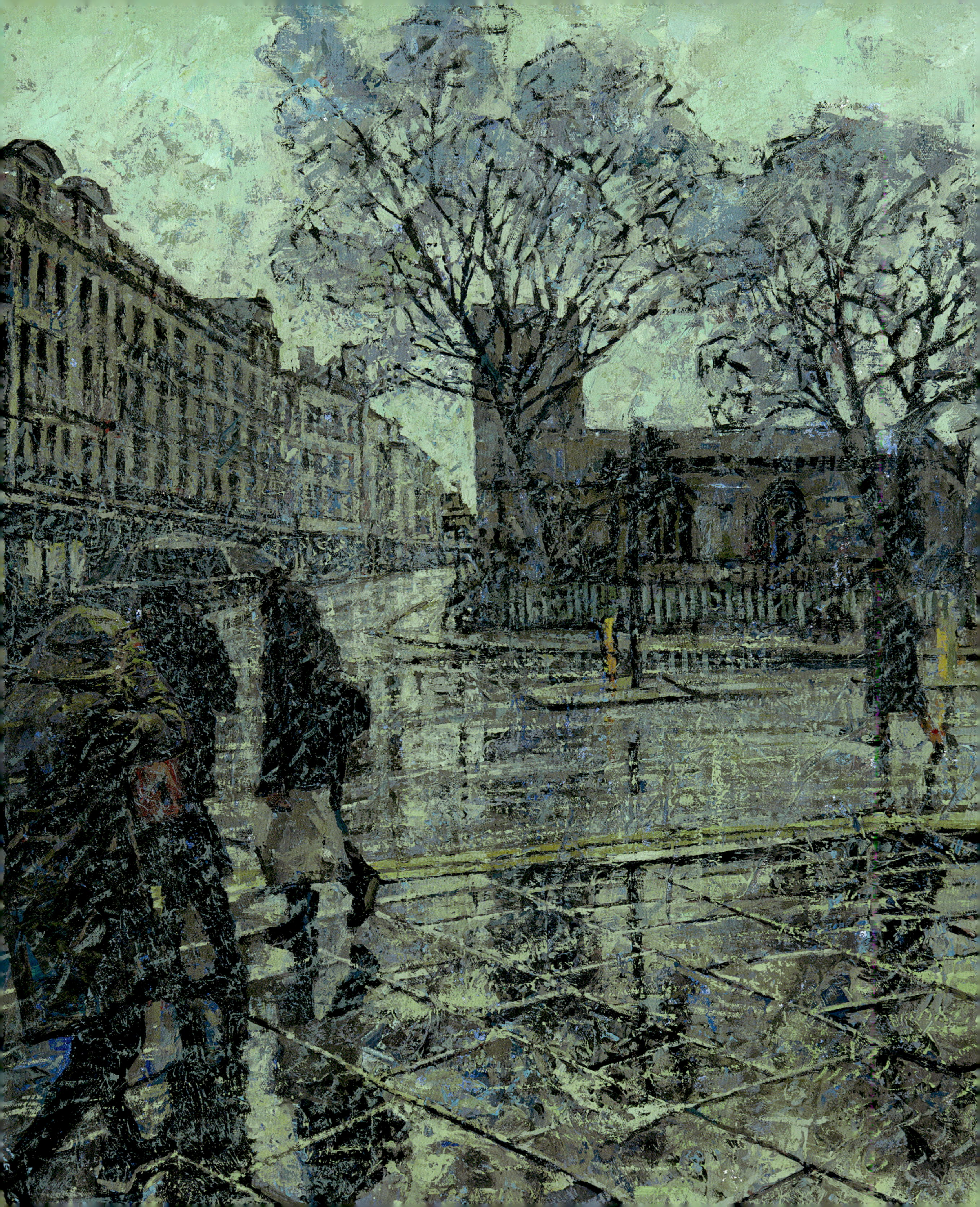

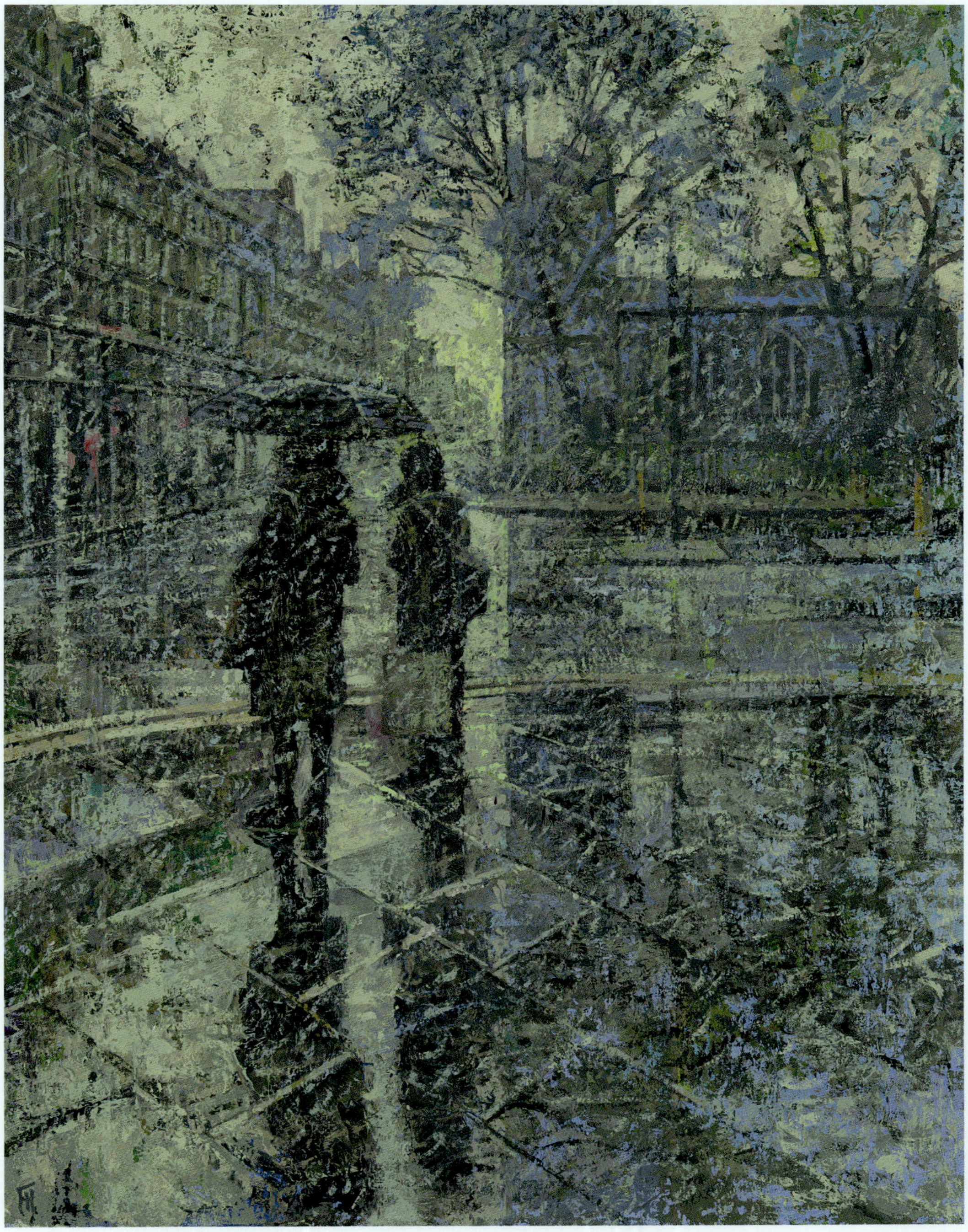

St Mary Magdalen from Broad Street
46 x 36 cm, oil on linen, 2024

Rain in Broad Street
46 x 36 cm, oil on linen, 2024

Beyond the canal, and a few warehouses, he could make out the Venetian water-tower of that church where Pamela was so fond of going. It was, from where he stood, the most impressive architectural monument in sight. A row of scruffy Edwardian shops; a lumpy hotel insultingly aping a classical manner; a railway bridge; the most hideous of office blocks, a cube of black glass: these were the campanile's only rivals for the eye's attention. The delicacy of pinnacles and spires, the grandeur of domes, the ingenuity of buttresses, the proportions of quadrangles, now intimate, now superb, for which the town was more noted in the imagination of travellers, were kept sensibly hidden from view.

A.N. Wilson, *The Healing Art,* 1980

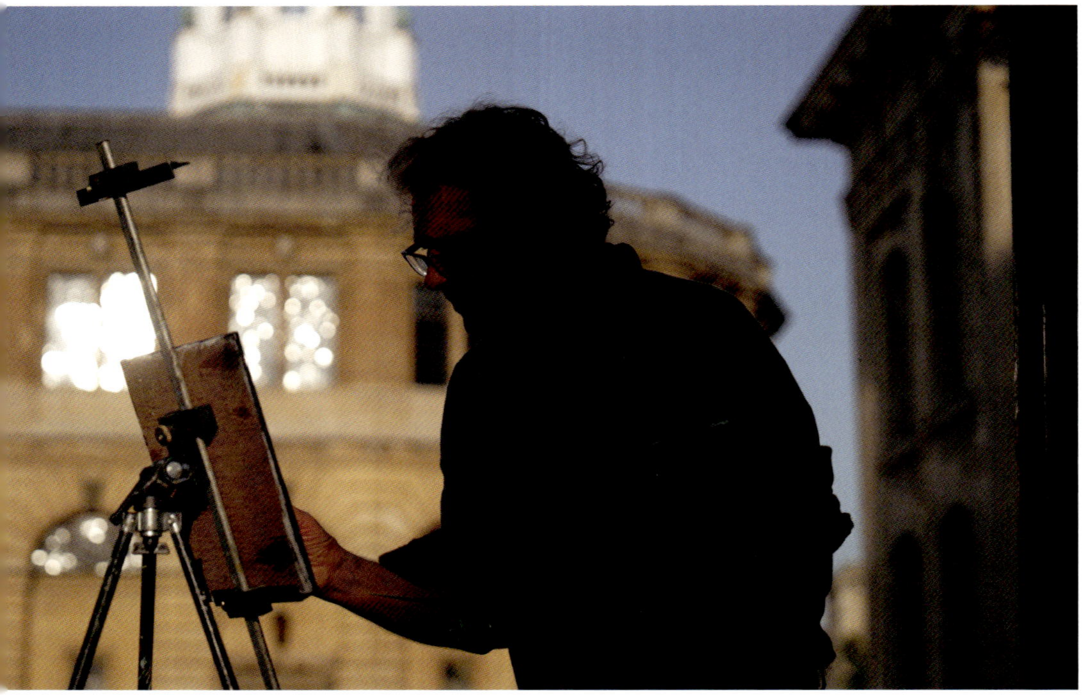

Exeter College and the Clarendon Building in Evening Sun (detail)
oil on panel, 2003

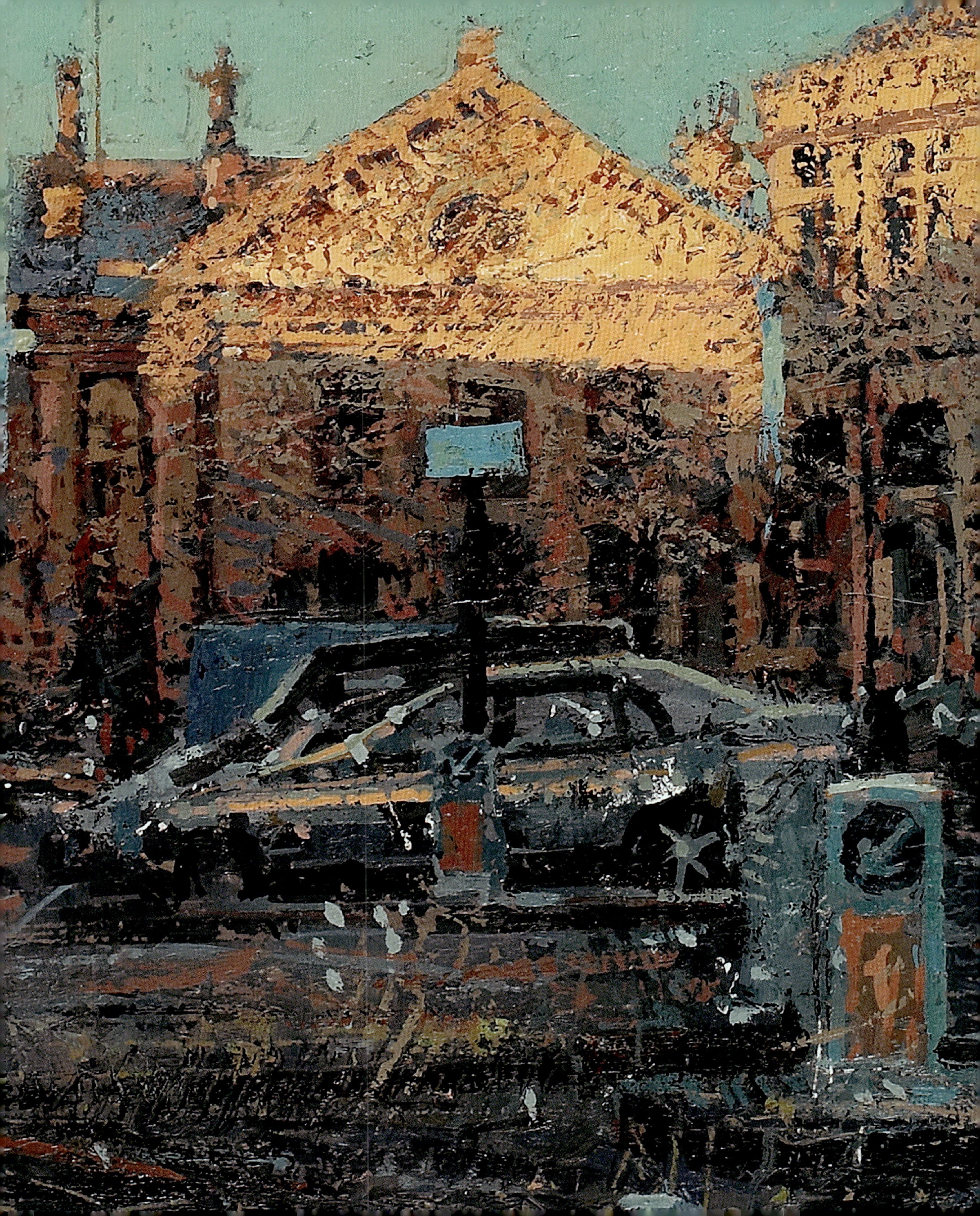

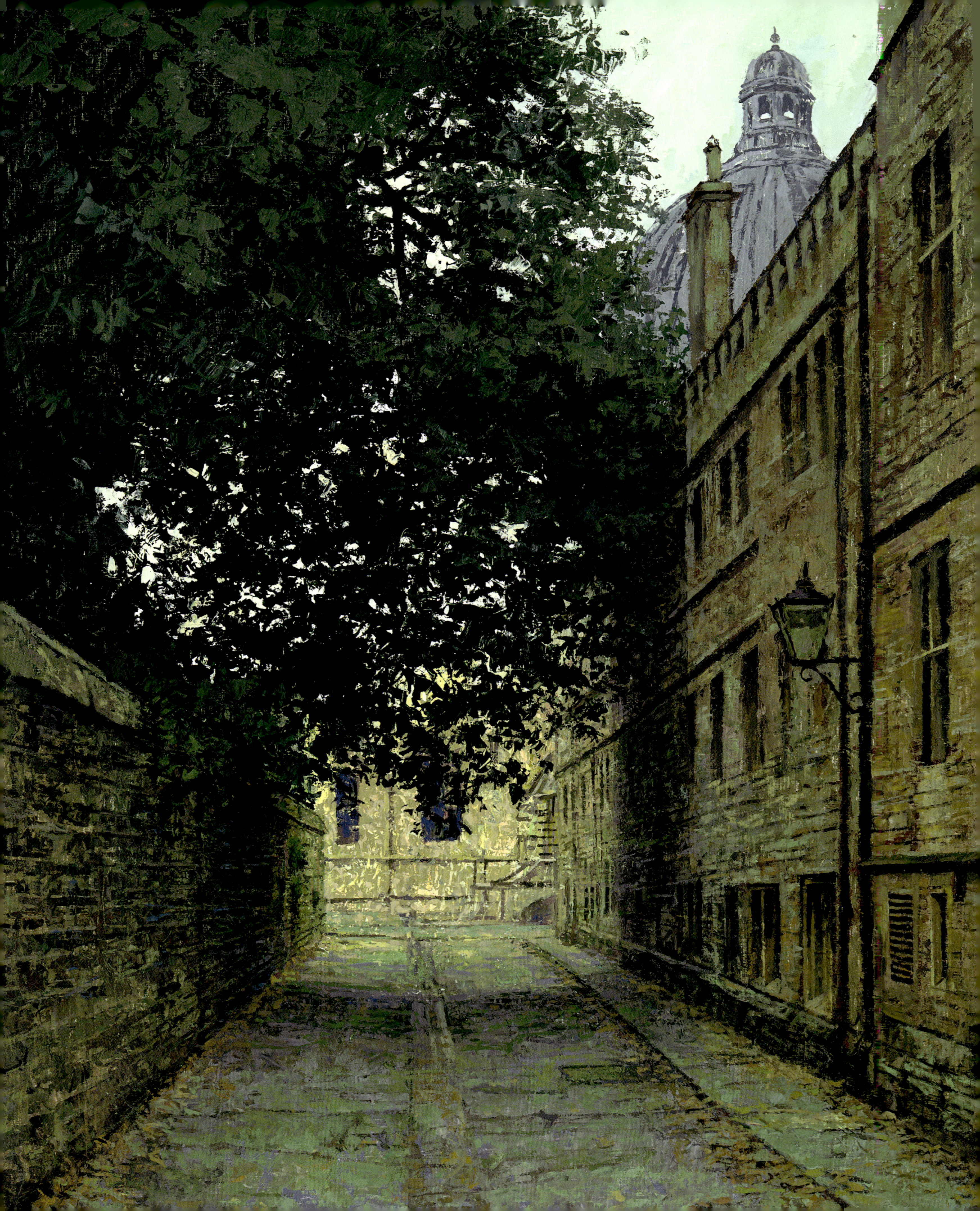

Jordan College was the grandest and richest of all the colleges in Oxford. It was probably the largest, too, though no one knew for certain. The buildings, which were grouped around three irregular quadrangles, dated from every period from the early Middle Ages to the mid eighteenth-century. It had never been planned; it had grown piecemeal, with past and present over-lapping at every spot, and the final effect was one of jumbled and squalid grandeur. Some part was always about to fall down, and for five generations the same family, the Parslows, had been employed full-time by the College as masons and scaffolders. The present Mr Parslow was teaching his son the craft; the two of them and their three workmen would scramble like industrious termites over the scaffolding they'd erected at the corner of the library, or over the roof of the Chapel and haul up bright new blocks of stone or rolls of shiny lead or baulks of timber.

The College owned farms and estates all over Brytain. It was said that you could walk from Oxford to Bristol in one direction and to London in the other and never leave Jordan land. In every part of the Kingdom there were dye-works and brick-kilns, forests and atomcraft-works that paid rent to Jordan and every Quarter-Day the Bursar and his clerks would tot it all up, announce the total to Concilium and order a pair of swans for the Feast. Some of the money was put by for re-investment – Concilium had just approved the purchase of an office-block in Manchester – and the rest was used to pay the Scholars' modest stipends and the wages of the servants (and the Parslows, and the other dozen or so families of craftsmen and traders who served the College), to keep the wine-cellar richly filled, to buy books and anbarographs for the immense Library that filled one side of the Melrose Quadrangle and extended, burrow-like, for several floors beneath the ground; and, not least, to buy the latest philosophical apparatus to equip the Chapel...

Philip Pullman, *Northern Lights*, 1995

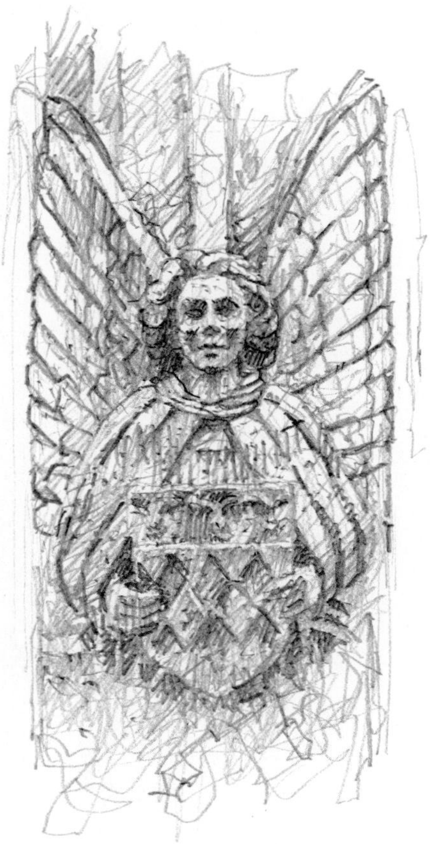

Brasenose Lane
122 x 90 cm, oil on linen, 2024

Philip Nicholas Outram Pullman (born 1946) read English at Exeter College. He counts himself lucky he got a third as fourth class degrees were only abandoned the previous year. As well as the *His Dark Materials* novels, other works include the *Sally Lockhart* and the *Book of Dust* series. In 2009 Pullman was honoured at *Encaenia* with a Doctor of Letters Honorary Degree.

Passing rapidly through London, with its roar of causes that have been won, and the suburbs, where they have no causes, and skirting the willowy Thames, glassy or silver, or with engrailed grey waves and brown ploughlands, elm-guarded, solitary, I approached Oxford. Nuneham woods made one great shadow on the land, one great shadow on the Thames. According to an old custom, it rained. But rain takes away nothing from Oxford save a few nice foot passengers. It transmutes the Franciscan habit of the city to a more Dominican cast; and if the foil of sky be faintly lighted, the rain becomes a visible beatitude.

One by one the churches of St Mary the Virgin and All Saints', and the pleasant spire of the Cathedral, appear; with the dome of the Radcliffe Camera, Tom Tower of Christ Church, and that old bucolic tower of Robert d'Oigli's castle on the west. For a minute several haystacks, a gasometer, and the engine smoke replace them. But already that one cameo from February's hand has painted and lit and garnished again that city within the heart, which is Oxford. I think, when I see an old woodcut of a patron holding his towered foundation in his hand, about to bestow it as a gift, as William of Wykeham is depicted, holding Winchester, that even so Oxford gives to us the stones of church and college, the lawns and shrubs of gardens, and the waters of Isis, to be stored in the chambers of the soul – "Mother of Arts!"....

But the dark entry to the city, on the western side, suddenly changed my thoughts. It is well known. It is the most contemptible in Europe. It consists of a hoarding, a brewery, and suitable appurtenances.... On the north and east the approach is not worse, consisting, as it does, of sermons in brick, arranged in perfect successful imitation of Tooting.

Edward Thomas, *Oxford,* 1903

The Turl in the Rain
51 x 38 cm, oil on panel, 2012

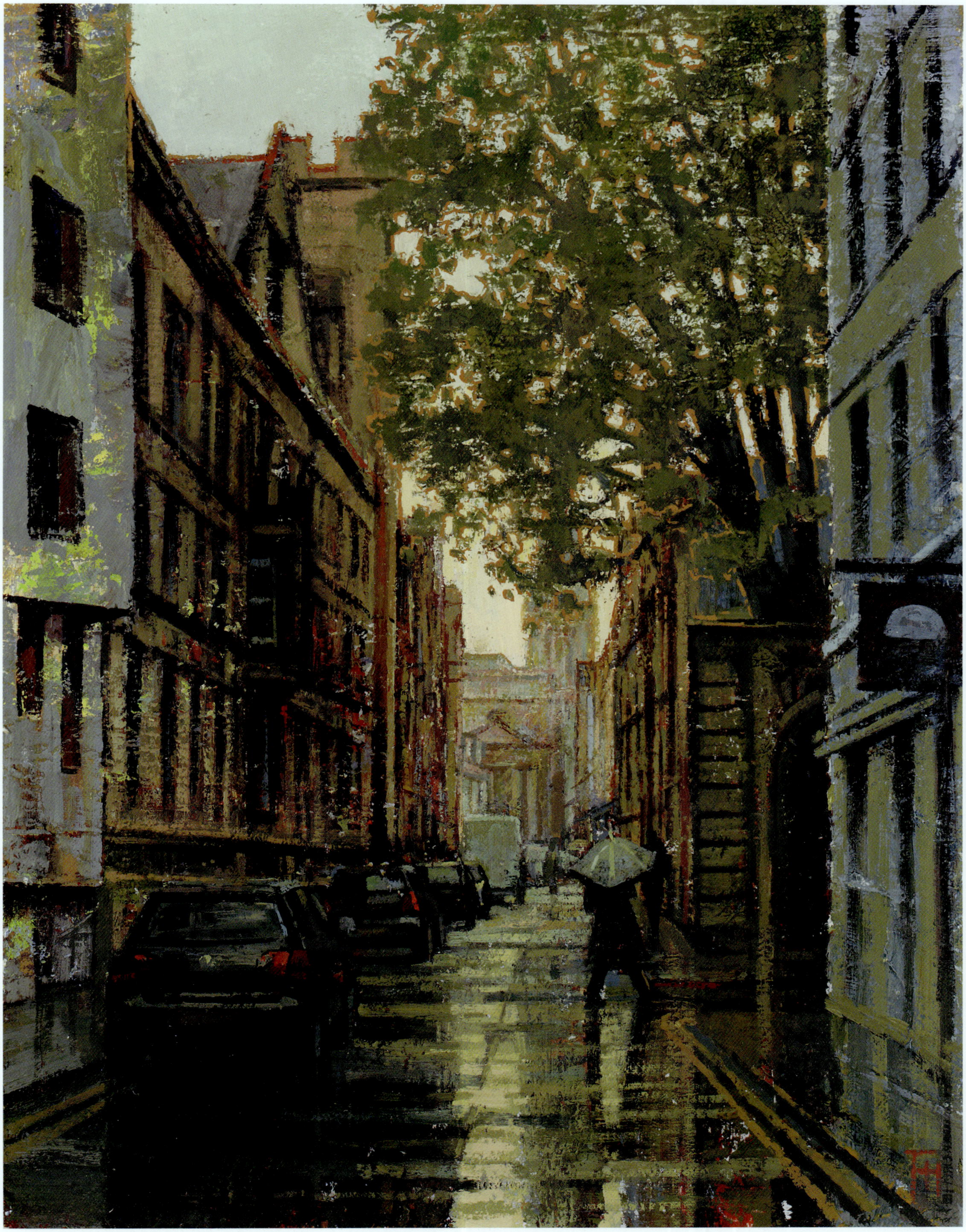

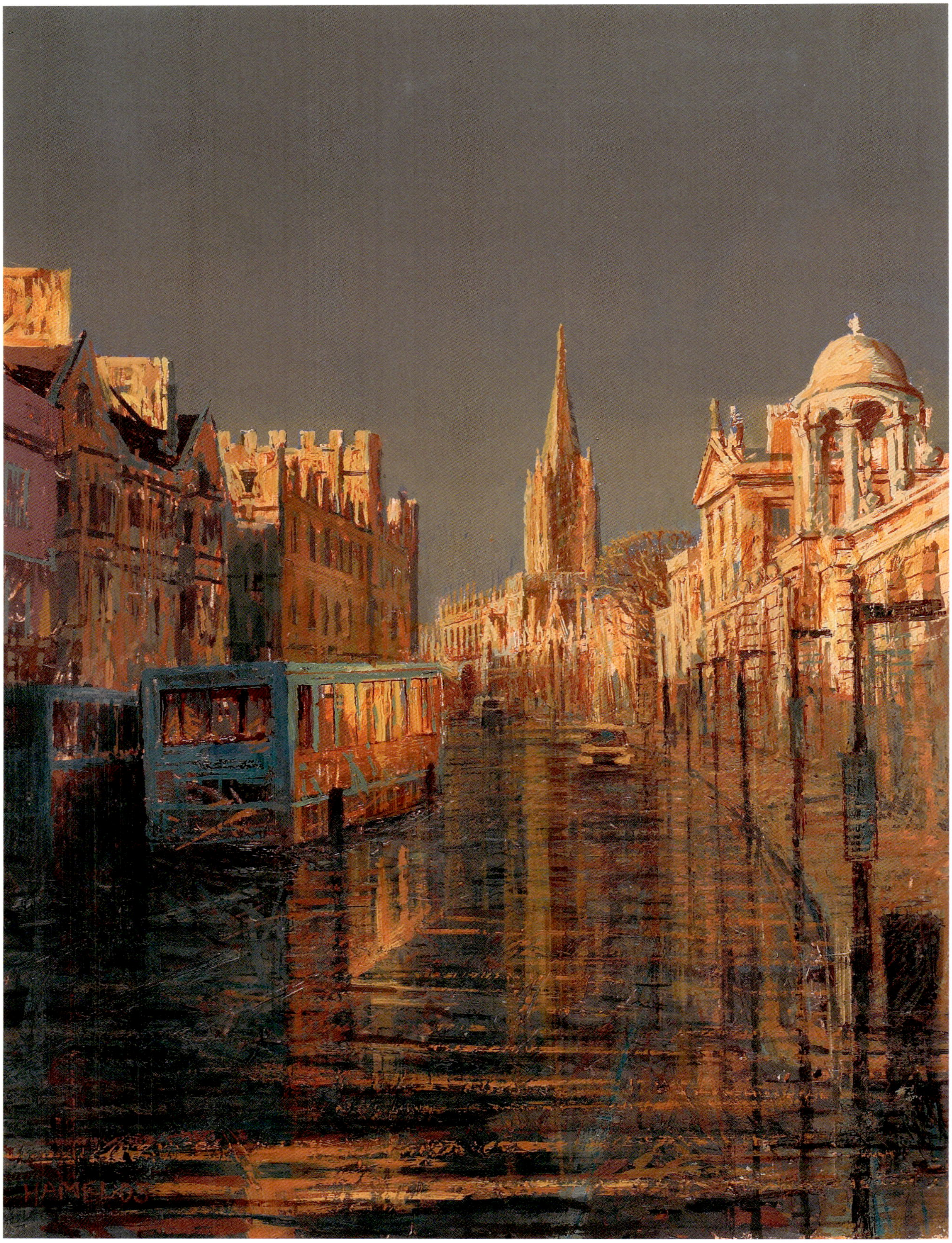

Ye sacred Nurseries of blooming Youth!
In whose collegiate shelter England's Flowers
Expand, enjoying through their vernal hours
The air of liberty, the light of truth;
Much have ye suffered from Time's gnawing tooth:
Yet, O ye spires of Oxford! domes and towers!
Gardens and groves! your presence overpowers
The soberness of reason; till, in sooth,
Transformed, and rushing on a bold exchange
I slight my own beloved Cam, to range
Where silver Isis leads my stripling feet;
Pace the long avenue, or glide adown
The stream-like windings of that glorious street –
An eager Novice robed in Fluttering gown!

William Wordsworth, *Oxford*, 1820

University College and The Queen's College with Rain, The High Street
50 x 38 cm, oil on panel, 2002

William Wordsworth (1770–1850) a graduate of Cambridge University, along with Samuel Taylor Coleridge, he introduced Romanticism into British literature with *Lyrical Ballads* in 1798. *The Prelude*, now considered his major work, was published in the year of his death and made little impact at the time. Wordsworth was Poet Laureate and is the only person to have held the post without writing a single line of official verse.

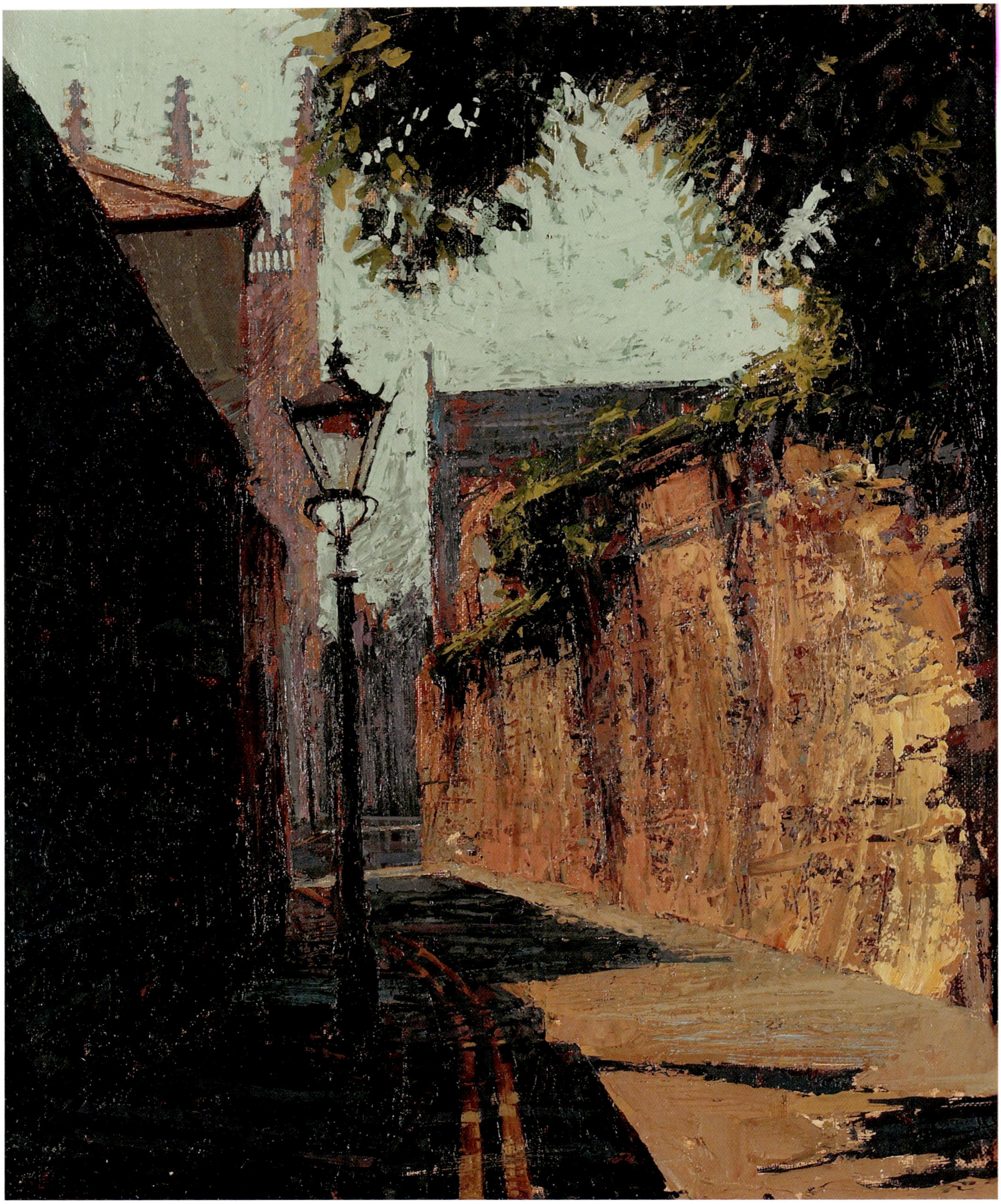

To the university of Oxford I acknowledge no obligation, and she will as cheerfully renounce me for a son, as I am willing to disclaim her for a mother.

Edward Gibbon, 1792

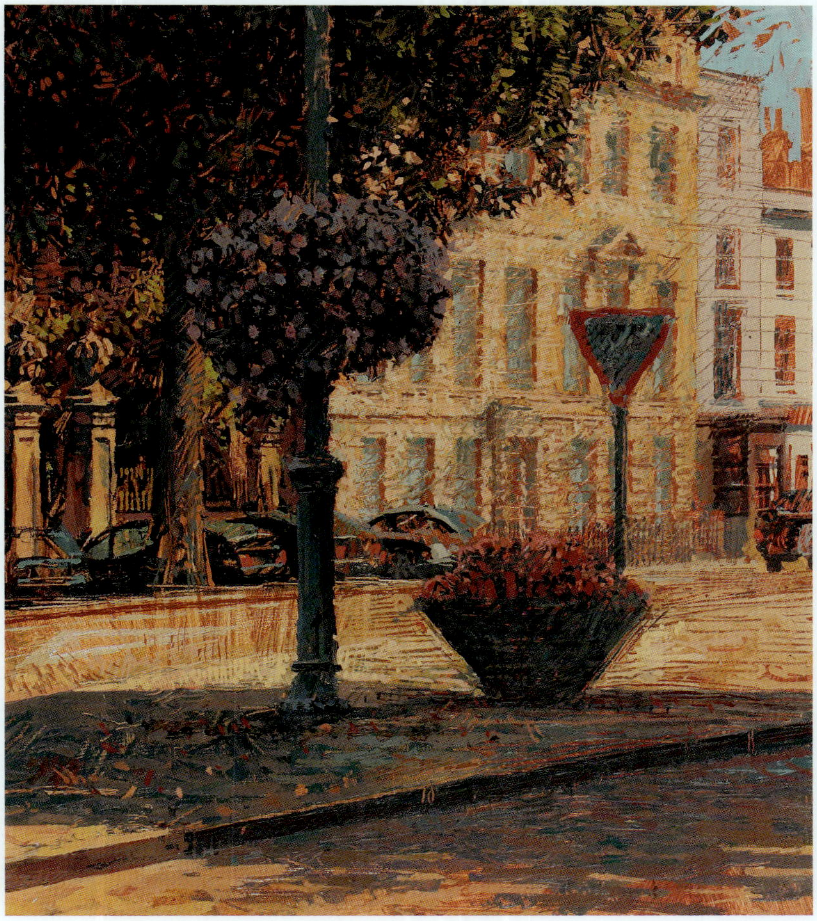

Magpie Lane Looking towards Merton Chapel
38 x 30.5 cm, oil on panel, 2003

St Giles' in Summer with Petunias
32 x 27 cm, oil on panel, 2002

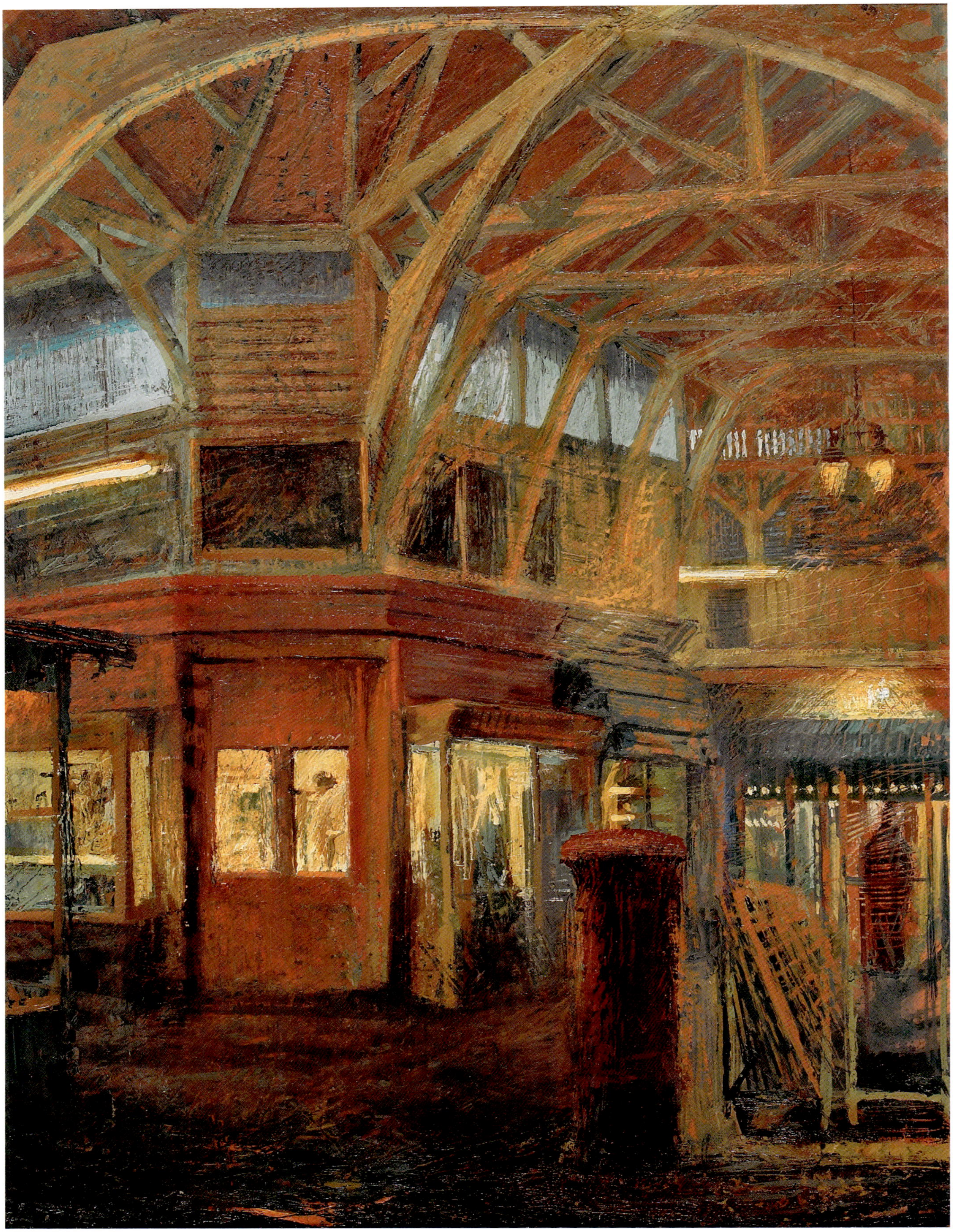

One of the greatest English carols has its origins in an incident when a student of The Queen's College was attacked by a boar on Shotover Hill. The quick-thinking student deployed his weapon of defence – apparently a thick volume of Aristotle (we're not told which particular work) – and stuffed it into the jaws of the attacking boar while crying out "*Graecum Est*".

This incident is remembered by a feast where a boar's head is brought into the hall and a carol sung:

Hey, hey, hey, hey, the borrys hede is army'd gaye;

The borrys hede in hond I brynge,

The borys hede ye furst mes.

The borys hede, as I yow say,

He takes his leyfe and gothe his way,

Gone after ye xij tweyl ffyt day, With hey.

The Boar's Head

The Covered Market
50 x 38 cm, oil on panel, 2002

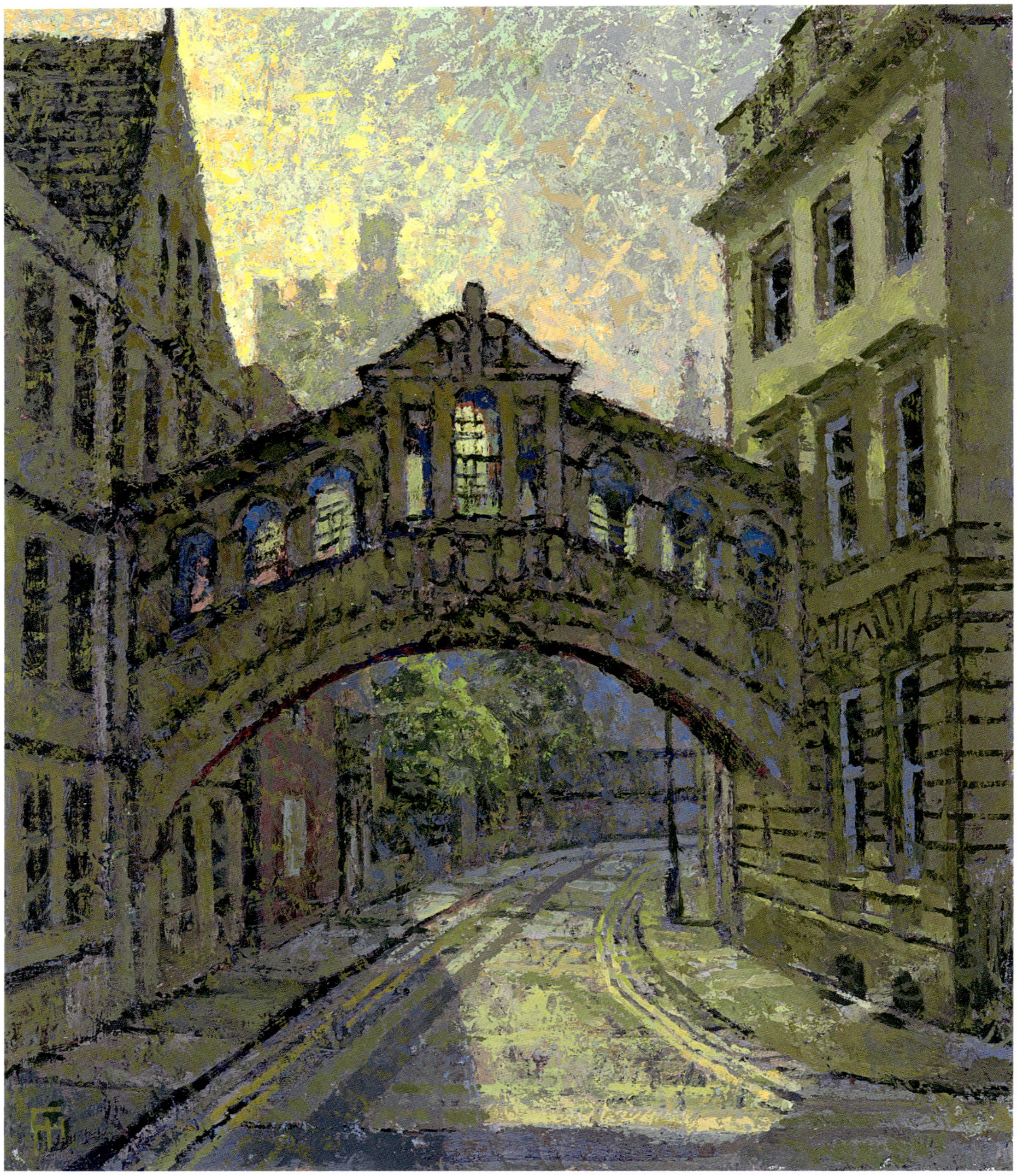

The Bridge of Sighs, Hertford College
30 x 25 cm, oil on linen, 2024

The Radcliffe Camera from St Mary's Passage
26 x 22 cm, oil on linen, 2024

Here on either side of the boulevards planted with chestnuts, is some of the most remarkable domestic architecture in Europe. Towering yellow brick piles, embellished with purbeck shafts and freestone copings, house the theological colleges... In a quarter of an hour's walk the student can observe examples of almost every kind of gothic window: Angevin, Venetian, Spanish and more. Square and saddleback towers abound. Further up, there are red-brick mansions, several which claim Ruskin as their architect, and show each some notable feature, such as a carved pediment to a porch, or a lavish display of dog-tooth ornament.

Robert Liddell, *The Last Enchantments,* 1948

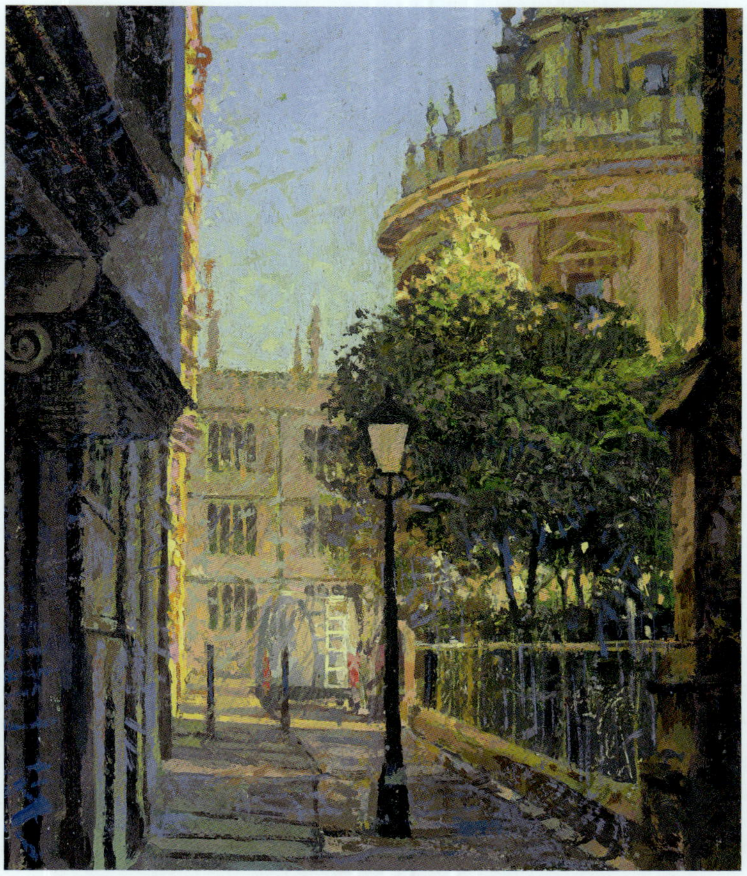

Robert Liddell (1908–1992) was a novelist, poet, travel writer, literary critic and academic, he read Classics at Corpus Christi College. After a period working at the Bodleian, he worked for the British Council, taught at Cairo and Alexandria Universities and then lead the English Department at Athens University. Liddell was friends with Barbara Pym, Constantine Cavafy, Ivy Compton Burnett, Olivia Manning and Elizabeth Taylor, all of whom feature in his works. Patrick White described Liddell as "one of those novelists who sit quietly writing classics over a lifetime."

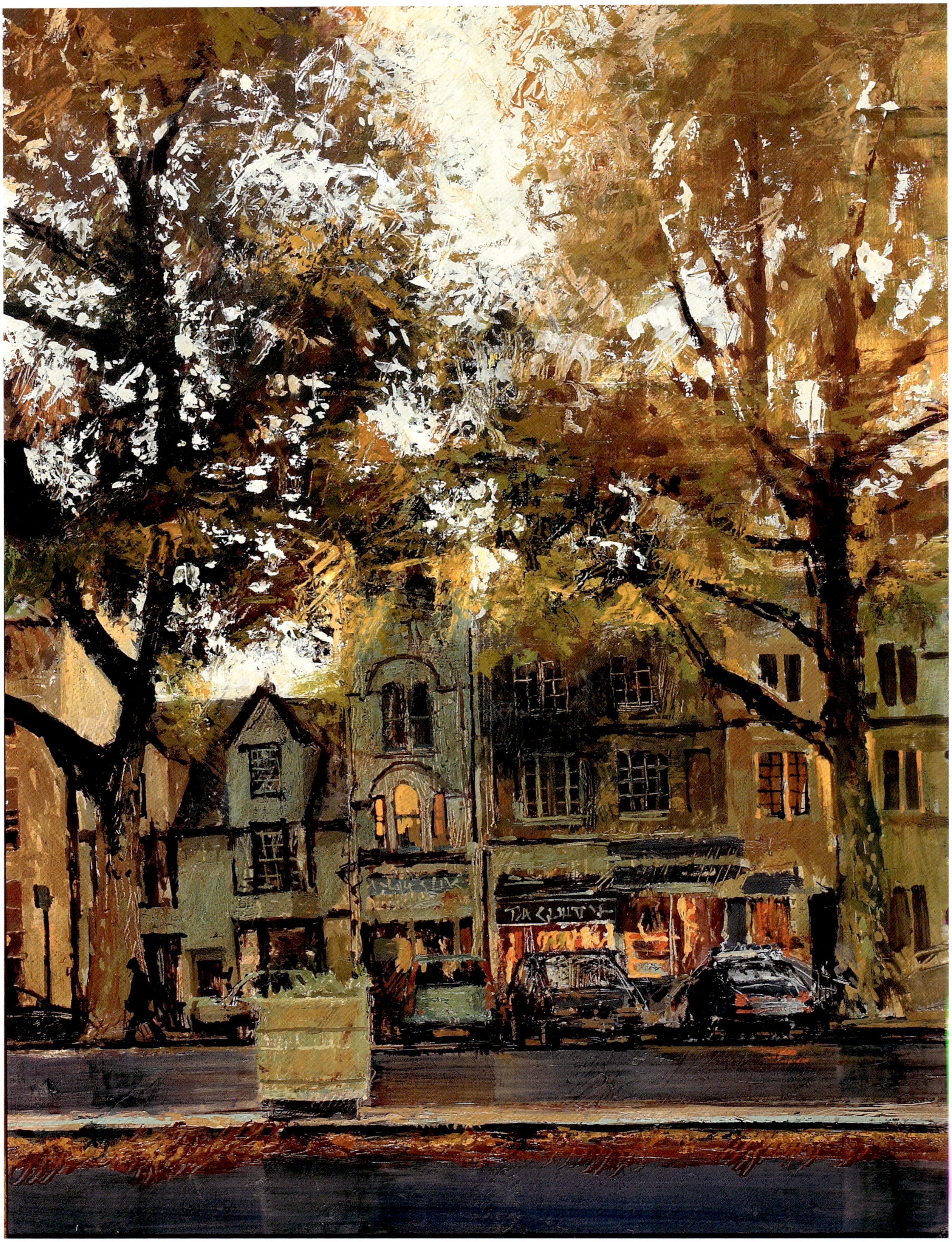

It's at this time of year, after the clocks have gone back, and the evenings draw closer, that I like to don my coat and scarf and set off for a night walk around the streets of old Oxford. Once the day trippers have gone, the students are safely ensconced in their college rooms and the kebab vans have shut up shop, I can often find myself on my own, the velvety darkness shot through with shafts of muted streetlight. When the moon is full, or the turrets and towers are swathed in mist it is especially atmospheric. But for me whatever the conditions, to saunter at night through the cobbled squares and streets, down the ancient alleyways, past the aged walls of the medieval buildings will always remain mysterious and beautiful.

It is on these walks that I find it not at all surprising that so many writers of fantasy fiction have come from within the city. As Philip Pullman, for whom Oxford stands as a central character in *His Dark Materials* trilogy, once wrote, "I put it down to the mists from the river which have a kind of solvent effect on reality. A city.... where the Magdalen gargoyles climb down at night and fight with those from New College or catch a fish under a bridge is a place where likelihood evaporates. A place where past and present jostle each other on the pavement."

Most certainly. It is not hard to imagine those bearded philosopher heads outside the Sheldonian in heated discussions after the witching hour, or the playful grotesques laughing as you turn your back. They and the hundreds of other stone statues, muses, virtues, kings, queens and beasts of all incarnations, whose gaze follows you everywhere, peering down from on high and from every corner. Curious but harmless spirits having fun while most slumber. I am after all just another nighttime wanderer come to bathe in their thousand-year-old history.

Occasionally I will spot a late-night reveller bottle still in hand, swaying back to their lodgings with the inbuilt wiring of a homing pigeon; an intimate couple oblivious to everything and promising themselves to each other, at least until the following morning; I once spied a bunch of rowdy drinkers all dressed as Father Christmas heading into Queens College in the early hours. And this year there are the Deliveroo drivers bombing through the backstreets on bikes to unburden themselves of somebody's midnight feast. But generally, it's still just me; me and the ghosts of Oxford town.
And I like it that way.

Arabella Warner, *Street Life: A Night Walk in Old Oxford*, November 2024

St Giles' at Dusk
51 x 37 cm, oil on panel, 2002

Arabella Warner (born 1958) lives in the centre of Oxford and writes her weekly blog *The Oxford Sausage*, a spicy mix of Oxford stories from a house once belonging to a city sausage maker.

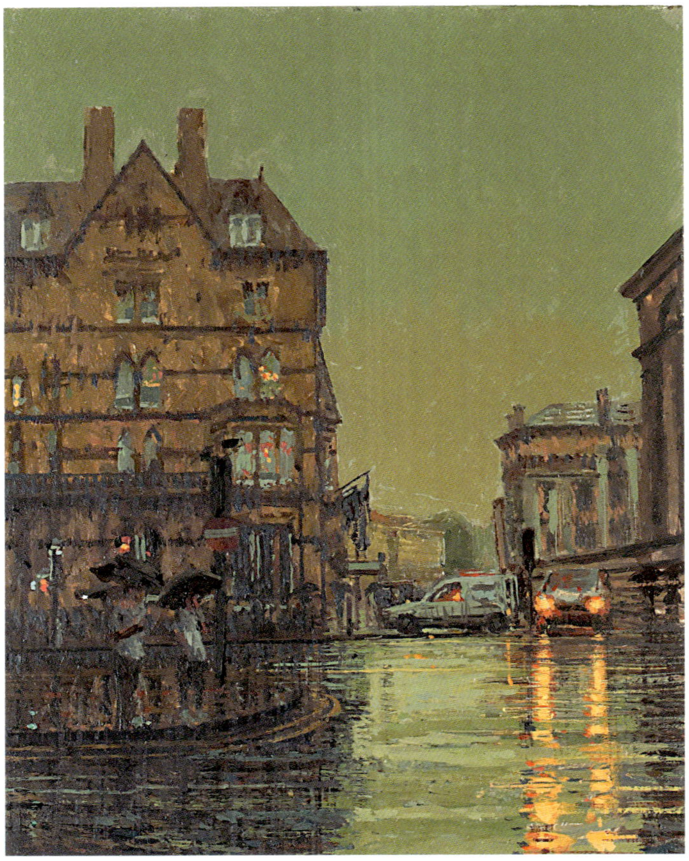

Thomas, Lord Fairfax of Cameron, Lord Generall of the Parliament armie. When Oxford was surrendred, the first thing General Fairfax did was to sett a good guard of soldiers to preserve the Bodleian Library. "Tis said there was more hurt donne by the Cavaliers (during their garrison), by way of embezilling and cutting off chaines of bookes, then there was since. He was a lover of learning, and had he not taken this speciall care, that noble library had been utterly destroyed, for there were ignorant senators enough who would have been contented to have had it so.

The Scandal and Credulities of John Aubrey,
London, 1931

The Randolph in the Rain
45 x 35 cm, oil on panel, 2014

Broad Street in the Rain
31 x 23 cm, oil on panel, 2012

John Aubrey (1626–1697), antiquary, natural philosopher and early archaeologist, he studied at Trinity College, but did not complete his degree due to the disruptions caused by the Civil War. He recorded neolithic sites most notably Avebury and Stonehenge and began, but mostly failed, to complete a range of books on local history, place names and folklore. His *Brief Lives* is a catalogue of the lives and peccadilloes of the great and the good of his time.

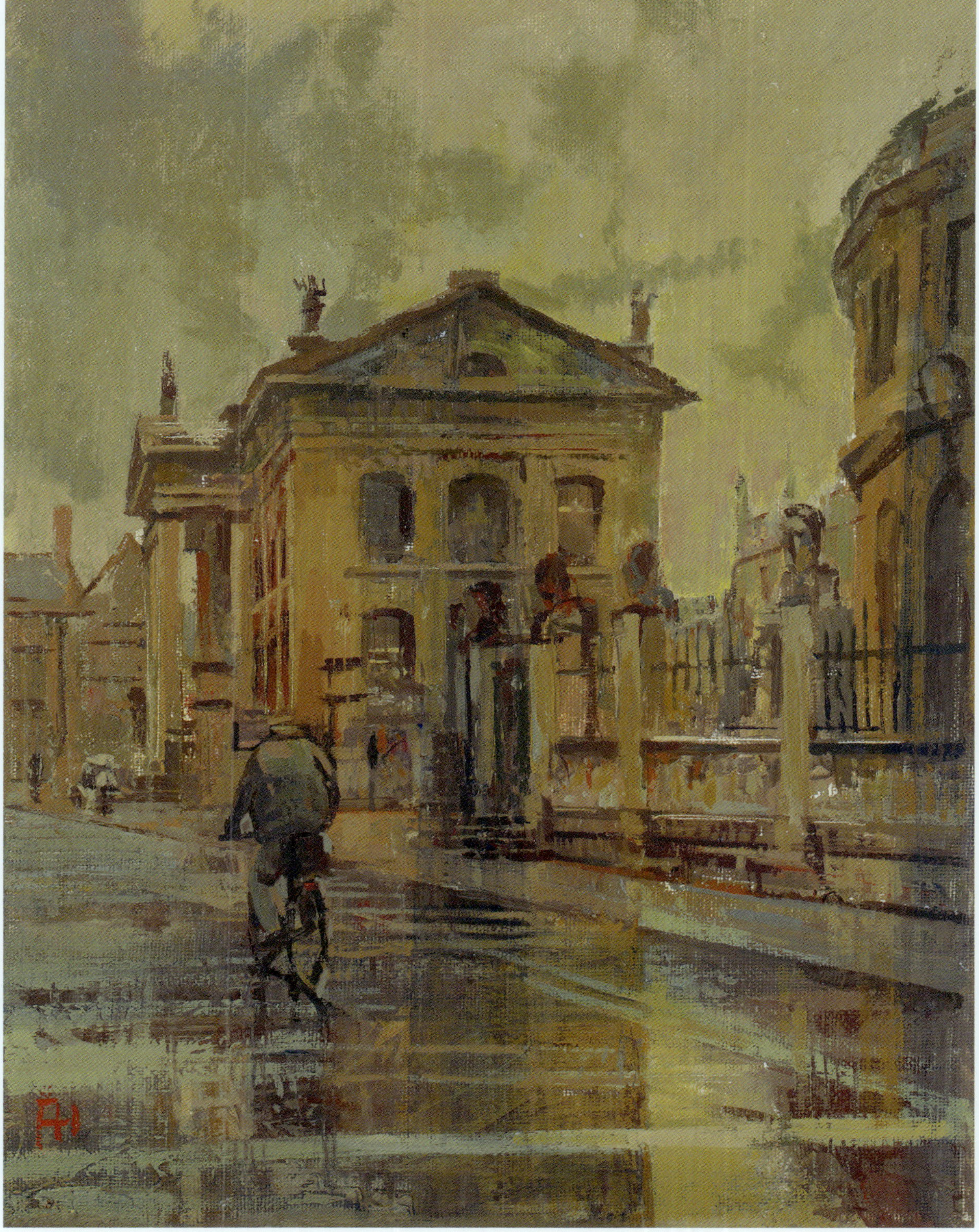

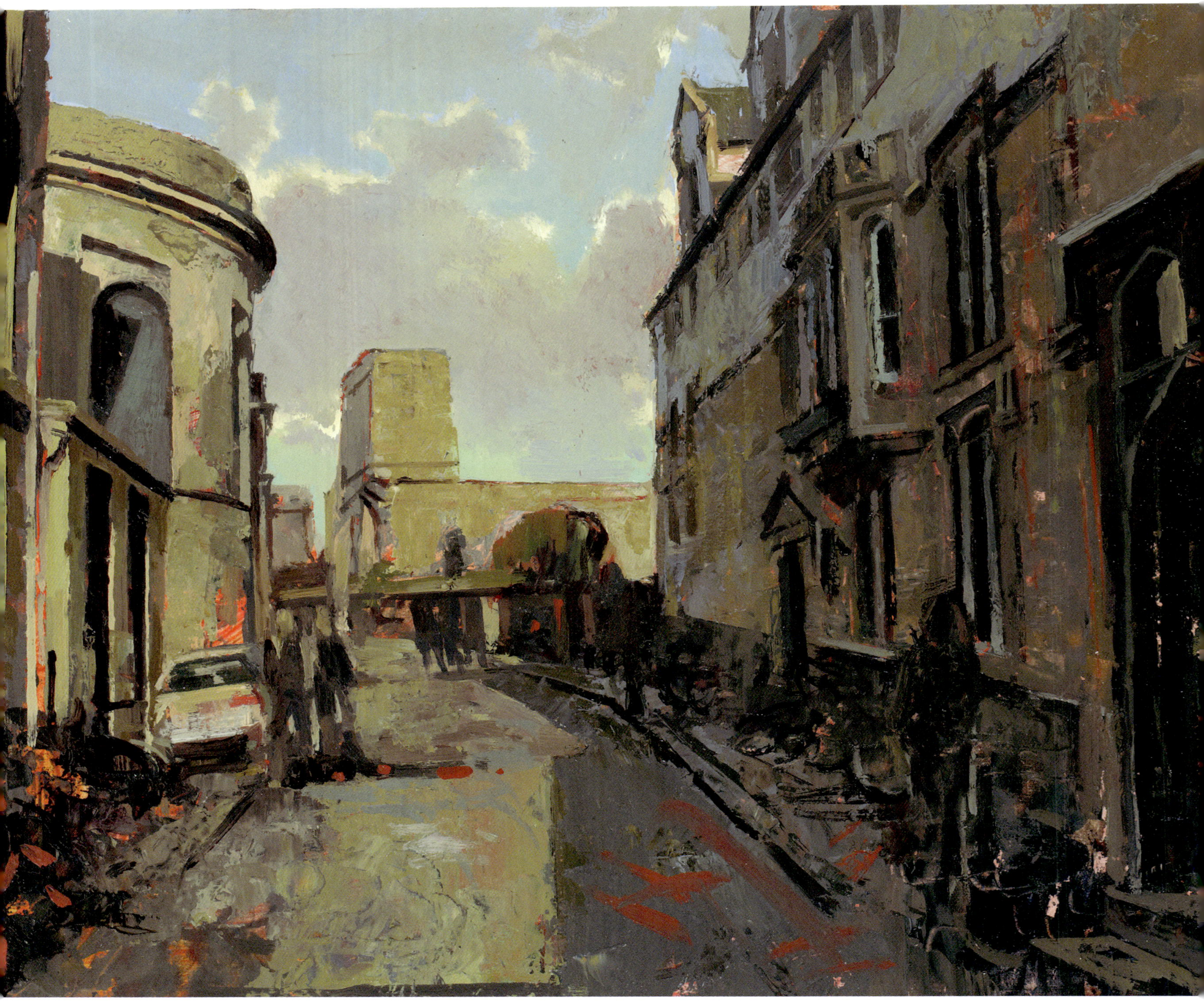

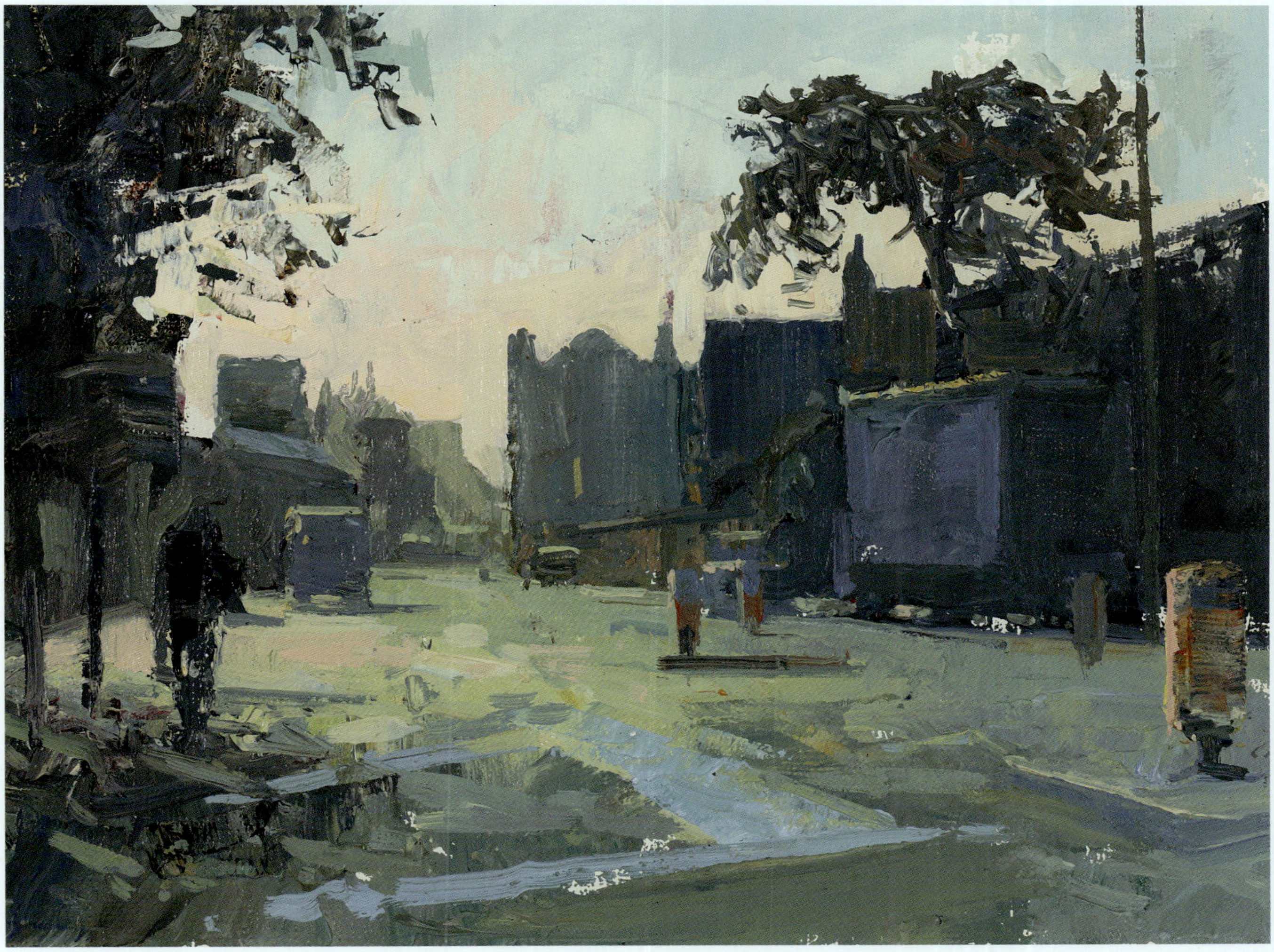

Queen's Lane and St Edmund Hall
28 x 36 cm, oil on panel, 2012

Woodstock Road, Cyclist
20 x 25 cm, oil on panel, 2012

Yesterday Morning, at two Clock, the Duke of Beaufort (who is of Univ. Coll.) rid out of Town with that vicious, loose Fellow, Mr Ward (commonly call'd Jolly Ward) of Univ. Coll... It is said they had sate up 'till that time drinking. Ward was so drunk that he vomited four times between Queen's Coll. Lane & East Gate.

Thomas Hearne, Diaries, 15th December 1722

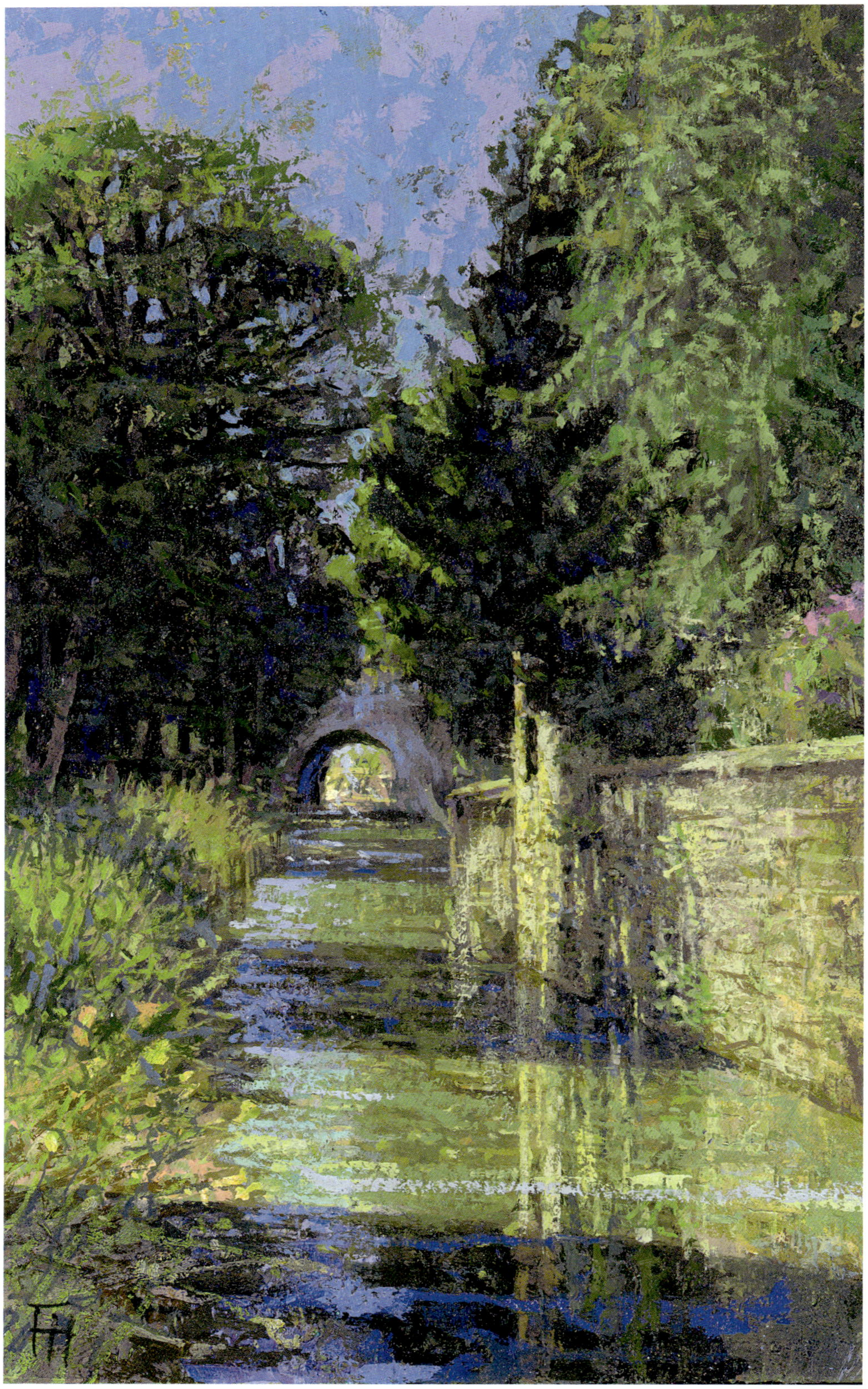

The man, who, stretch'd in Isis' calm retreat,
To books and study gives seven years complete,
See! strew'd with learned dust, his nightcap on,
He walks, an object new beneath the sun!
The boys flock round him, and the people stare:
So stiff, so mute! some statue, you would swear,
Stepp'd from its pedestal to take the air!

Alexander Pope, *Horace's Epistles,* 1734

About a mile before I reached Oxford, all the Night bells toll'd, in different notes; the Clocks of every College answered one another; and told me in a deeper, some in a softer voice, that it was eleven a clock. All this was no ill preparation to the life I have led since; among these old walls, venerable Galleries, Stone Portico's, studious walks & solitary scenes of the University, I wanted nothing but a black Gown and a Salary, to be as meer a Bookworm as any there.

Alexander Pope, Letter from the autumn of 1717 to his friends Teresa and Martha Blount of Mapledurham, describing his arrival for a short stay in Oxford.

Alexander Pope (1688–1744), poet, translator and satirist, his works include *The Rape of the Lock*, *An Essay on Criticism*, *The Dunciad* and translations of *Homer*. As a Catholic, Oxford was closed to Pope, as were Cambridge, Trinity College, Dublin and the Scottish Universities – something of an advertisement for self-education.

Magdalen, Tributary of the Cherwell
33 x 21 cm, oil on linen, 2024

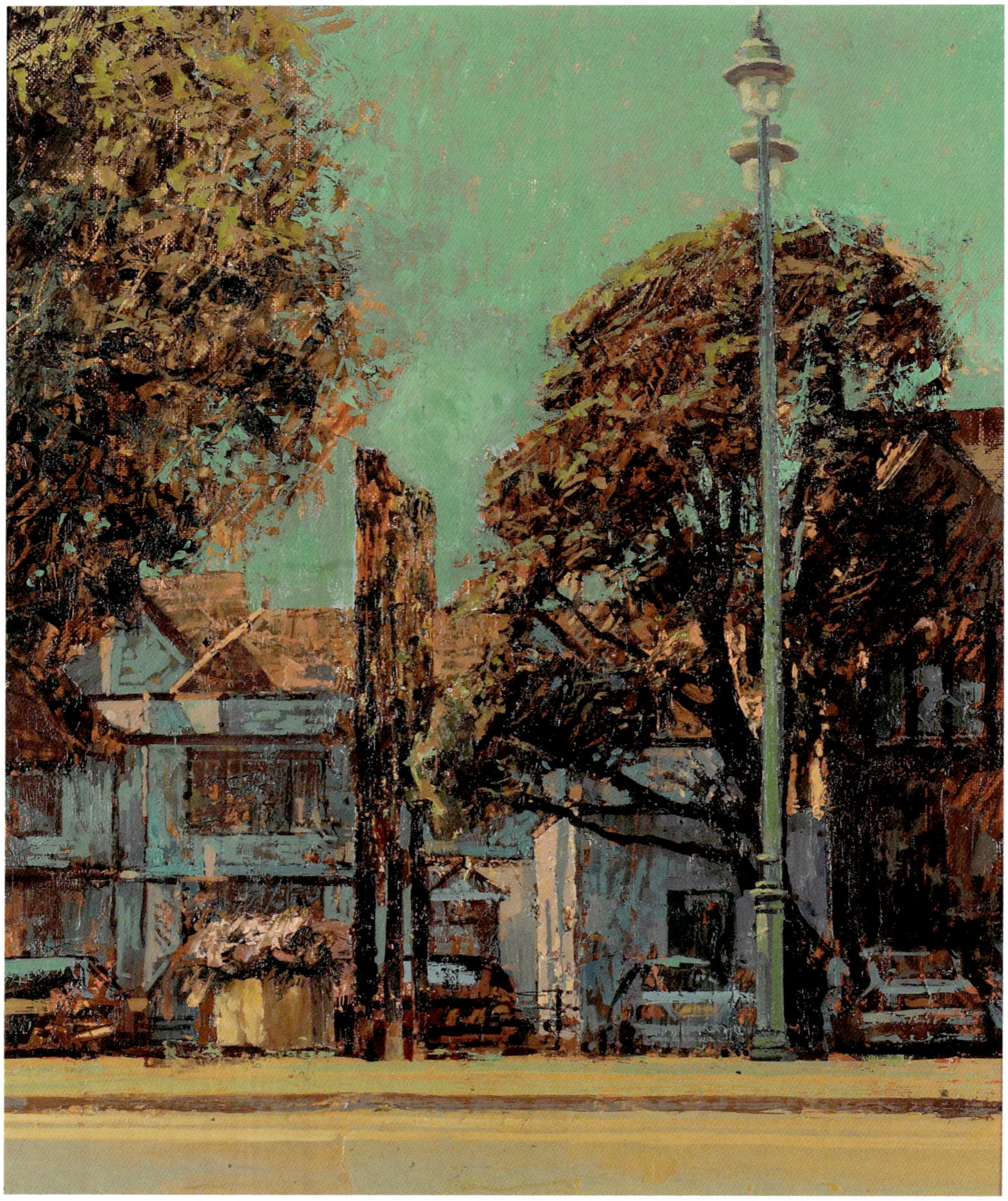

Study as if you were to live for ever; live as if you were to die tomorrow.

Edmund of Abingdon c.1174–1240

Edmund of Abingdon (c 1174–1240), an early proponent of Aristotle, lectured in Dialectics and Mathematics at Paris and Oxford Universities. His promotion to the see of Canterbury immersed him in a power struggle with Henry III and the Pope – never a happy position for the poor cleric in the middle. He died in Pontigny in France, is buried there and was canonized in 1246.

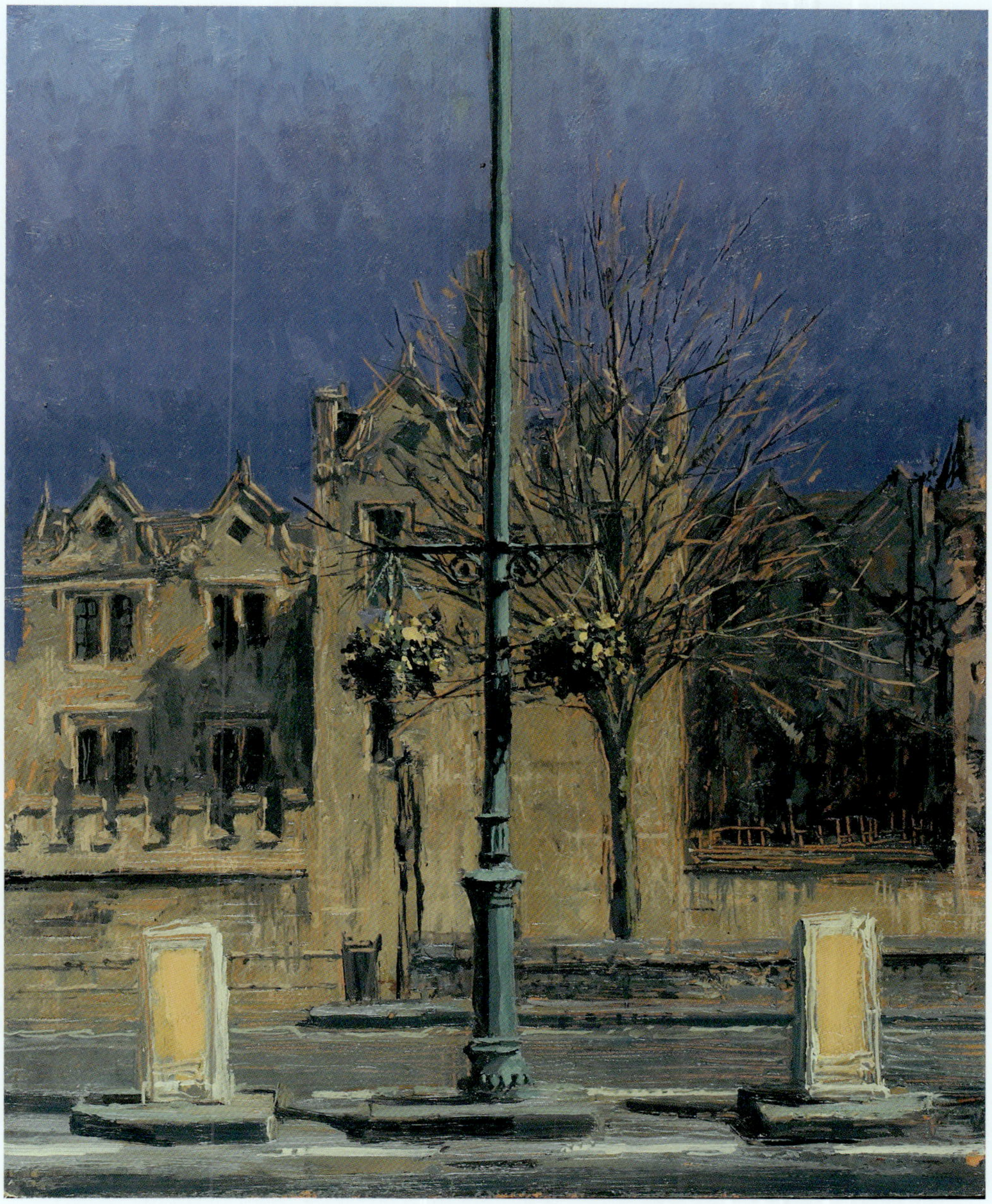

St Giles' in Late Afternoon
37 x 30.5 cm, oil on panel, 2003

St Giles' in Afternoon Sunshine, St John's and Balliol
28 x 38 cm, oil on panel, 2012

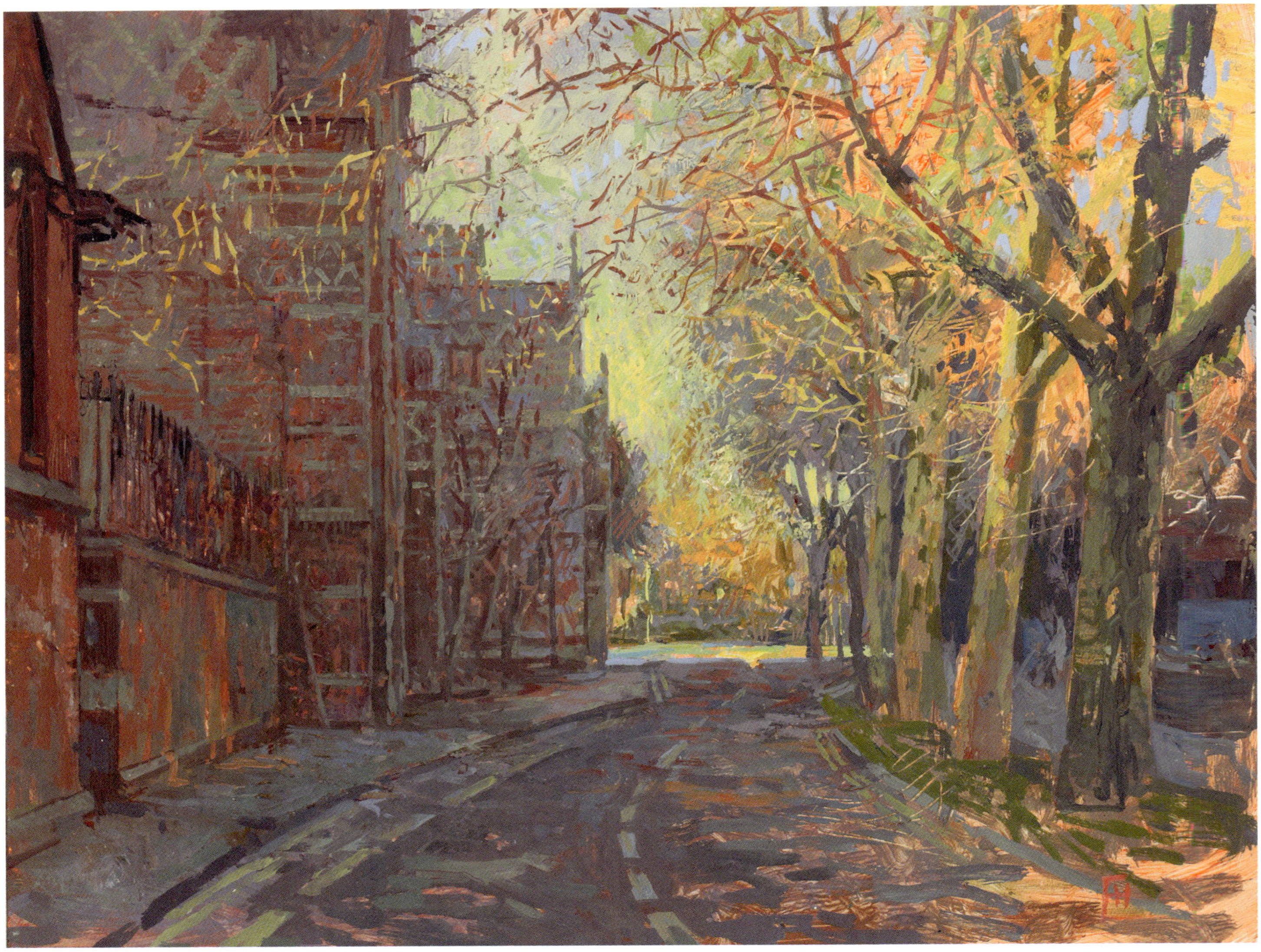

"... you are now about to embark upon a course of studies which will occupy you for two years. Together, they form a noble adventure. But I would like to remind you of an important point. Some of you, when you go down from the University, will go into the Church, or to the Bar, or to the House of Commons, or to the Home Civil Service, or the Indian or Colonial Services, or into various professions. Some may go into the Army, some into industry and commerce; some may become country gentlemen. A few – I hope a very few – will become teachers or dons. Let me make this clear to you. Except for those in the last category, nothing that you will learn in the course of your studies will be of the slightest possible use to you in after life – save only this that if you work hard and intelligently you should be able to detect when a man is talking rot, and that, in my view, is the main, if not the sole, purpose of education."

Harold Macmillan in *The Times*, 1965

Recalling J.A. Smith, Professor of Moral Philosophy, opening a lecture course in 1914.

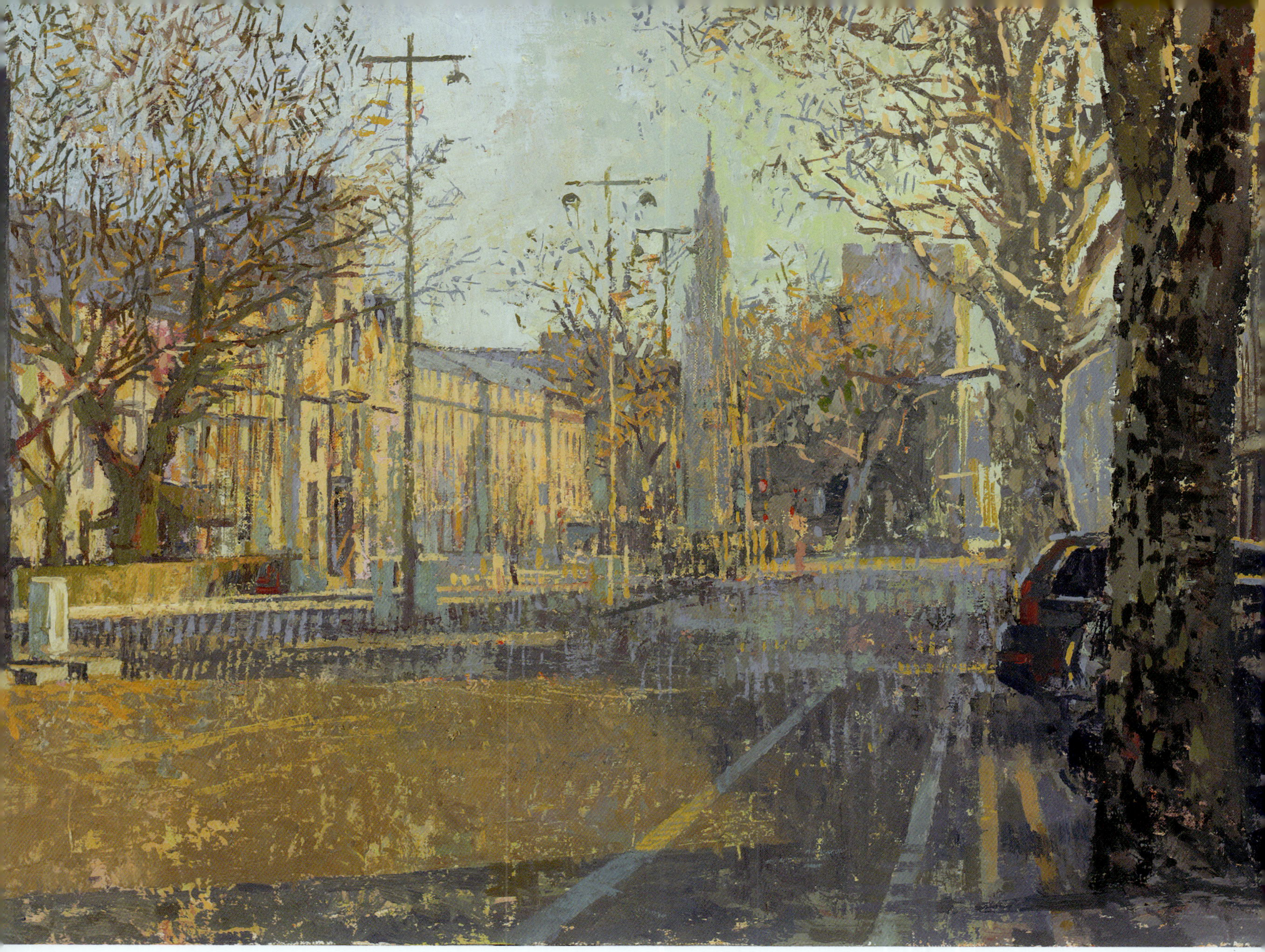

Harold Macmillan (1894–1986) read Classics at Balliol taking a First in Mods. War ended Macmillan's Oxford career: the effects of Army service meant he could not face returning. Despite being a Conservative MP from 1924 he was out of sympathy with the leadership and was left on the backbenches. His rebellions culminated in voting against Chamberlain in the Norway Debate in 1940 which effectively brought Chamberlain down. After that, there was no stopping Macmillan: he ended World War II as Minister Resident in the Mediterranean, he was then Minister for Housing, Minister of Defence, Foreign Secretary, Chancellor and finally Prime Minister. Macmillan was a chameleon – happy to portray himself as the descendant of a Scottish crofter, as a businessman, an aristocrat, an intellectual, a soldier, as a Whig, as a romantic Tory, as the last Edwardian – intersectionality would not have been a new concept for him. Not having a degree did not stop Macmillan becoming Chancellor of the University of Oxford.

J.A. Smith (1863–1939) was an idealist philosopher who taught at Balliol for 14 years before moving to Magdalen College when he was appointed Waynflete Professor of Moral and Metaphysical Philosophy. Smith was one of the leading advocates of creating the School of Modern Greats (Politics, Philosophy and Economics).

Keble
28 x 36 cm, oil on linen, 2012

St John's from St Giles'
32 x 25 cm, oil on linen, 2012

Oxford... must remain its own sole expression; and those whose sad fortune it may be never to behold it have no better resource than to dream about grey, weather-stained, ivy-grown edifices, wrought with quaint Gothic ornament, and standing around grassy quadrangles, where cloistered walks have echoed to the quiet footsteps of twenty generations, lawns and gardens of luxurious repose, shadowed with canopies of foliage, and lit up with sunny glimpses through archways of great boughs, spires, towers, and turrets, each with its history and legend, dimly magnificent chapels, with painted windows of rare beauty and brilliantly diversified hues, creating an atmosphere of richest gloom, vast college halls, high-windowed, oaken-panelled and hung around with portraits of the men in every age whom the University has nurtured to be illustrious, long vistas of alcoved libraries, where the wisdom and learned folly of all time is shelved, kitchens (we throw in this feature by way of ballast, and because it would not be English Oxford without its beef and beer) with huge fireplaces, capable of roasting a hundred joints at once, and cavernous cellars, where rows of piled-up hogsheads seethe and fume with that mighty malt-liquor which is the true milk of *Alma Mater*: make all these things vivid in your dream, and you will never know nor believe how inadequate is the result to represent even the merest outside of Oxford.

Nathaniel Hawthorne, *Our Old Home*, 1863

Nathaniel Hawthorne (1804–1864) was an American novelist and short story writer. He was US Consul in Liverpool for the four years of his friend Franklin Pierce's tenure as US President, the position was highly lucrative, and followed Hawthorne writing a positive campaign biography of his old college buddy Pierce.

The Cherwell, University Parks
30 x 41 cm, oil on linen, 2012

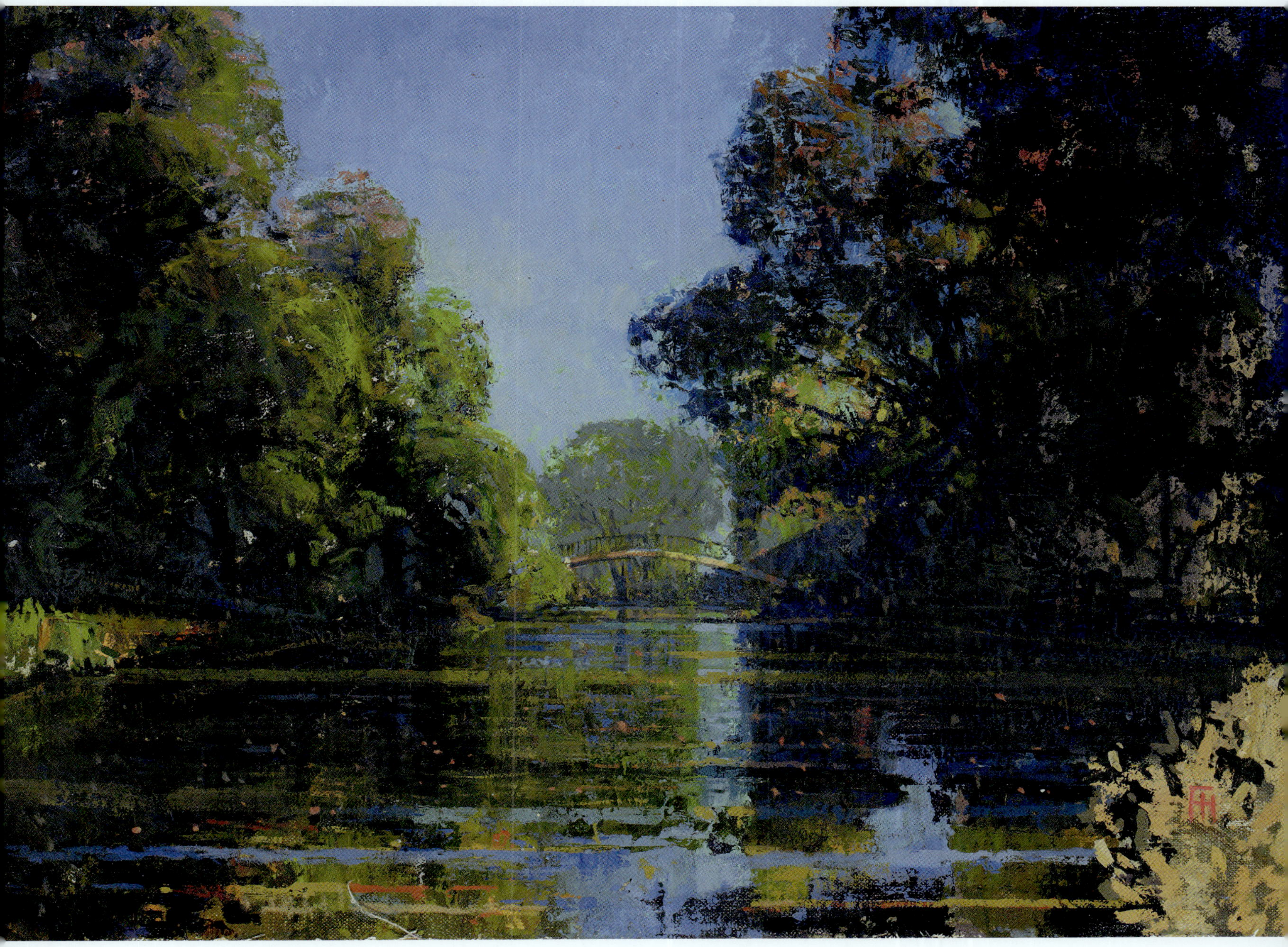

I tried to work myself up to a little enthusiasm, and took a draught of the water of Isis so much celebrated in poetry, but all in vain.

James Boswell, Journal, 1763

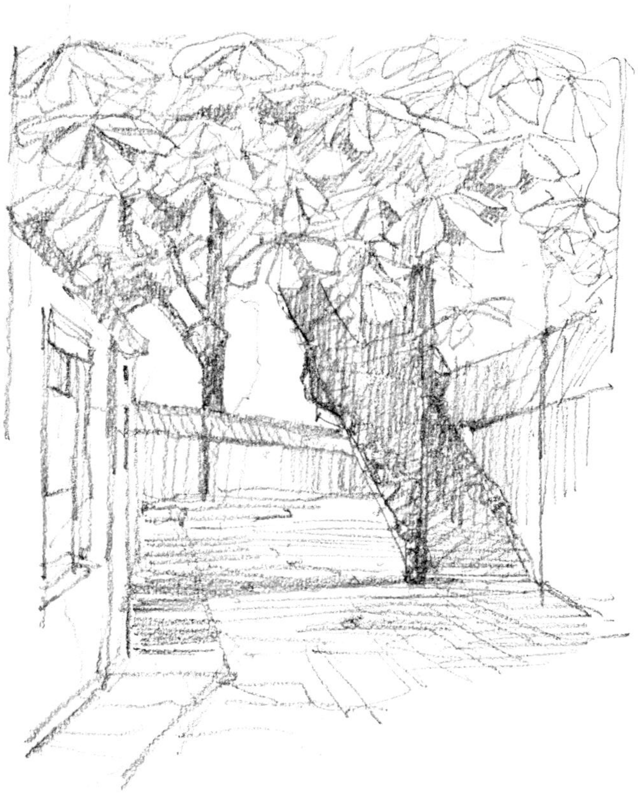

James Boswell (1740–1795) biographer, diarist and lawyer, studied at Glasgow, Edinburgh and Utrecht Universities. He practised Law both in Edinburgh and London and failed in both. It is calculated that Boswell could only have spent 250 days with Dr Johnson – but he made great use of the time and his biography has been through innumerable editions and beat hands down at least four Johnson biographies which preceded it.

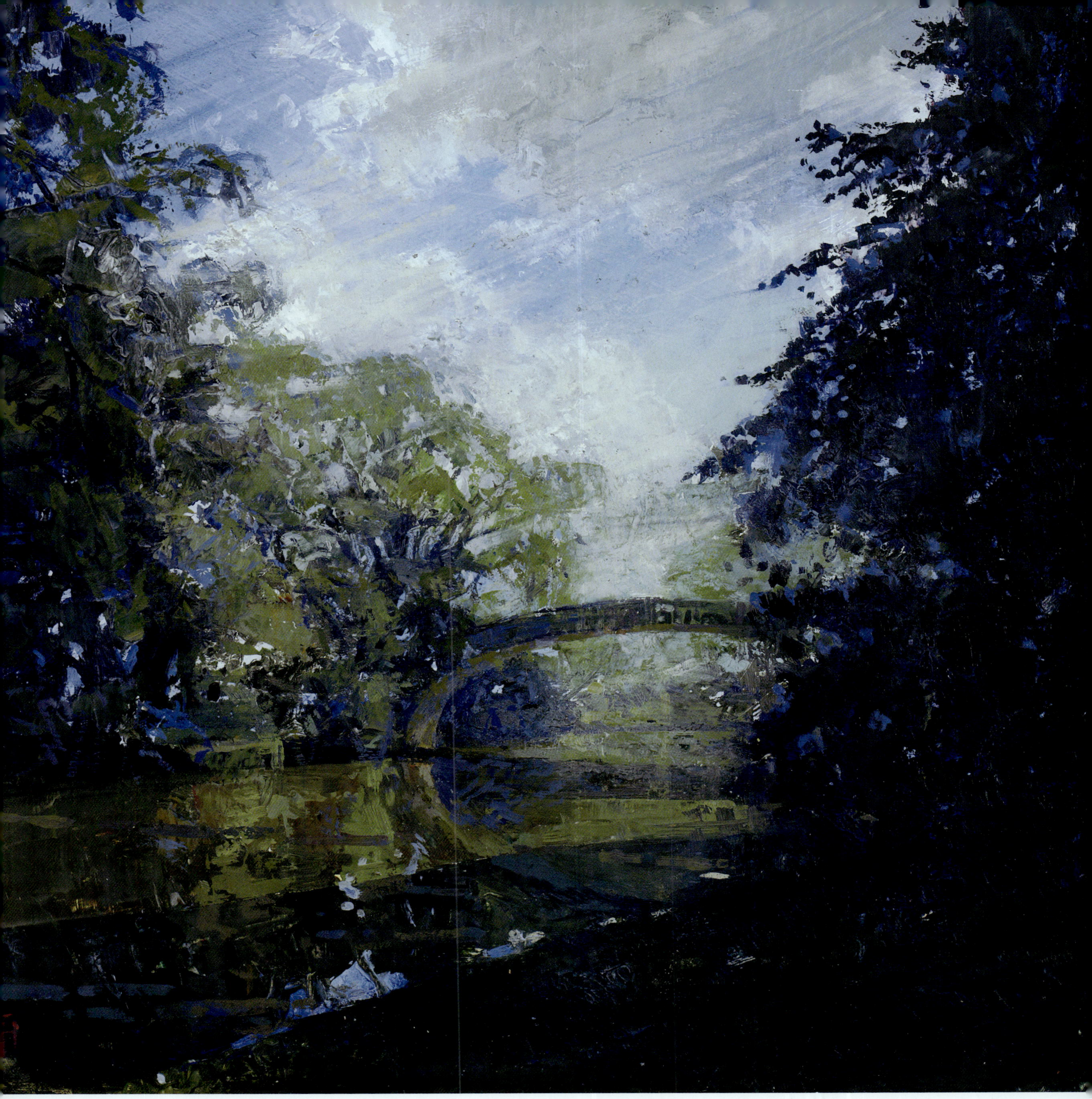

Rainbow Bridge, University Parks
30 x 30 cm, oil on panel, 2012

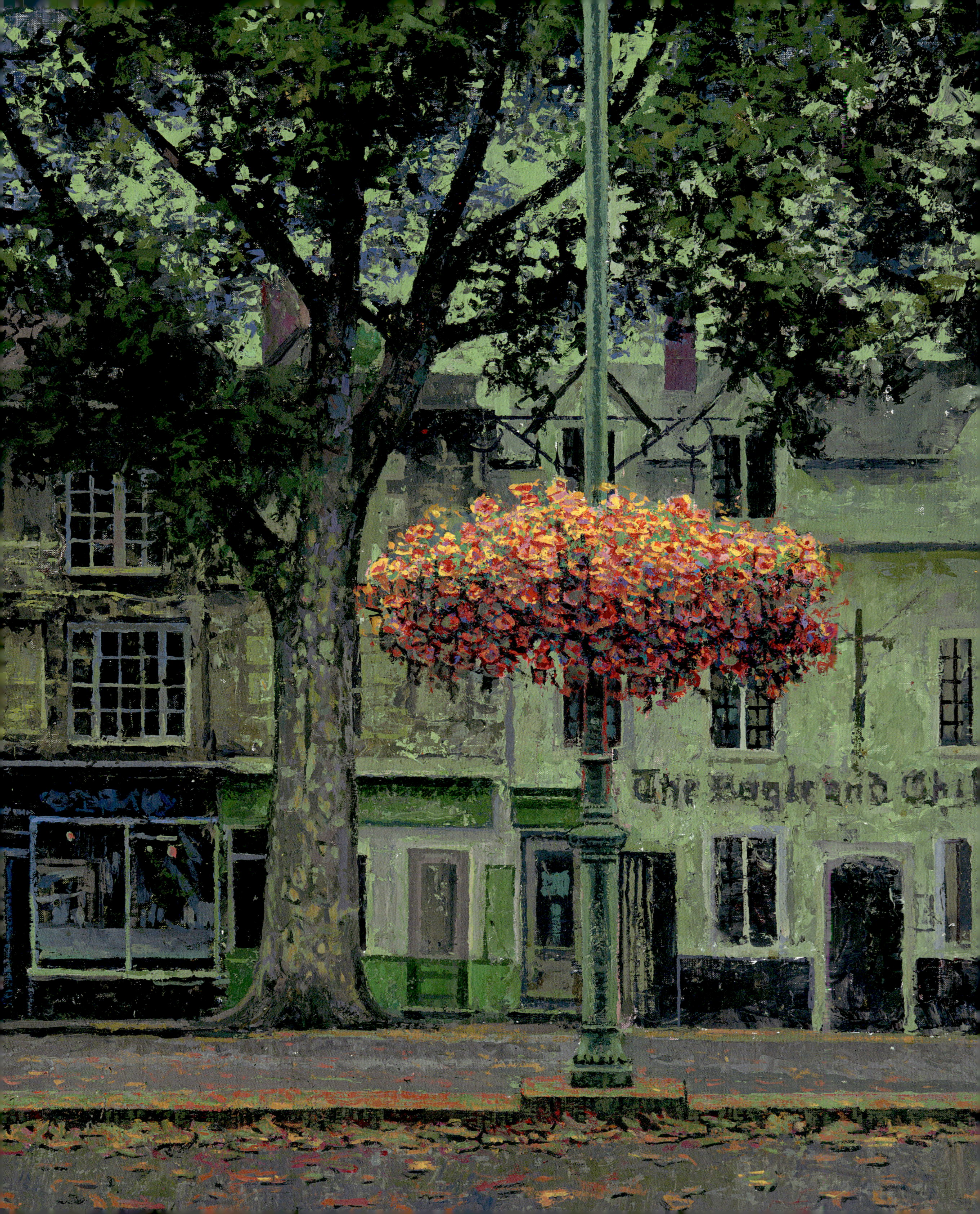

4 Eastbourne Rd

...I enjoyed this last term – though perhaps it wasn't such unalloyed heaven as my first term. I saw more of the seamy side of Oxford – and it's certainly a pretty vicious place in some ways. Also I had much too much to do and nearly had a nervous breakdown a few weeks before the end of term. However I stayed up a week and worked in the Ashmolean library – a well of silence – and recovered. My emotional life gives me trouble too – I find myself quite astonishingly interested in the opposite sex, and capable of being in love with about six men all at once – which gives rise to complications and distresses. And too many people are in love with me just at present which though pleasing to my vanity, is also liable to be annoying and difficult.

But on the whole I find life, if not a sweet flower garden with endless vistas of roses, at any rate a very rich, lively, interesting place, and not without hope and promise, though not for me as an individual...

Iris Murdoch, Letter to Ann Leech, early April 1939
Living on Paper: Letters from Iris Murdoch, 1934–1995

The Eagle and Child, Hanging Basket
61 x 51 cm, oil on linen, 2024

Iris Murdoch (1919–1999), civil servant, academic and novelist, read Greats at Somerville returning to teach Philosophy at St Anne's before resigning to concentrate on writing. She was part of a group including Philippa Foot and Elizabeth Anscombe who worked on Moral rather than Analytical Philosophy. A member of the Communist Party, she regularly dropped off documents from her work at the Treasury during the war to her handler. Unsurprisingly the Americans were wary of issuing her a visa to study at Vassar or indeed to enter the country.

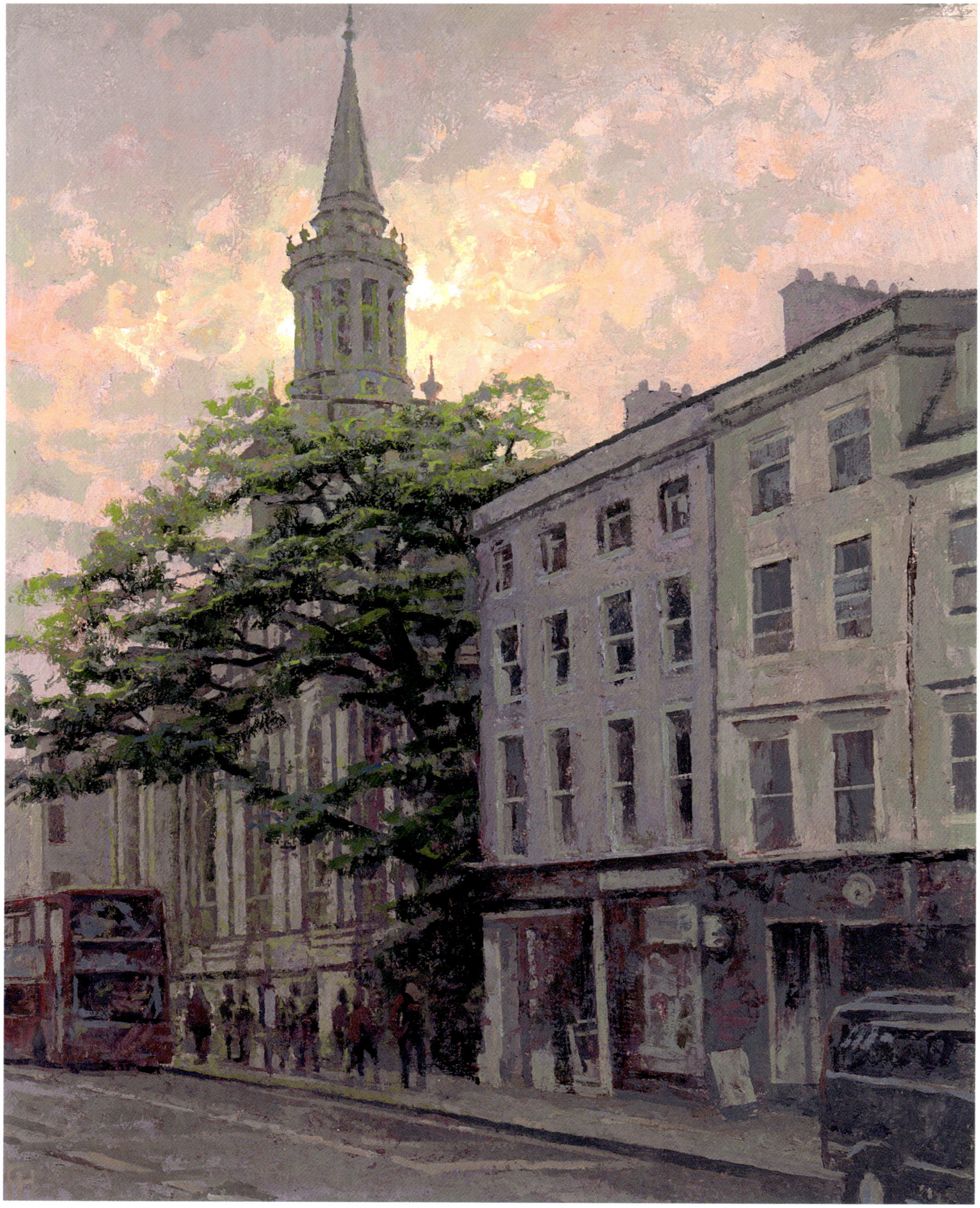

That old bell, presage of a train, had just sounded through Oxford station; and the undergraduates who were waiting there, gay figures in tweed or flannel, moved to the margin of the platform and gazed idly up the line. Young and careless, in the glow of the afternoon sunshine, they struck a sharp note of incongruity with the worn boards they stood on, with the fading signals and grey eternal walls of that antique station, which, familiar to them and insigni1cant, does yet whisper to the tourist the last enchantments of the Middle Age.

At the door of the first-class waiting-room, aloof and venerable, stood the Warden of Judas. An ebon pillar of tradition seemed he, in his garb of old-fashioned cleric. Aloft, between the wide brim of his silk hat and the white extent of his shirt-front, appeared those eyes which hawks, that nose which eagles, had often envied. He supported his years on an ebon stick. He alone was worthy of the background.

Came a whistle from the distance. The breast of an engine was described, and a long train curving after it, under a flight of smoke... Into the station it came blustering, with cloud and clangour. Ere it had yet stopped, the door of one carriage flew open, and from it, in a white travelling-dress, in a toque a-twinkle with fine diamonds, a little and radiant creature slipped nimbly down to the platform.

A cynosure indeed! A hundred eyes were fixed on her, and half as many hearts lost to her. The Warden of Judas himself had mounted on his nose a pair of black-rimmed glasses. Him espying, the nymph darted in his direction. The throng made way for her. She was at his side.

'My dear Zuleika', he said, 'welcome to Oxford.'

Max Beerbohm, *Zuleika Dobson*, 1911

Max Beerbohm (1872–1956) was an essayist, caricaturist, parodist, novelist, dandy and humorist he was an undergraduate at Merton College, but left without taking a degree, "I was a modest, good-humoured boy", he recalled. "it was Oxford that has made me insufferable." He was part of the group around Oscar Wilde, ("The gods have bestowed on Max the gift of perpetual old age" Wilde teased) Frank Harris and Aubrey Beardsley and he knew just about everyone who mattered. Despite living in Italy for the better part of 50 years, he chose never to learn Italian.

Acacia Tree by Lincoln College Library
46 x 36 cm, oil on linen, 2024

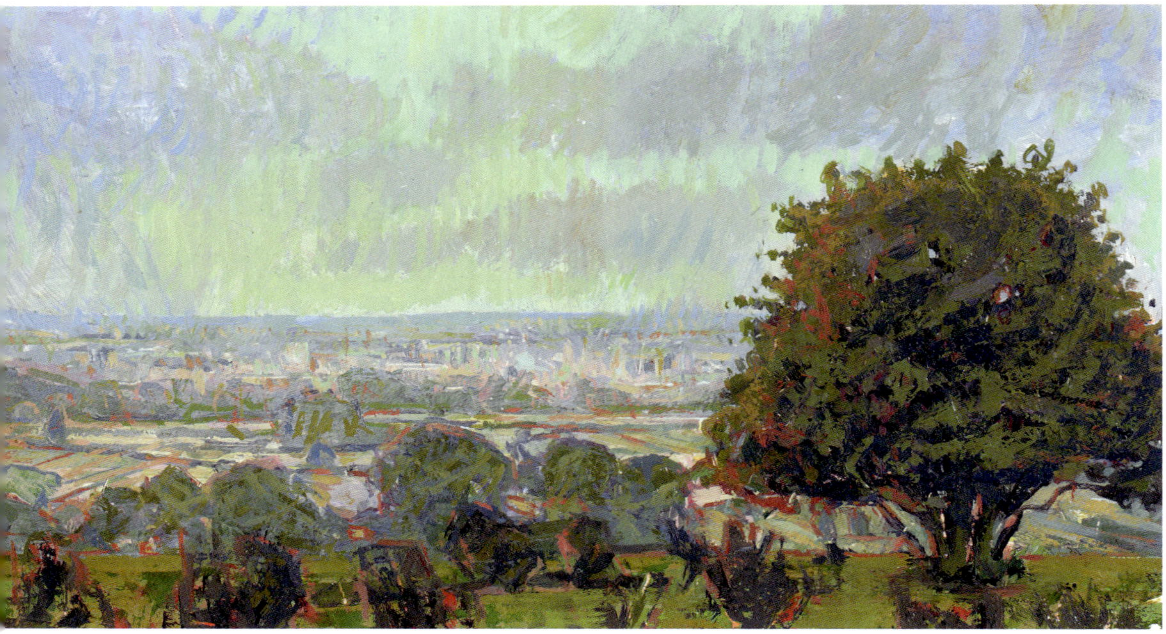

Sebastian entered dove-grey flannel, white crêpe de Chine, a Charvet tie, my tie as it happened, a pattern of postage stamps "Charles – what in the world's happening at your college? Is there a circus? I've seen everything except elephants. I must say the whole of Oxford has become most peculiar suddenly. Last night it was pullulating with women. You're to come away at once, out of danger. I've got a motor-car and a basket of strawberries and a bottle of Château Peyraguey which isn't a wine you've ever tasted, so don't pretend. It's heaven with strawberries..."

Beyond the gate, beyond the winter garden that was once the lodge, stood an open, two-seater Morris-Cowley. Sebastian's teddy bear sat at the wheel. We put him between us – "Take care he's not sick" – and drove off. The bells of St Mary's were chiming nine; we escaped collision with a clergyman, black-straw-hatted, white-bearded, pedalling quietly down the wrong side of the High Street, crossed Carfax, passed the station, and were soon in open country on the Botley Road; open country was easily reached in those days.

Evelyn Waugh, *Brideshead Revisited*, 1945

Oxford from Boar's Hill
16 x 28 cm, oil on panel, 2012

Turl Street in Sunshine
38 x 28 cm, oil on linen, 2012

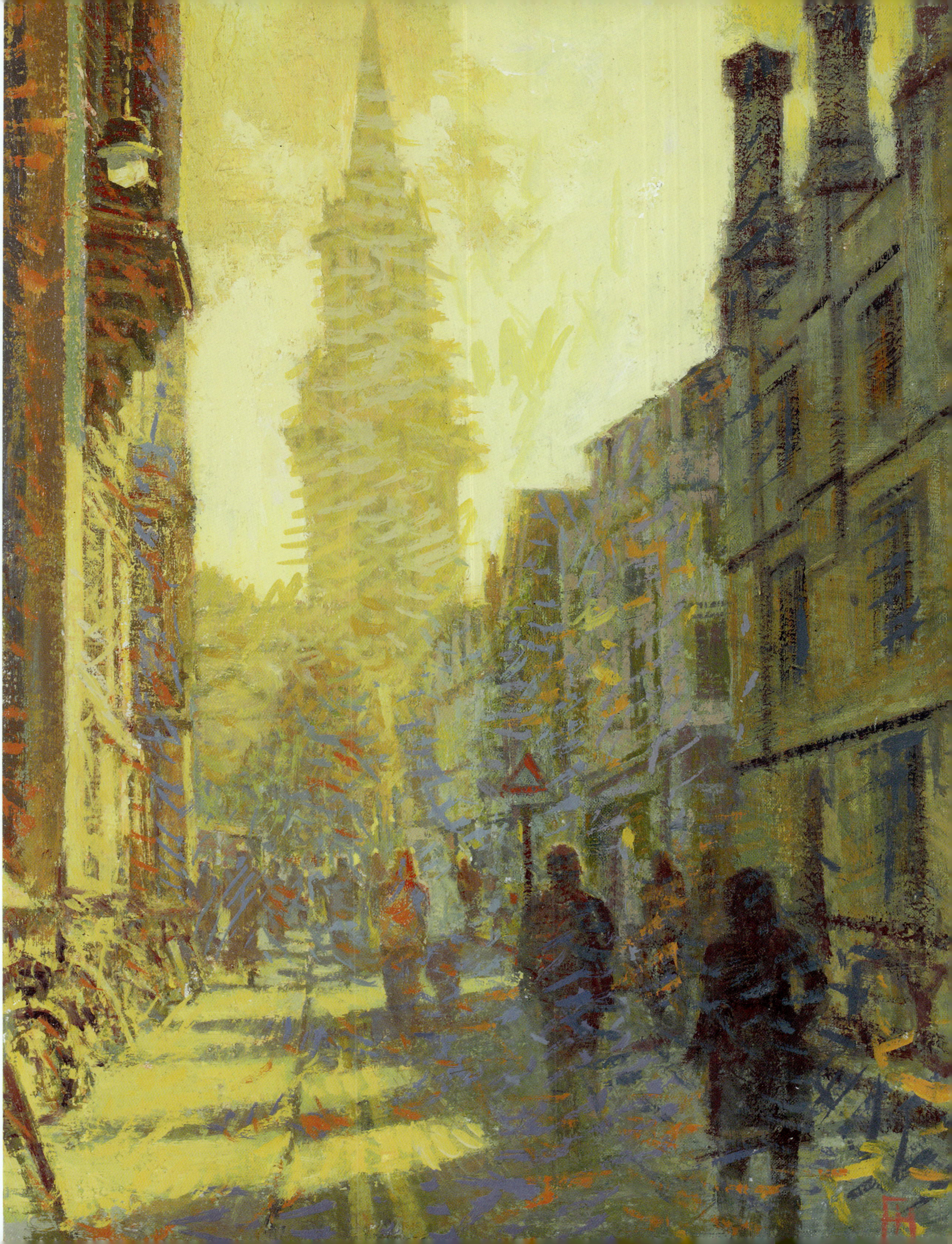

Standing at Carfax, and occasionally moving step to one side or another, I see with my eyes, indeed, the west front of Christ Church, with Tom Tower; the borders of All Saints' and St Mary's; and that grim tower of St Michael's; and the handsome curves of High Street and St Aldate's, which are part of the mere good fortune of Oxford: but, especially if a dawn light recall the first dim shining, or a sunset recall the grey and golden splendour of its maturity, I may also see the past of the University unrolled again. For at Carfax I am in sight of monuments on which is implied or recorded all its history. On the south, above Folly Bridge, is the gravelly reach that formed the eponymous ford; between that and Christ Church was the old south gate; and, through Wolsey's gateway, lies the Cathedral, speaking of St. Frideswide, the misty, original founder, King's daughter, virgin, martyr, saint, and, with its newly revealed Norman crypt, which perhaps held the University chest in the beginning, representative of Oxford's piety and generosity.

On the east, in the High Street, University College and St Mary's and Brasenose speak clearly, although falsely, of King Alfred. There, by St Peter's in the East, was the old east gate; and in sight of these is Merton, the fount of the collegiate idea. On the north, in Cornmarket Street, St Michael's marks the place of the north gate, and while it is one of the oldest, is by far the oldest-looking place in Oxford, rising up always to our surprise, like a piece of substantial night left by the dark ages, yet clothed with green in June. On the west, the Castle tower, twin made with St Michael's by the first Norman lord of Oxford, lies by the old west gate; and the quiet, monstrous mound beyond recalls the days of King Alfred's daughter's supremacy in Mercia.

At Carfax itself there was a St. Martin's church, of which only the tower remains, a descendant of the one whose bells in the Middle Ages and again in the seventeenth century, called the city to arms against the University, but long ago deprived of its insolent height of tower, because the citizens pelted the scholars therefrom.

Edward Thomas, *Oxford*, 1903

Cornmarket in the Rain
51 x 38 cm, oil on panel, 2012

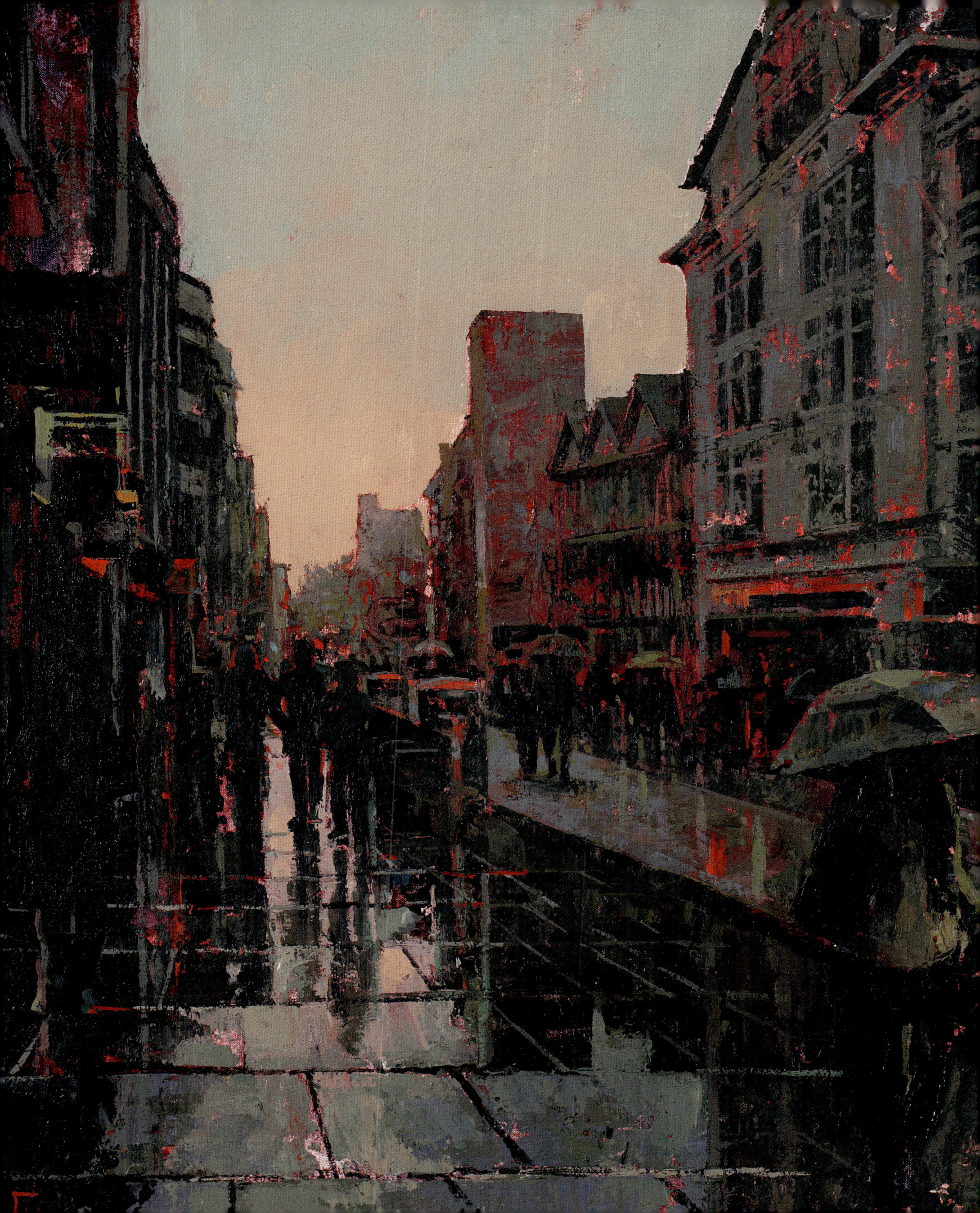

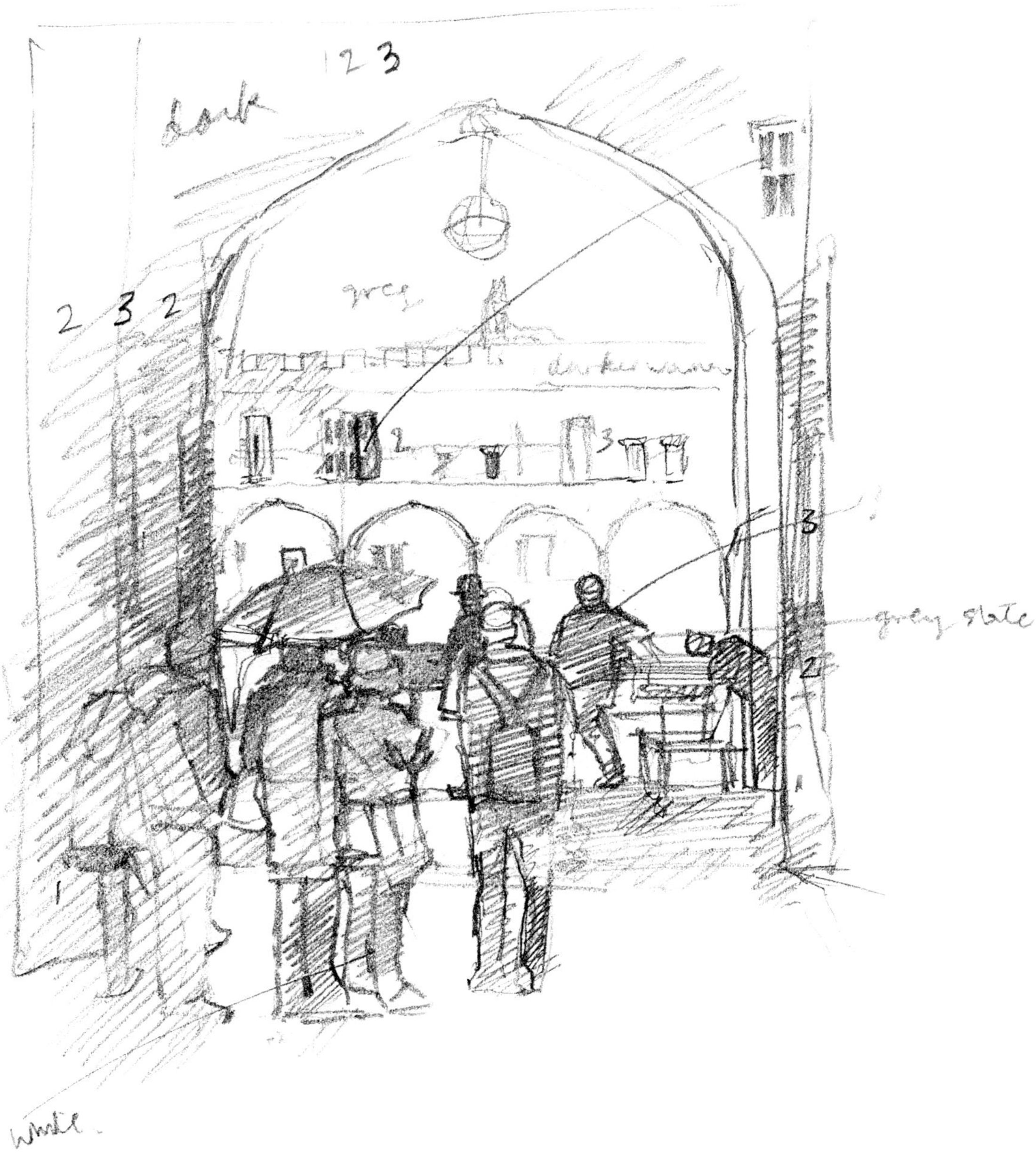

The Entrance to Christ Church

26 x 20 cm, oil on panel, 2012

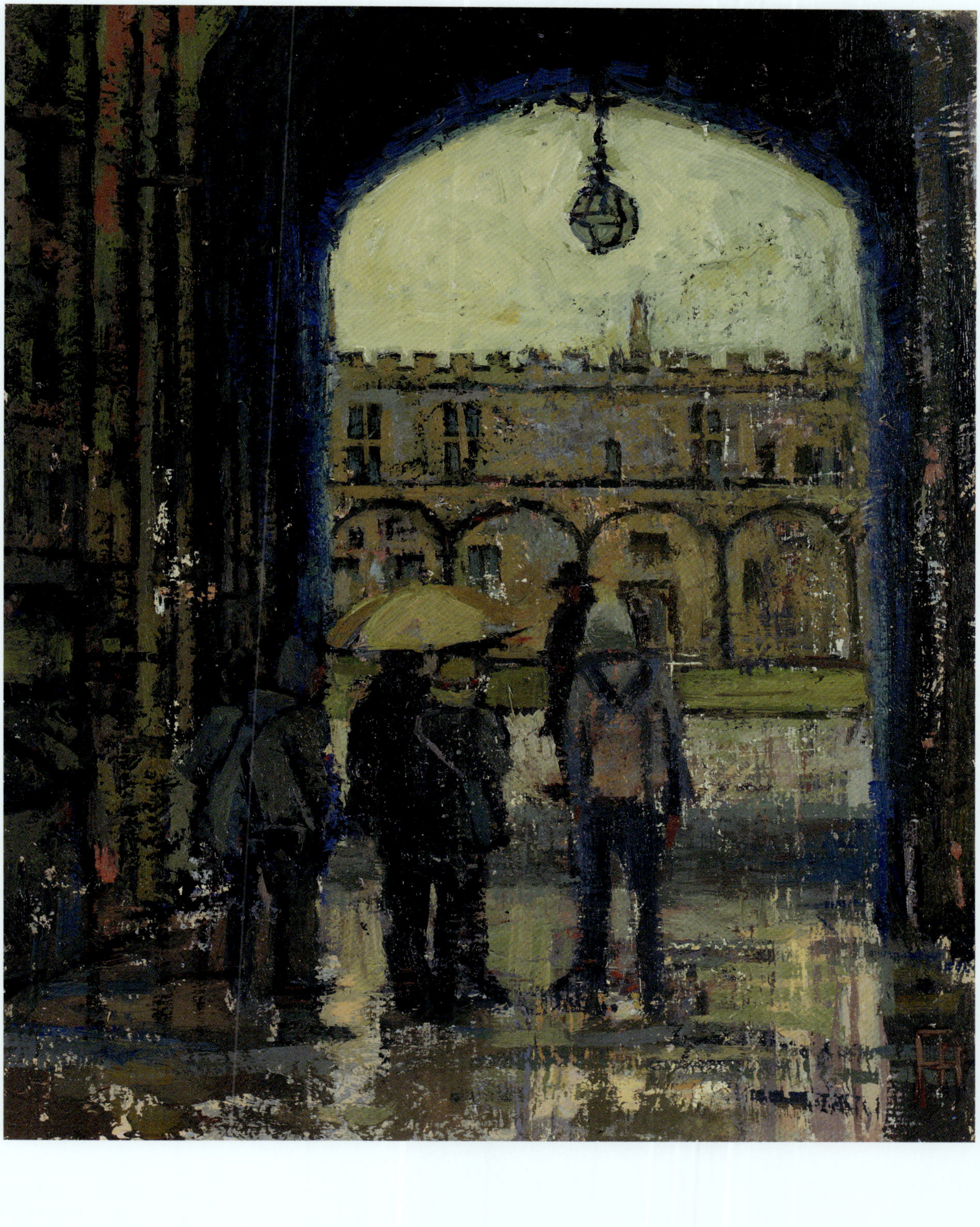

A land of waters green and clear,
Of willows and of poplars tall,
And, in the spring-time of the year,
The white may breaking over all;
And Pleasure quick to come at call,
And summer rides by marsh and wold,
And Autumn with her crimson pall
About the towers of Magdalen rolled;
And strange enchantments from the past,
And memories of the friends of old,
And strong Tradition, binding fast
The 'flying terms' with bands of gold.

Andrew Lang, *Almae Matres,* 1887

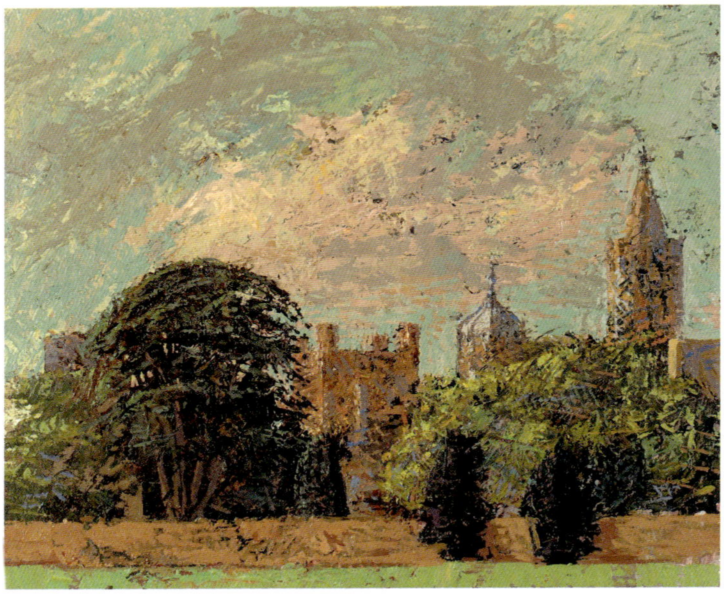

Andrew Lang (1844–1912) studied at St Andrew's University and Balliol College before becoming a fellow at Merton College. He was a classical scholar, historian, anthropologist, editor of both Walter Scott and Charles Dickens, biographer, researcher into the paranormal and a collector of fairy and folk stories. His output was simply prodigious – producing more books than the years he lived.

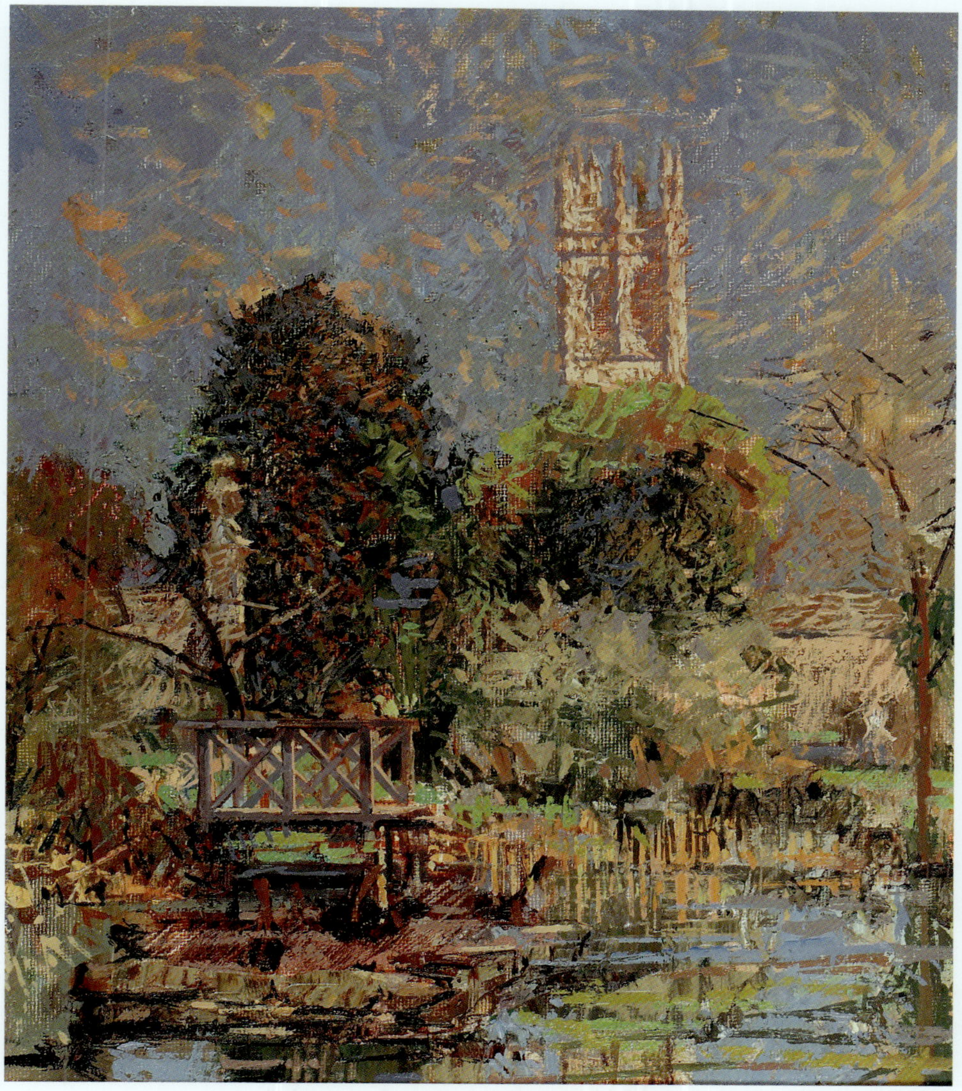

Christ Church from the Meadow
25.5 x 30.5 cm, oil on panel, 2003

Magdalen from the Botanical Gardens
30 x 25 cm, oil on panel, 2002

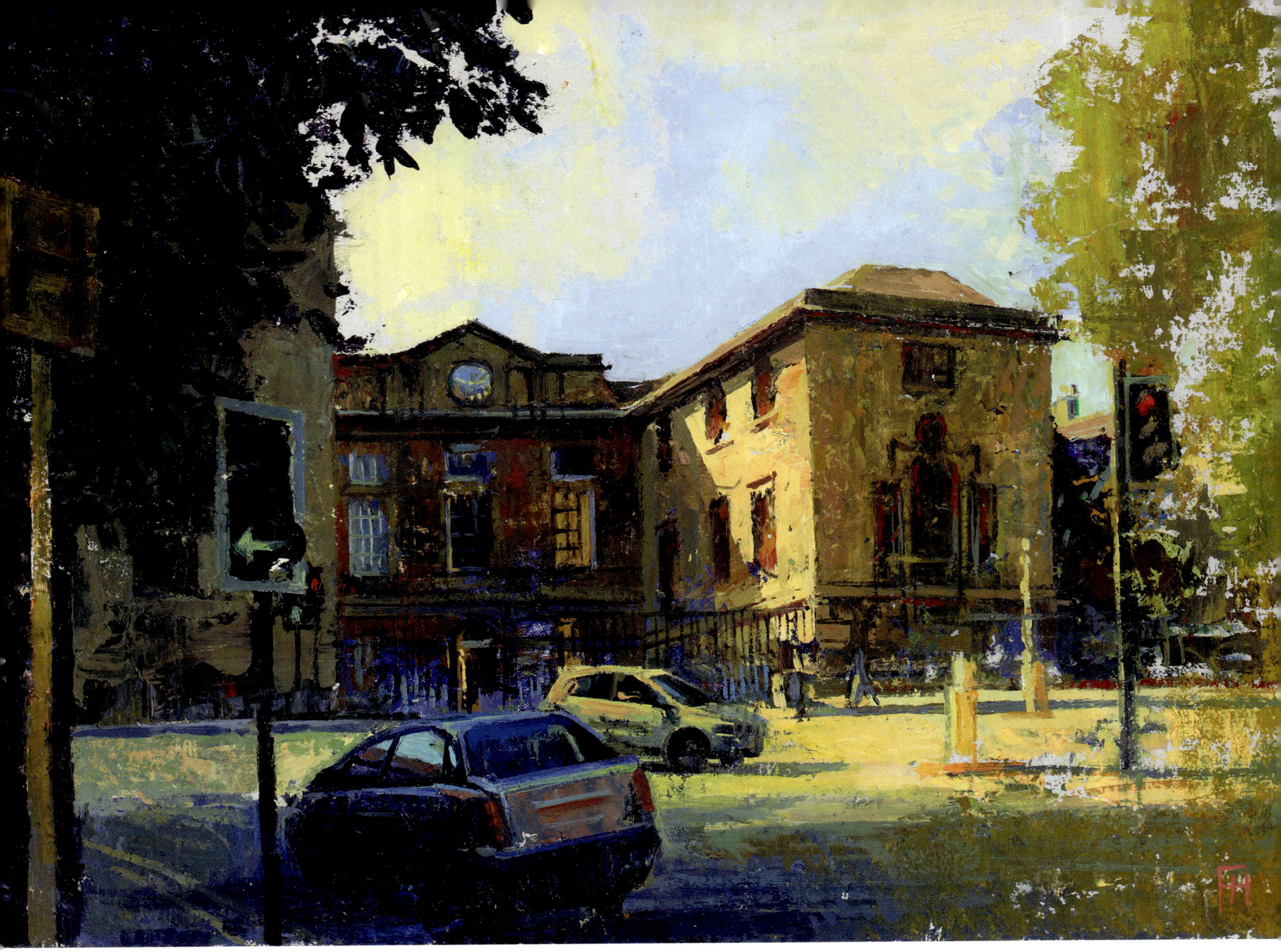

One night at a Vice-Chancellarian dinner-party a lady sitting next to him plied him with questions… 'Pray, Master,' she said, 'how are Heads of Colleges chosen?' Dr. Jeune (the Master), if I may trust to my imagination or my instinct, did not approve of ladies who asked questions; … 'Madam,' he said (and again I let my imagination picture his handsome and imposing figure at the head of his own table), 'the Fellows of a College meet together and choose the best-looking among their number to be their Head.' The lady was not satisfied. 'Oh, Master,' she said, 'are you sure that is true? I feel that there must be a mistake somewhere, for I dined with the Provost of Worcester last week.' Dr. Jeune was equal to the occasion. 'Madam,' said he, 'of course I am sure of my facts. You may have dined last week with the Provost, but you have not, I think, met the Fellows of Worcester.'"

J C Masterman, *To Teach the Senators Wisdom*, 1952

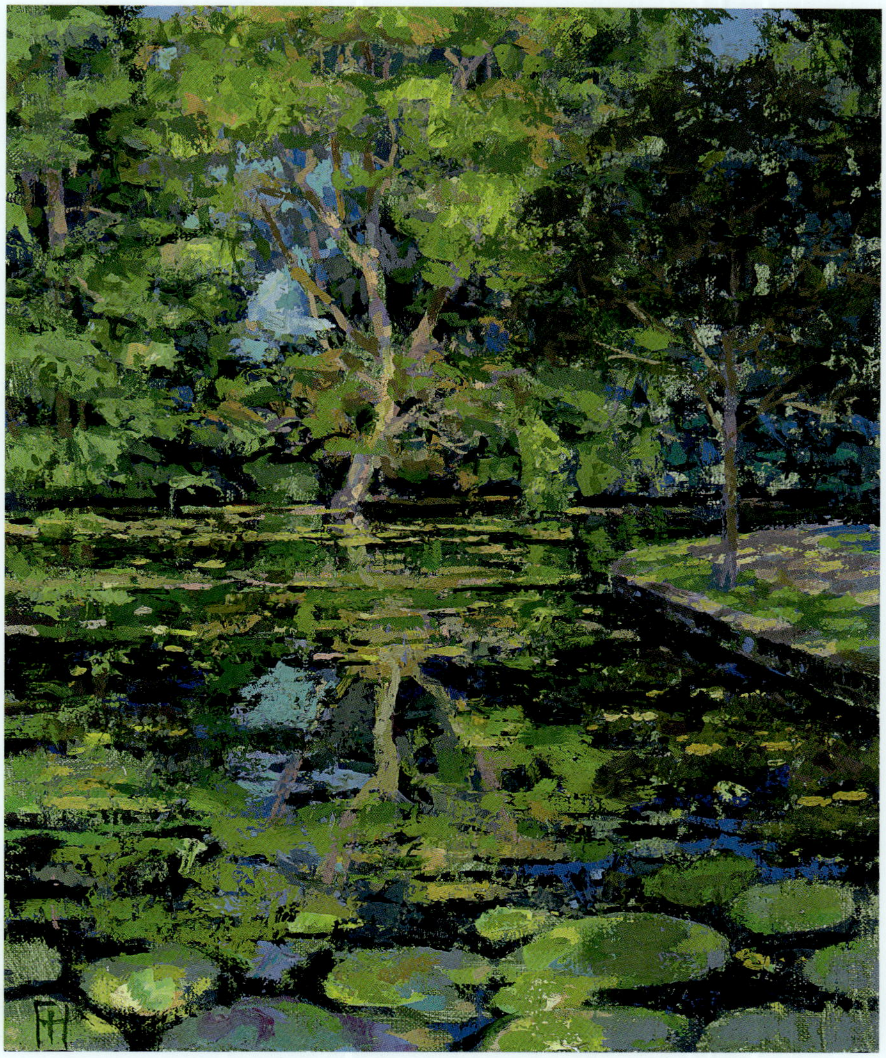

Worcester
28 x 38 cm, oil on linen, 2012

**Worcester College,
The Lake**
20 x 25 cm, oil on linen, 2024

By the Elizabeth Jennings Way bridge, a man in a panama hat is playing a loutar. Here, the city begins. Grand terraces back onto the canal, with smooth lawns on which ducks are dozing. The wild dog rose is upstaged by rambling roses that tumble over garden trellises and gazebos dressed with fancy ironwork furniture. The bridge is named after a writer who haunted Oxford from her time here as a student, and for a while held down a job in the city's Central Library. Poetry was Elizabeth Jennings' 'temporary home', her 'fulcrum' in a peripatetic life. She wore a duffle coat to be honoured by the Queen for her contribution to British Poetry at Buckingham Palace, a style that now seems ahead of the trend. But this once-beloved writer has fallen out of fashion since her death in 2001. Unkindly called 'the bag lady of the sonnets, and even described as 'ramshackle' by her biographer Dana Greene, that reputation rests on an all-too-common story: a good landlord dies, the tenant is evicted by a new unscrupulous landlord, and searches for permanent residence while drifting between temporary addresses. Greene quotes the unpublished poem On the Move Again, in which Jennings writes that she considered herself 'a parcel, sent to and fro, stamped with 'not known here'. She posted notices around town: 'Elizabeth Jennings has nowhere to live. Can you help?' I warm to the tone of sardonic humour in her shameless appeal, knowing all too well the desperation it may have masked.

There are still traces of Jennings in the city, and I often feel her presence in Jericho, where she would visit the cinema in the afternoons and work on translations of Michelangelo's sonnets in cafés late into the evenings, lingering over a glass of wine until she could no longer delay going back to her lodgings. There are living ghosts here too, people whose stories I know (or guess) without knowing the people, really, or them knowing me. Characters whose paths cross mine over and over, like the septuagenarian heavy metal giant wearing skinny black jeans, with silver skull rings on his fingers. The tall man sporting state-of-the-art headphones, shambling down the towpath after his golden retriever, is a respected humanitarian and former BBC foreign correspondent, whose chisel face once stared from the screen to a background of missiles over Belgrade and Baghdad. We give each other the hint of a smile. The parent teaching her children.

Nancy Campbell, *Thunderstone,* 2022

Jericho
34 x 31 cm, oil on panel, 2002

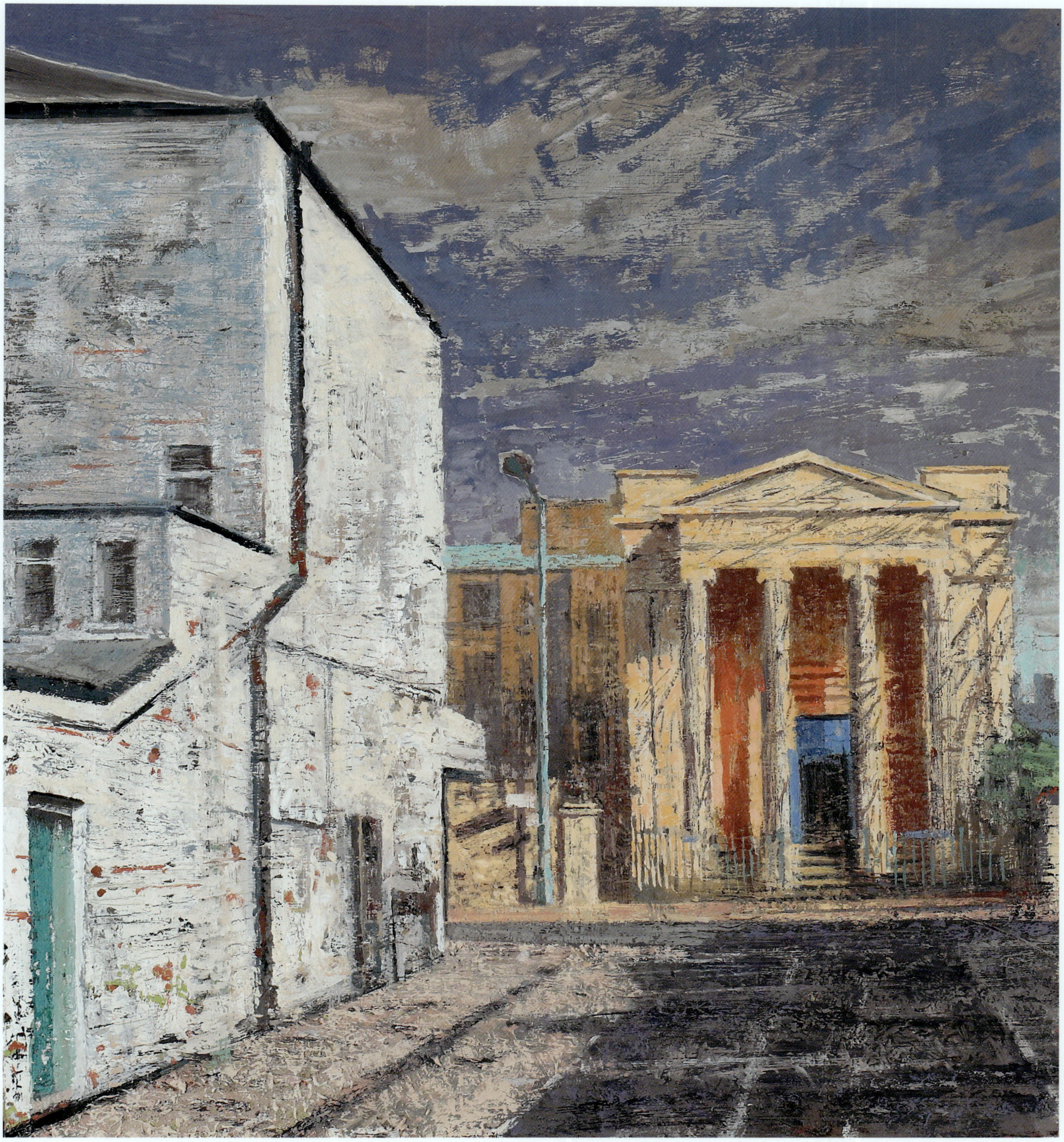

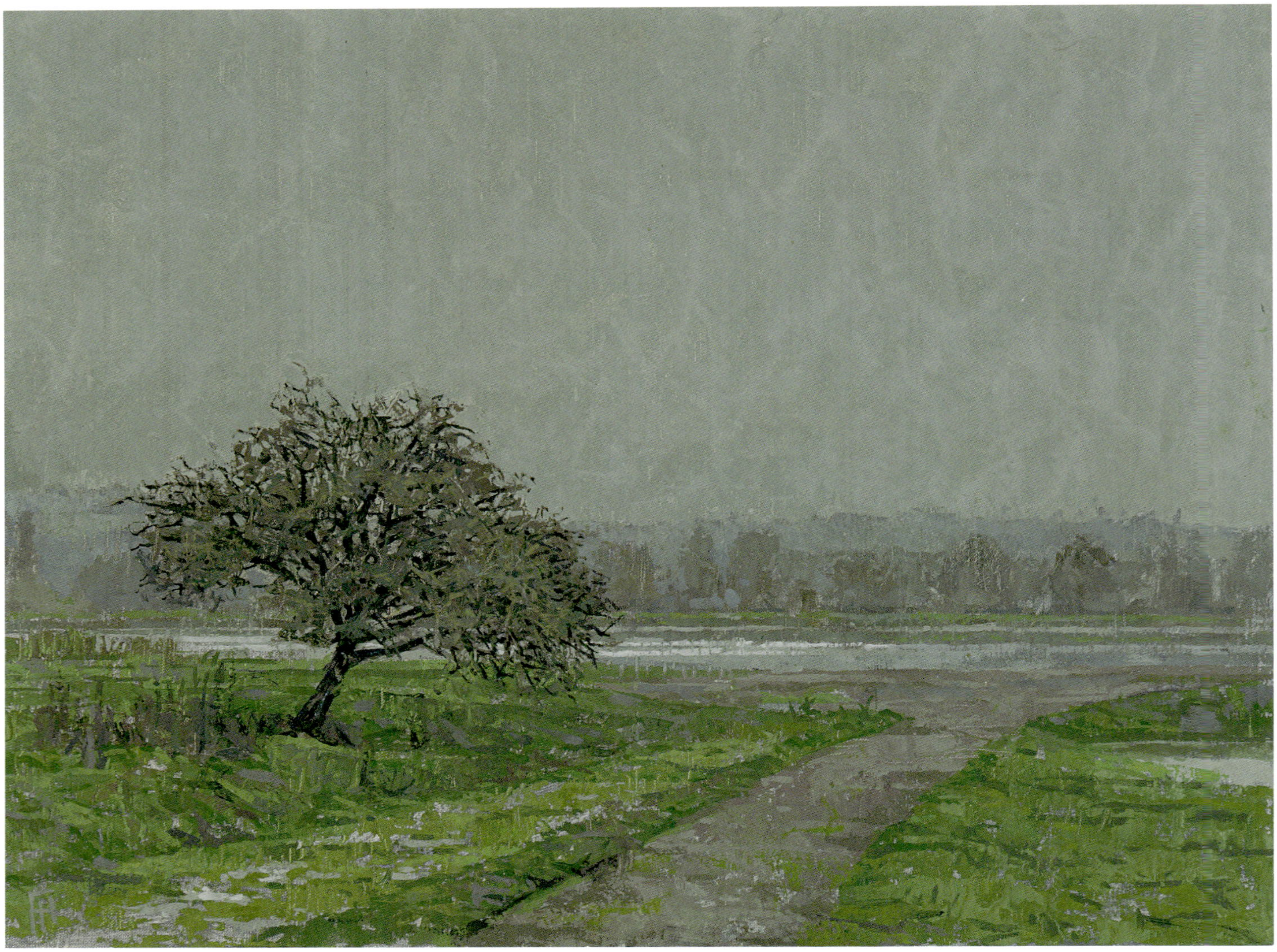

Hawthorn Tree on Port Meadow
35 x 45 cm, oil on linen, 2024

The Marina on Port Meadow
35 x 46 cm, oil on linen, 2024

Behind me is a great meadow,
It is rich with stllness and the feeling
Of wide open spaces. At night
Trains rush through it, but they are only a shadow.
In the morning it always has a different light.

I can tune it to children-their games-or else
Remember it at winter with the happy skaters.
I feel as if I could feel its pulse.
The warmth of the morning comes later.

There is a river beside it and a duck-pond.
This is the children's element, I think.
Above it is wide, wide sky.
I feel uplifted, I want to learn to fly,
To be beyond
This edge of life, this tremulous brink.

Elizabeth Jennings, ***Port Meadow,*** **1969**

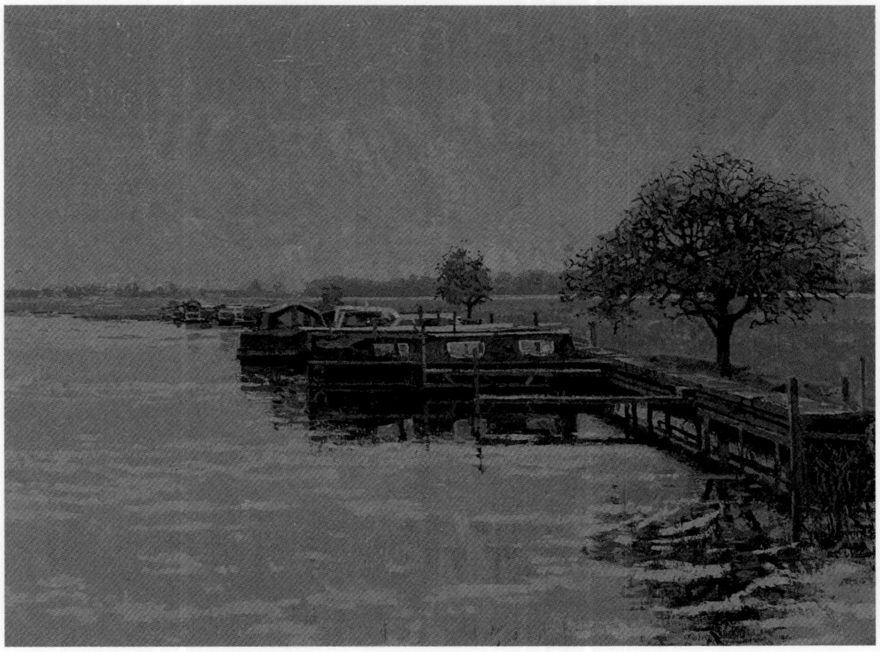

Elizabeth Jennings (1926–2001) read English at St Anne's College. After a career in copy-editing in London she returned to Oxford to take up a full-time post as a librarian. She worked briefly at Chatto and Windus before becoming a full-time poet, her deeply held Roman Catholicism coloured much of her work. She is buried in Wolvercote Cemetery, Oxford.

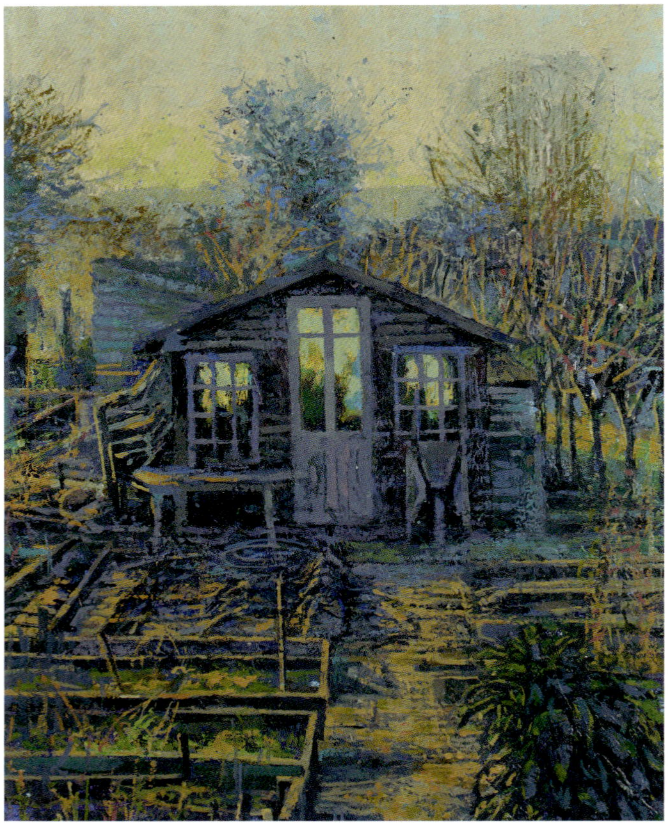

At the beginning of 1854 Ned wrote a letter to his father which indicates clearly the 'unmanageable' nature of his need for beauty that winter. 'I have just come in from my terminal pilgrimage to Godstow and the burial place of Fair Rosamund. The day has gone down magnificently; all by the river's side I came back in a delirium of joy, the land was so enchanted with bright colours, blue and purple in the sky, shot over with a dust of golden shower, and in the water, a mirror'd counterpart, ruffled by a light west wind and in my mind pictures of the old days, the abbey, and long crosiers, gay knights and ladies by the river bank, hawking parties and all the pageantry of the golden age it made me feel so wild and mad I had to throw stones into the water to break the dream. I never remember having such an unutterable ecstasy, it was quite painful with intensity, as if my forehead would burst. I get frightened of indulging now in my dreams, so vivid that they seem recollections rather than imaginings, but they seldom last more than half an hour; and then the sound of earthly bells in the distance, and presently the wreathing of steam upon the trees where the railway runs, called me back to the years I cannot convince myself of living in.'

Penelope Fitzgerald, *Edward Burne-Jones*, 1975

Penelope Mary Fitzgerald (1916–2000) attended Somerville College, where she emerged with a congratulatory first. Born into an extraordinary family, her father a successful humourist and editor of *Punch*, her uncles were Ronald Knox (Catholic priest, writer of apologetics, translator and crime writer); Dilwyn Knox (classics scholar and cryptographer); Wilfred Knox (biblical scholar) ; and her Aunt Winifred Peck (novelist and biographer). Her husband, Desmond Fitzgerald, despite winning a Military Cross in the North Africa Campaign returned from the war an alcoholic. She lived a somewhat rackety life working to support her family. Her first book was published when she was 58 and was followed by a series of novels – one of which won the Booker Prize. Her only University novel is unfortunately set in Cambridge.

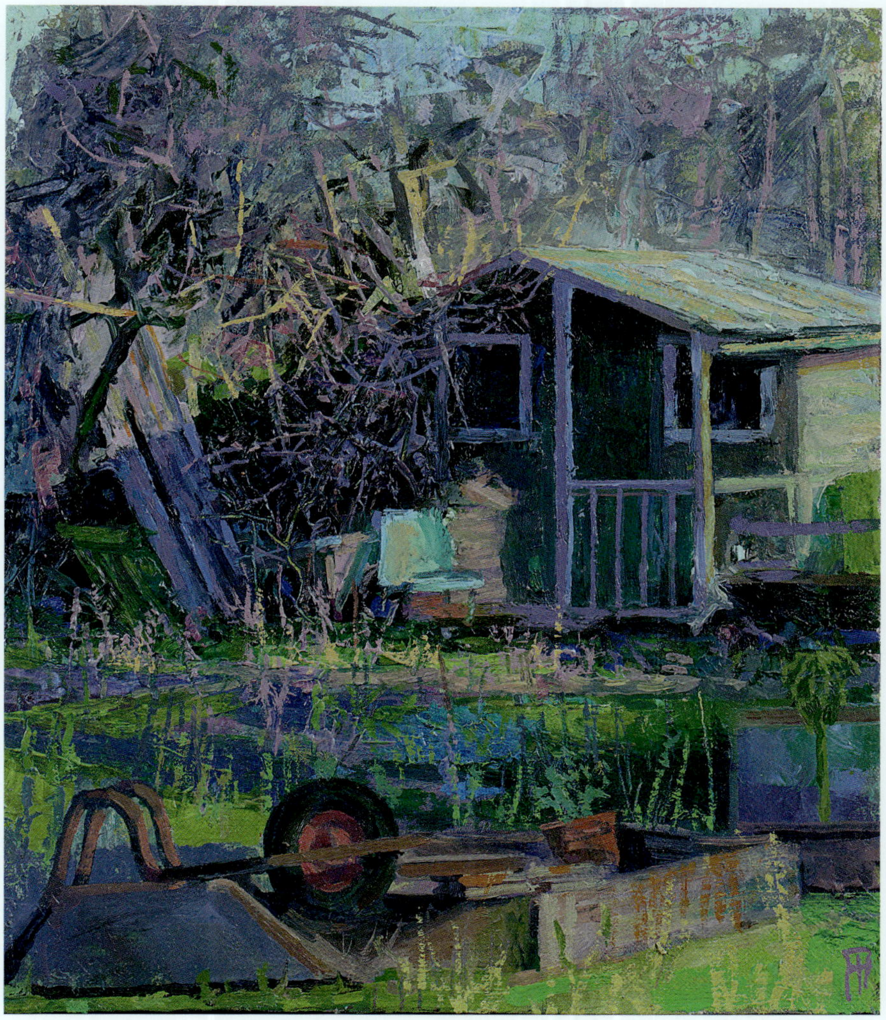

The Trap Ground Allotments, Temple
31 x 22.5 cm, oil on linen, 2023

The Trap Ground Allotments, Wheelbarrow study
25 x 20 cm, oil in linen, 2023

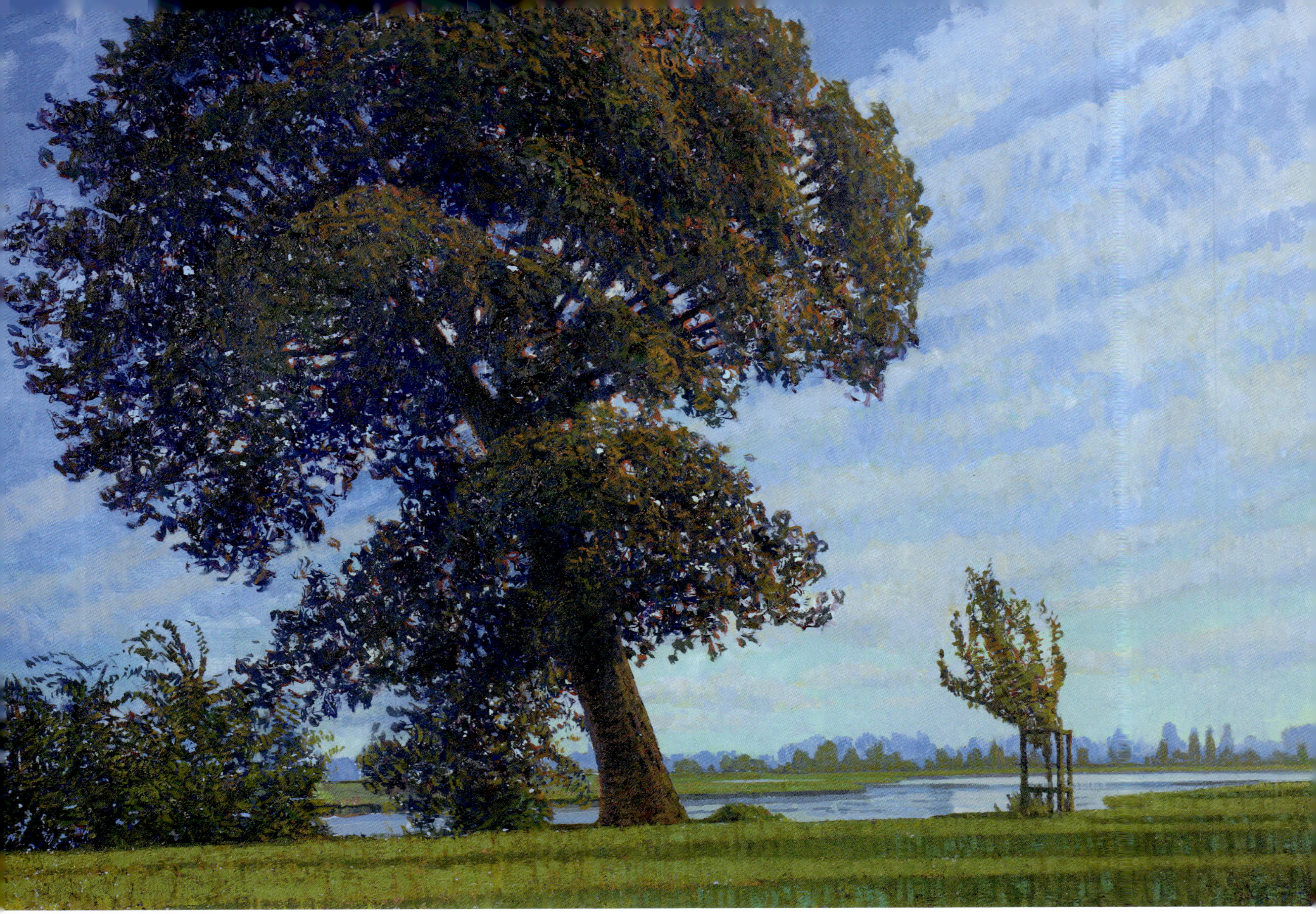

My aspens dear, whose airy cages quelled,
Quelled or quenched in leaves the leaping sun,
All felled, felled, are all felled;
Of a fresh and following folded rank
Not spared, not one
That dandled a sandalled
Shadow that swam or sank
On meadow and river and wind-wandering weed-winding bank.

O if we but knew what we do
When we delve or hew —
Hack and rack the growing green!
Since country is so tender
To touch, her being só slender,
That, like this sleek and seeing ball
But a prick will make no eye at all,
Where we, even where we mean
To mend her we end her,

When we hew or delve:
After-comers cannot guess the beauty been.
Ten or twelve, only ten or twelve
Strokes of havoc únselve
The sweet especial scene,
Rural scene, a rural scene,
Sweet especial rural scene.

Gerard Manley Hopkins, *Binsey Poplars*, 1879

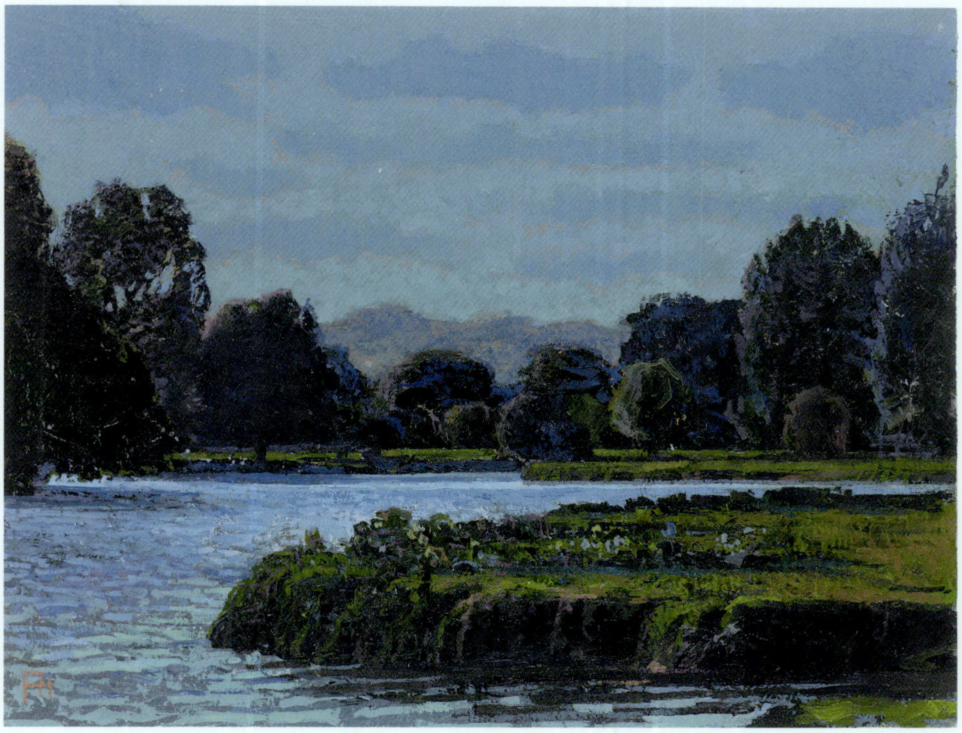

Binsey Poplars, Young and Old
61 x 91 cm, oil on panel, 2012

The Thames looking from Port Meadow to Wytham
36 x 46 cm, oil on panel, 2012

Gerard Manley Hopkins, SJ (1844–1889) poet and Jesuit priest, read Classics at Balliol where he was close friends with Robert Bridges, later Poet Laureate, and was taught by Walter Pater. After his conversion to Catholicism he trained to become a Jesuit, eventually being sent to Dublin where he became Professor of Classics at the new Catholic University. His poetry, with its radical use of what he termed sprung rhythm, was largely private in his lifetime – indeed he burned his poems when he entered the novitiate. It is fortunate that he had already sent copies of some of his poetry to his friend Robert Bridges who prepared the first edition in 1918, followed by an expanded selection in 1930 prepared by Charles Williams (an Inkling).

I tug back the bolt on the gate and walk down the lane with a rush of freedom. After months of matching my steps carefully to another's, I'm finding my own pace again. In the glade, spring is burgeoning into summer. Ivy scrambles up the trunks of alder and elder and ash, dressing the woods in uniform green. As I hack at the nettles with a blunt pair of garden shears, I consider my original plan to leave Oxford. Was it so absurd? I'm fond of this city, for all the lofty arrogance I've encountered at its academic heart. Even that cold core has its cosy spots. I recall the pub snugs once frequented by Iris Murdoch or J. R. R. Tolkien, spirits who trod the line between the university's strictures and the wild spaces of their own imaginations. Philip Pullman's description of Oxford in *The Subtle Knife* as a place where rifts in the fabric of this world might lead us into other worlds is not far from my own experience. I've found kindred spirits here, real and imaginary. I've speculated like Lyra with her alethiometer, trying to scry out some kind of future in dark times. I've meandered through unfamiliar neighbourhoods, discovering handy treasures: boxes of windfalls at the back gates of a convent, or jars of honey with a hopeful honesty box down a lavender path. Over the low walls of the most unkempt and mysterious front gardens I've browsed trestle tables exhibiting ('free to a good home') cuttings of saxifrage and sempervivums, miniature botanical gardens that hint at an orderly greenhouse hidden somewhere beyond the climbing roses and apple trees hung with Tibetan prayer flags. The main roads of the city branch out like the spokes of a mandala and between them run forgotten alleyways: Cuckoo Lane in the East, Jackdaw Lane in the South…

Nancy Campbell, *Thunderstone*, 2022

Rainbow Flag on Aristotle Lane Allotments
51 x 38 cm, oil on panel, 2002

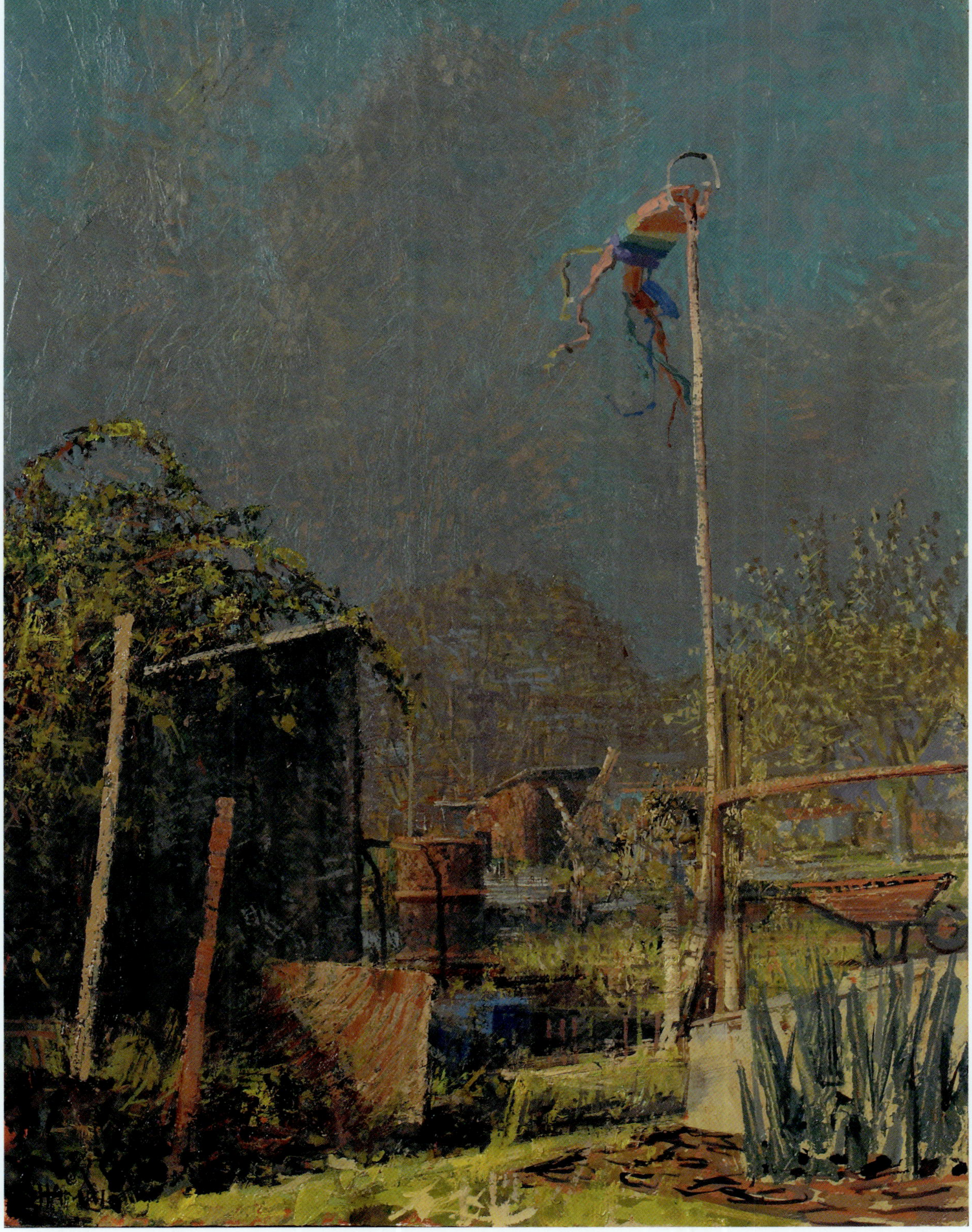

On my way to Hagley I dined at Park Place and lay at Oxford. As I was quite alone, I did not care to see it was dark I ventured anything; but as soon as out, and the moon rose as I was wandering among the colleges, and gave me a charming venerable Gothic scene, which was not lessened by the monkish appearance of the old fellows stealing to their pleasures... Oxford, my passion.... the whole air of the town charms me.

Horace Walpole, Letters, 1758

Horatio (Horace) Walpole, 4th Earl of Orford (1717-1797)
Man of Taste, Man of Letters and MP. Son of Britain's first Prime Minister, he occupied at least three sinecures and sat for a number of constituencies which he saw no need ever to visit. His 1764 *The Castle of Otranto* – allied with the building of Strawberry Hill House in Twickenham – launched the Gothic Revival. His letters to his many friends occupy 48 volumes.

Telephone Box in the Rain
38 x 26 cm, oil on panel 2002

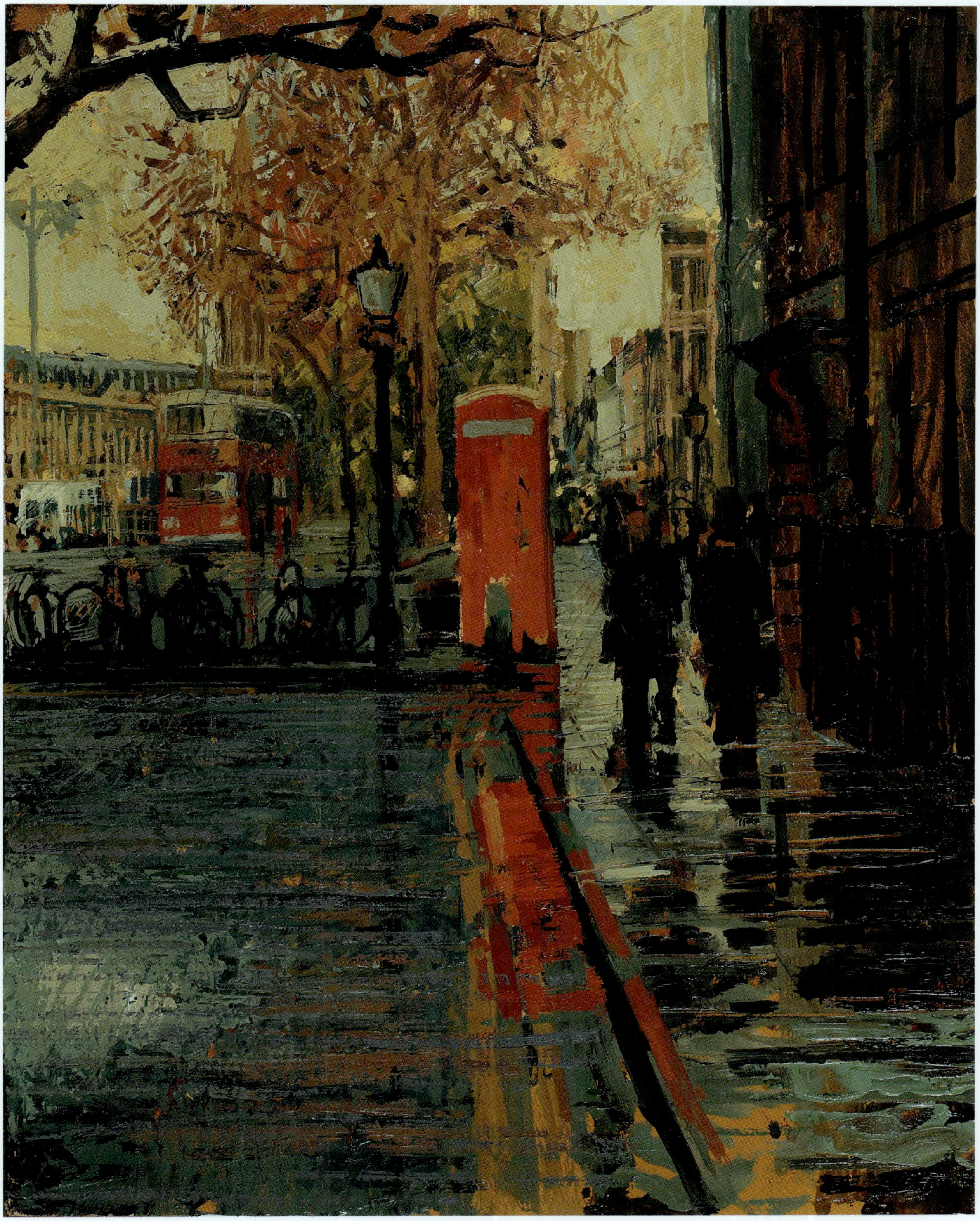

John Ruskin taught fine art at the university, and in his free hours he enjoyed exploring Oxfordshire on horseback. In 1874, he came up with a scheme that would improve conditions for villagers of Hinksey and help his privileged students understand manual labour. He planned to make improvements to a road, laying stones and creating a border with banks of flowers. Among the students who enlisted for the task was Oscar Wilde. It has been debated how late in the day he joined the troop, and how much labour he contributed, but he left this record of the experience:

"We were coming down the street – a troop of young men, some of them like myself only nineteen, going to river or tennis-court or cricket-field – when Ruskin going up to lecture in cap and gown met us. He seemed troubled and prayed us to go back with him to his lecture, which a few of us did, and there he spoke to us not on art this time but on life, saying that it seemed to him to be wrong that all the best physique and strength of the young men in England should be spent aimlessly on cricket ground or river, without any result at all except that if one rowed well one got a pewter-pot, and if one made a good score, a cane-handled bat. He thought, he said, that we should be working at something that would do good to other people, at something by which we might show that in all labour there was something noble. Well, we were a good deal moved, and said we would do anything he wished. So he went out round Oxford and found two villages, Upper and Lower Hinksey, and between them there lay a great swamp, so that the villagers could not pass from one to the other without many miles of a round. And when we came back in winter he asked us to help him to make a road across this morass for these village people to use.
So out we went, day after day, and learned how to lay levels and to break stones, and to wheel barrows along a plank – a very difficult thing to do. And Ruskin worked with us in the mist and rain and mud of an Oxford winter, and our friends and our enemies came out and mocked us from the bank. We did not mind it much then, and we did not mind it afterwards at all, but worked away for two months at our road.

And what became of the road? Well, like a bad lecture it ended abruptly – in the middle of the swamp Ruskin going away to Venice, when we came back for the next term there was no leader, and the 'diggers, as they called us, fell asunder."

Nancy Campbell, *Thunderstone*, 2022
and Oscar Wilde, *Art and the Handicraftsman*
in *Essays and Lectures,* 1908

John Ruskin (1819–1900) was a polymath, one of the most influential thinkers of his time and a more profound influence on British Socialism than Marx and Engels combined. His contemporaries would have been shocked at how little Ruskin is considered today. Studied at Oxford being awarded an honourary double fourth-class degree. First Slade Professor of Art at Oxford and founder of what became the Ruskin School of Art.

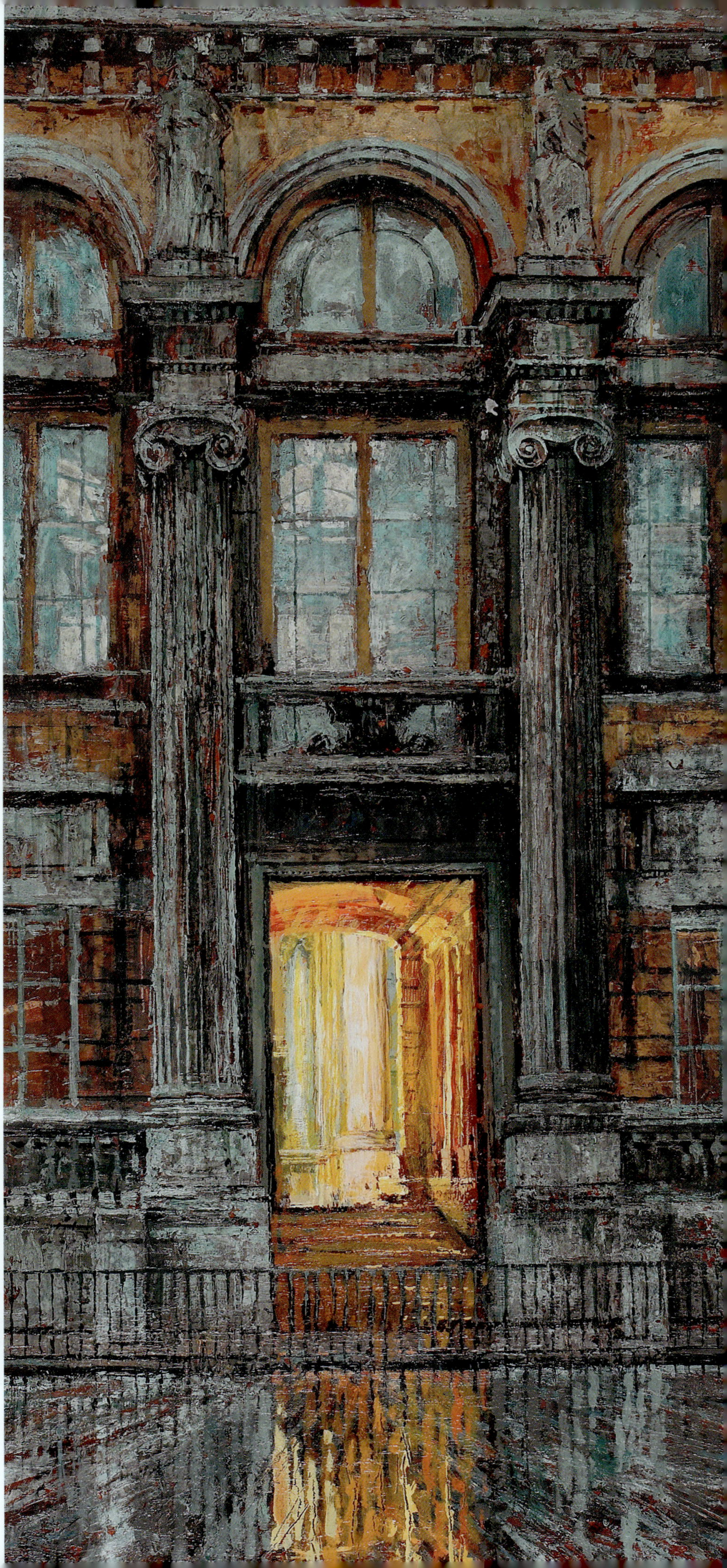

The Taylorian Institute and The Ashmolean
61 x 30 cm, oil on panel, 2001

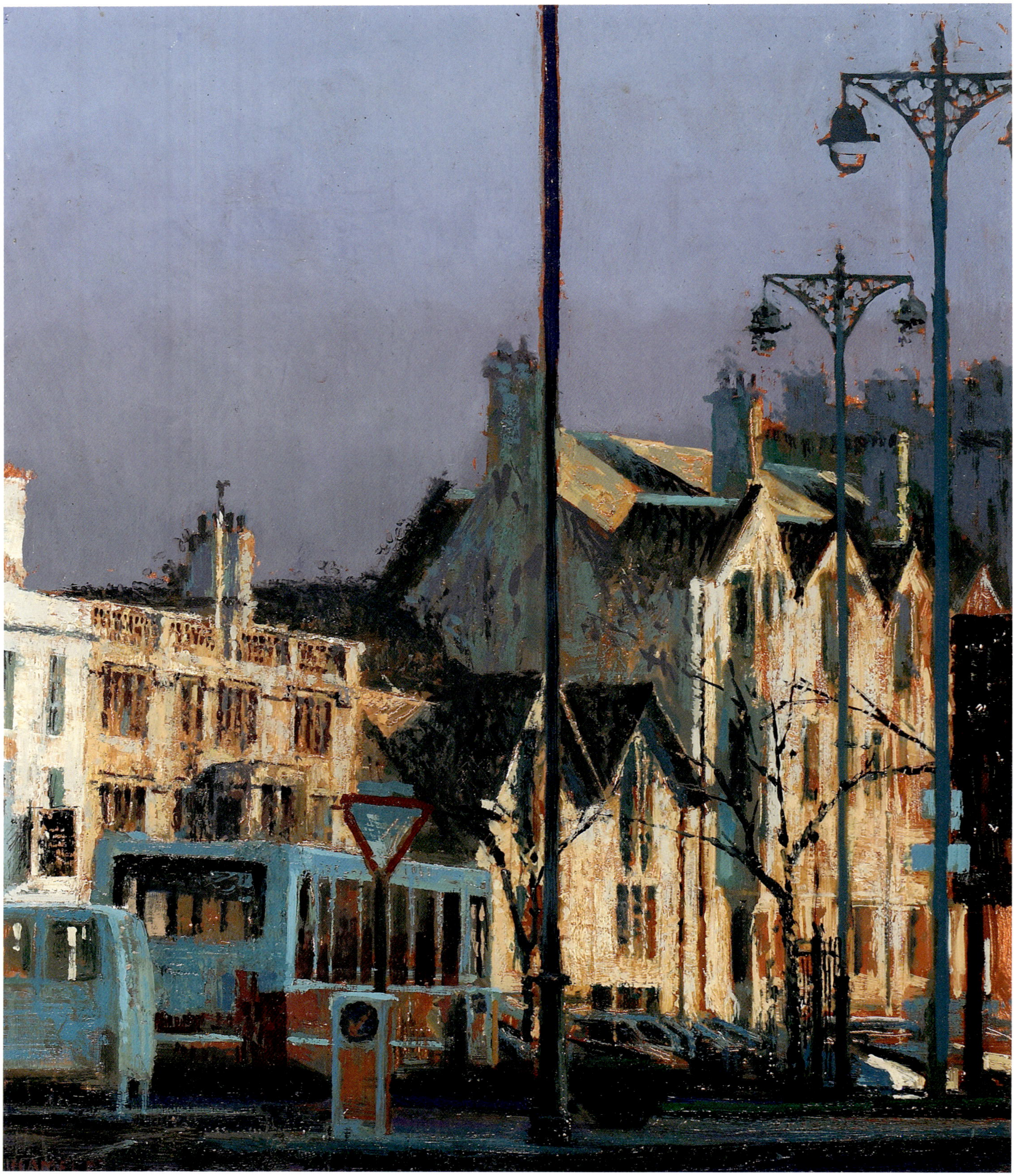

Mr Sniggs, the Junior Dean, and Mr Postlethwaite, the Domestic Bursar, sat alone in Mr Sniggs' room overlooking the garden quad at Scone College. From the rooms of Sir Alastair Digby-Vaine-Trumpington, two staircases away, came a confused roaring and breaking of glass. They alone of the senior members of Scone were at home that evening, for it was the night of the annual dinner of the Bollinger Club. The others were all scattered over Boar's Hill and North Oxford at gay, contentious little parties, or at other senior common-rooms, or at the meetings of learned societies, for the annual Bollinger dinner is a difficult time for those in authority.

It is not accurate to call this an annual event, because quite often the Club is suspended for some years after each meeting. There is tradition behind the Bollinger, it numbers reigning kings among its past members. At the last dinner, three years ago, a fox had been brought in in a cage and stoned to death with champagne bottles. What an evening that had been. This was the first meeting since then, and from all over Europe old members had rallied for the occasion. For two days they had been pouring into Oxford epileptic royalty from their villas of exile, uncouth peers from crumbling country seats; smooth young men of uncertain tastes from embassies and legations, illiterate lairds from wet granite hovels in the Highlands, ambitious young barristers and Conservative candidates torn from the London season and the indelicate advances of debutantes; all that was most sonorous of name and title was there for the beano.

"The fines!" said Mr Sniggs, gently rubbing his pipe along the side of his nose. "Oh my! the fines there'll be after this evening!"

Evelyn Waugh, *Decline and Fall,* 1928

St John's in Evening Sun
30.5 x 24.5 cm, oil on copper, 2002

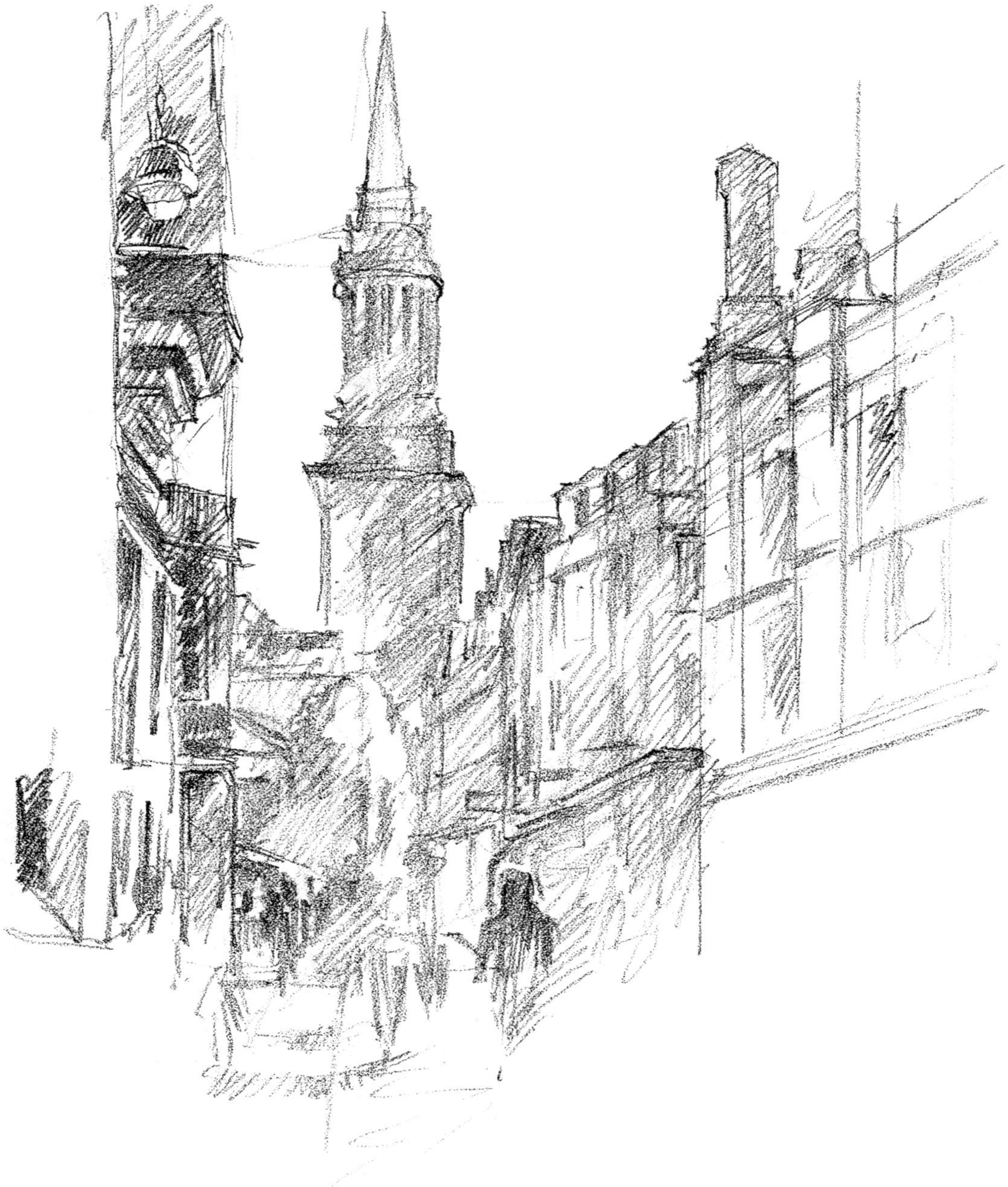

To make you merry, I'le tell you a story that Dr. Henry Birket told us t'other day at his cosen Mariet's, scilicet that about 1638 or 1640, when he was of Trinity College, Dr. Kettel, preaching as he was wont to doe on Trinity Sunday, told 'em that they should keepe their bodies chast and holy; but, said he, you fellows of the College here eate good comons, and drinke good double Beer, and breede Seede, and that will gett-out. How would the good old Dr. have raunted and beat-up his kettle-drum, if he should have seen such Luxury in the college as there is now! *Tempora mutantur.*

John Aubrey, *The Scandal and Credulities*, 1931

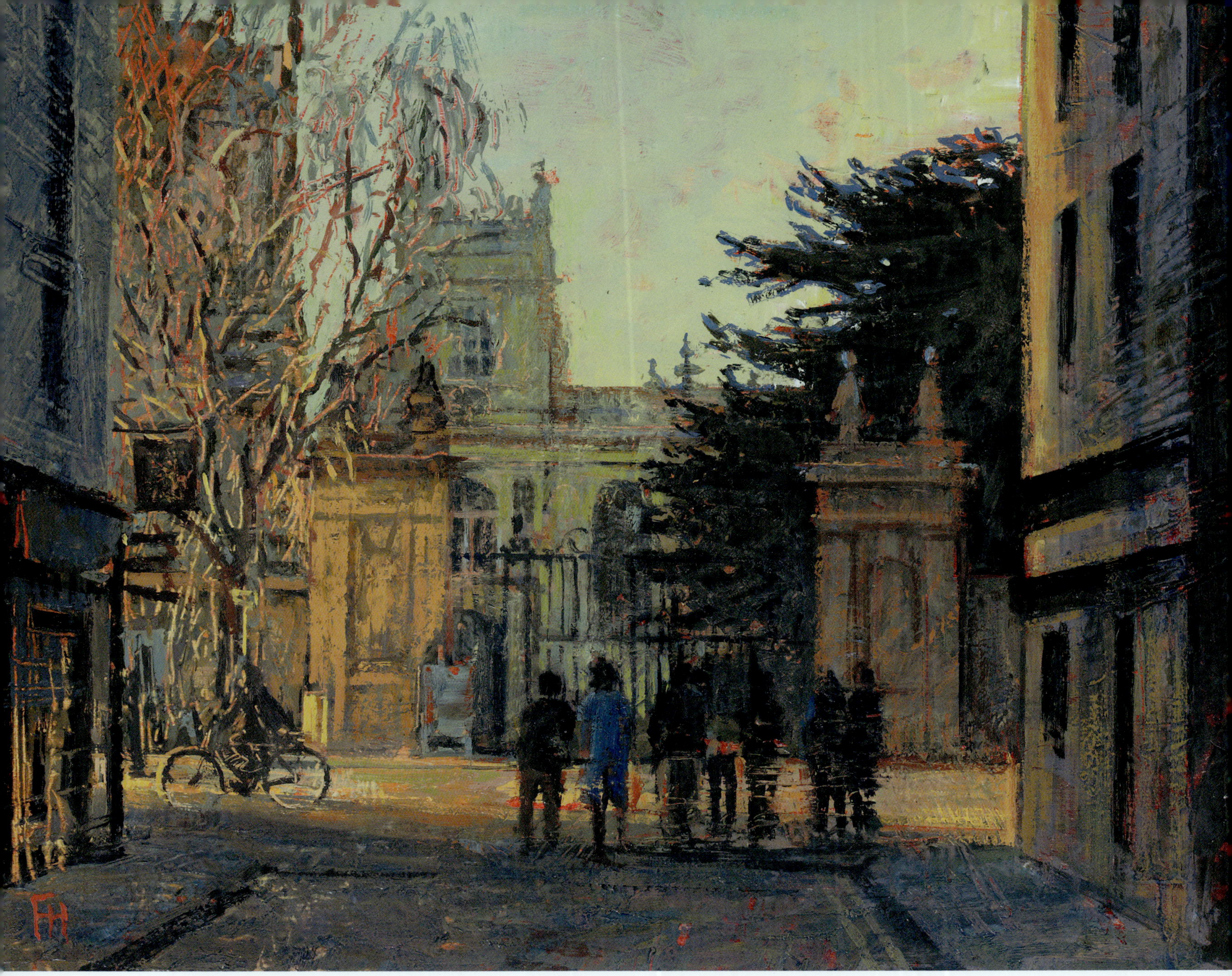

Trinity in Evening Sun
28 x 36 cm, oil on panel, 2012

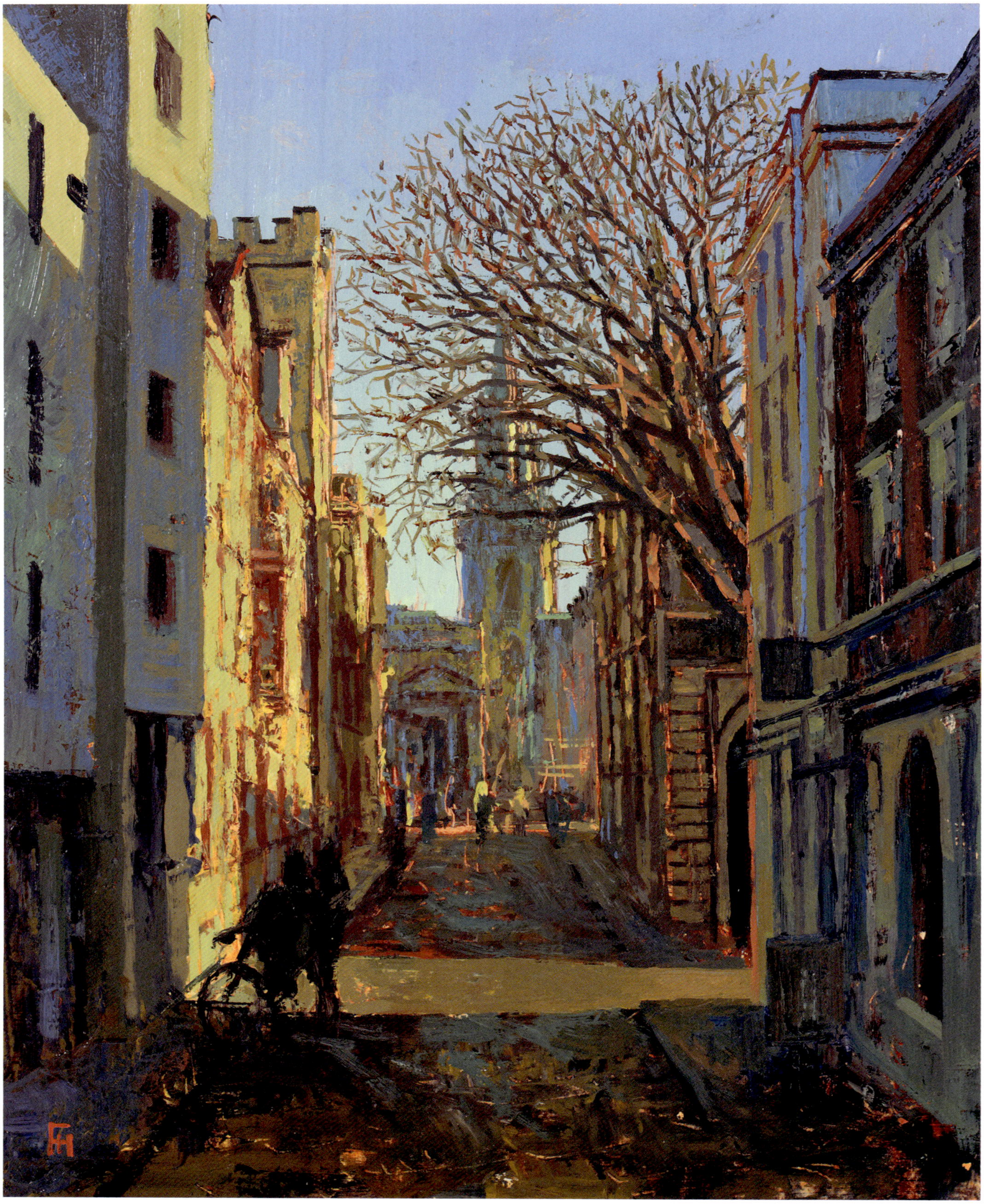

I dine at All Souls, where there are only three Fellows present. We have coffee afterwards in the quad, and the sun sinks gently over St Mary's and the Bodleian. I gaze with love at those dear buildings, wondering whether they will be assailed by one of the Baedeker raids, and whether I shall ever see them again. We walk to Balliol, where I deliver an address on Franco-British relations. I am amused that de Gaulle has sent down two officers and one of his Foreign Department to spy upon me. I have a large audience and the speech goes well. There is a reception afterwards, and I return in the lovely warm night to the Randolph. Dear Oxford.

Harold Nicolson, Diary, 5th June 1942

I dined with John Sparrow as I wanted consoling. He is fussed about his future. He would like to be Warden of All Souls, but it seems that the Fellows do not think him old enough or young enough or something. Anyhow he realises that he would not be elected. So he is now tempted to apply for the Librarianship of the Bodleian. I said that this was not the moment to make such a decision. Without realising it, he was probably overtired and overworked, and that through the cold of London the firelight playing on the books acquired a disproportionate beauty. But to be Librarian at the Bodleian meant much more than firelight on books. It meant dining at Worcester high-table on Sunday off cold pork; it meant walking in the Parks with the sub-Librarian; it meant a little house in North Oxford, and a bicycle. Wouldn't it be better just to go back to the Chancery Bar, to hunt books in the Charing Cross Road, to stand for Parliament, to become Solicitor, or even Attorney-General, or even Lord Chancellor Hawke or Sparrow Hawke if he liked? He could always end up in North Oxford if the worst came to the worst.

Harold Nicolson, letter to his sons, 26th January 1945

Harold George Nicolson (1886–1968) was a diplomat, historian, biographer, diarist, novelist, journalist, broadcaster, Member of Parliament and gardener. He emerged from Balliol with a third shortly before coming second in the entry exams for the Foreign Office. Nicolson was briefly excited by Oswald Mosley's New Party and edited the Party's newspaper. Mosley's move towards fascism saw Nicolson leave for the National Labour Party becoming an MP and a vocal critic of Appeasement. Alongside this he was a prolific writer about literature and history and a columnist for various publications – notably *The Spectator*. In 1930 his wife, Vita Sackville-West, acquired Sissinghurst and together they created the gardens.

The Turl in Afternoon Sun,
Exeter, Jesus and Lincoln Colleges
36 x 28 cm, oil on panel, 2012

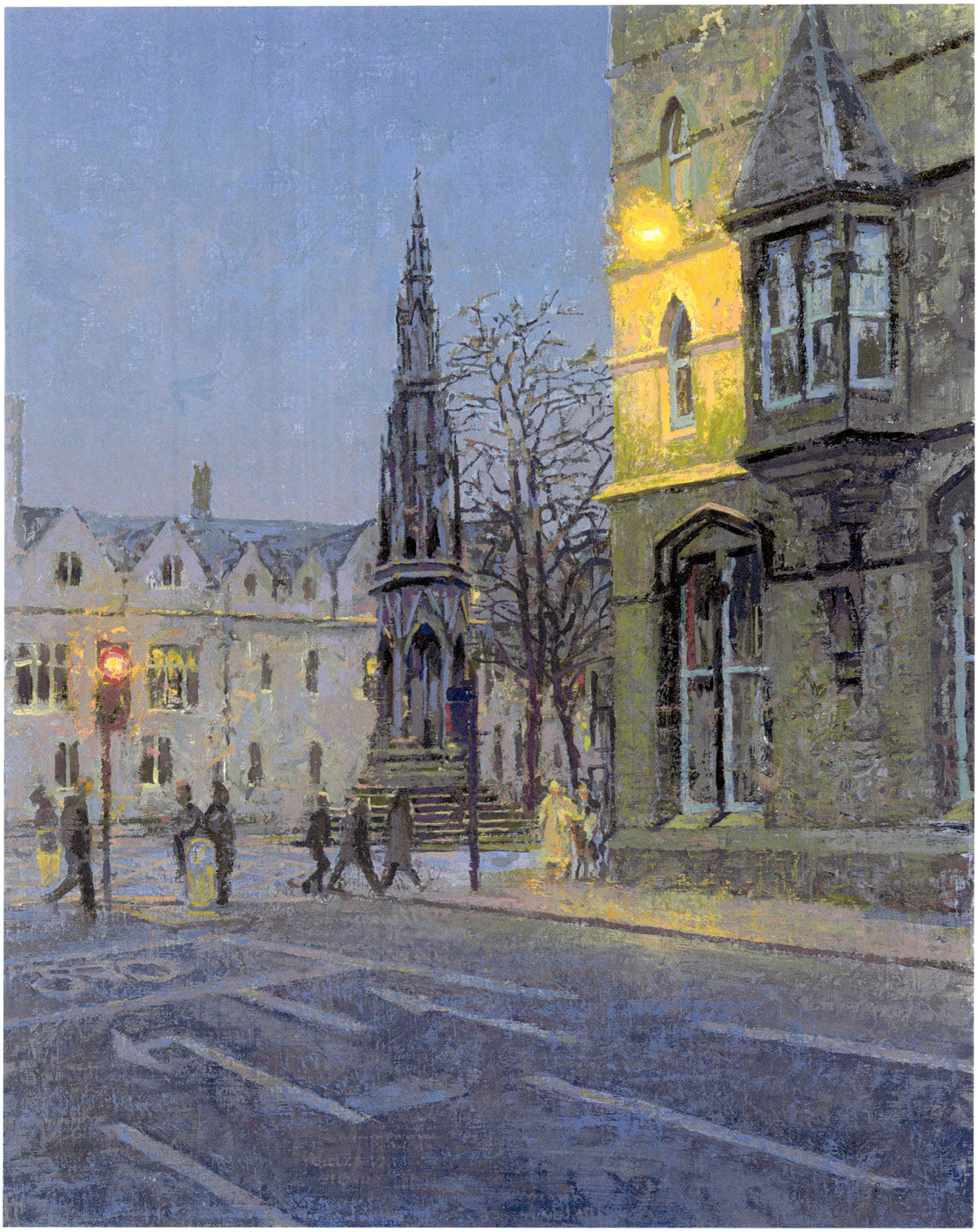

It was literally teeming, stratified, with the shades of human groups, who had met there for tragedy, comedy, farce; real enactments of the intensest kind. At Fourways men had stood and talked of Napoleon, the loss of America, the execution of King Charles, the burning of the Martyrs, the Crusades, the Norman Conquest, possibly of the arrival of Caesar. Here the two sexes had met for loving, hating, coupling, parting; had waited, had suffered, for each other; had triumphed over each other; cursed each other in jealousy, blessed each other in forgiveness.

He began to see that the town life was a book of humanity infinitely more palpitating, varied, and compendious than the gown life. These struggling men and women before him were the reality of Christminster, though they knew little of Christ or Minster. That was one of the humours of things. The floating population of students and teachers, who did know both in a way, were not Christminster in a local sense at all.

Thomas Hardy, *Jude the Obscure,* 1895

Thomas Hardy (1840–1928), novelist and poet, despite being recognised as one of the greatest English novelists – *Far from the Madding Crowd, Tess of the d'Urbervilles, The Return of the Native* – *Jude the Obscure,* published in 1898, was his last novel and until his death 30 years later he stuck to poetry. Just as well, he is now recognised as one of the greatest English Poets. Philip Larkin's *Oxford Book of Twentieth Century English Verse* contained 27 poems by Hardy, nine by T S Eliot and even fewer by W B Yeats.

The Randolph, Winter Evening
46 x 36 cm, oil on linen, 2024

Each year the *Magdalen College Record* drops through my letter box to tell me about the doings of what Professor Niall Ferguson once christened the 'Magdalen Empire'. News of the College's fellowship and present students and of the Old Members who write from all corners of the earth to communicate honours, promotions, marriages, divorces, new books, new films, new children, new spouses. For almost three decades I've wanted to write a letter letting Old Members know that after a few good years – and I mean really good years – out in Colombia I am presently in a maximum security prison for the foreseeable.

Having evergreen memories of Magdalen, I wanted to ensure that Old Members knew how much I would welcome a visit from any of them if they found themselves at a loose end in Bogota.

Ronald J Caffrey, 2024

Broad Street in the Early Morning Sun
46 x 36 cm, oil on linen, 2024

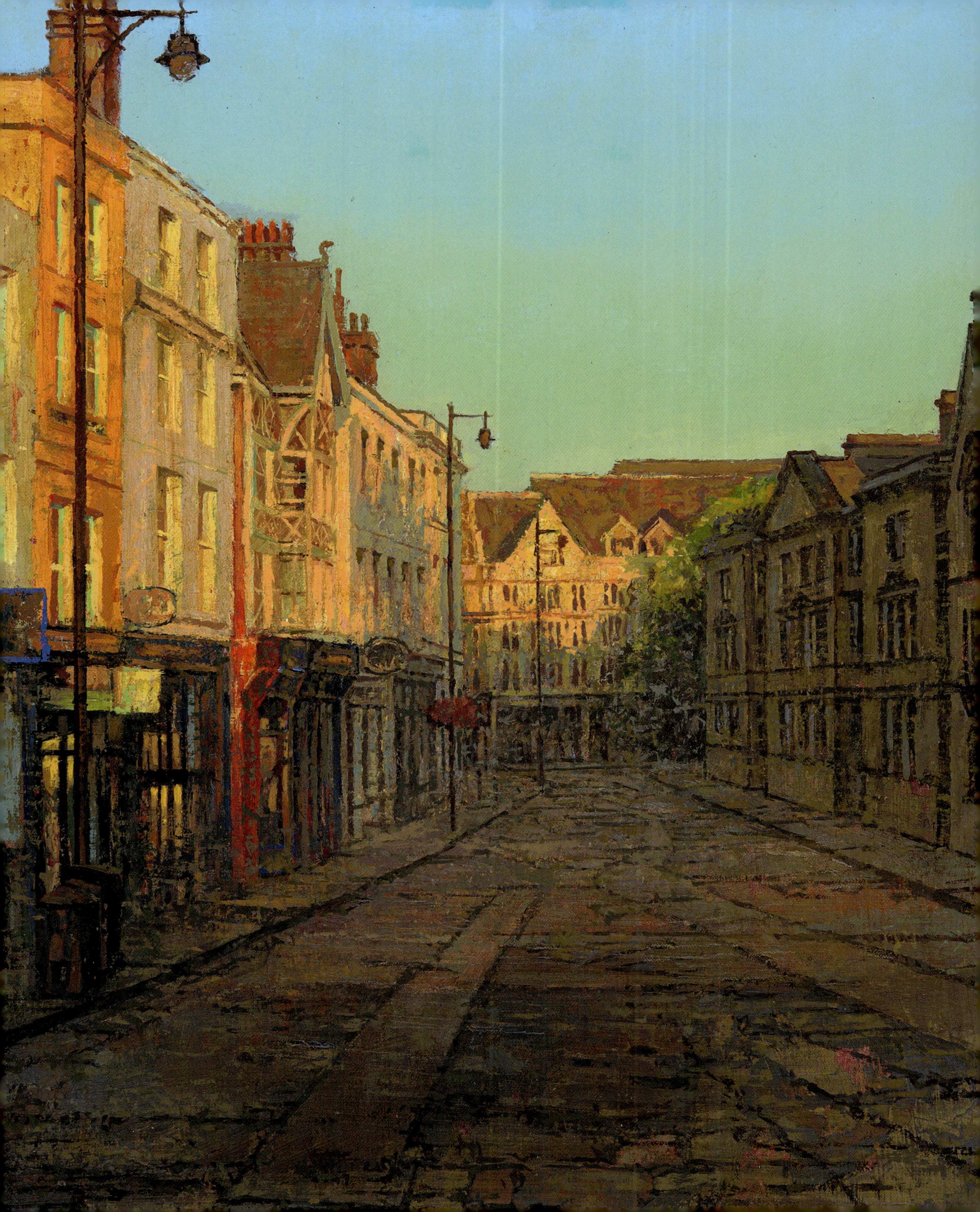

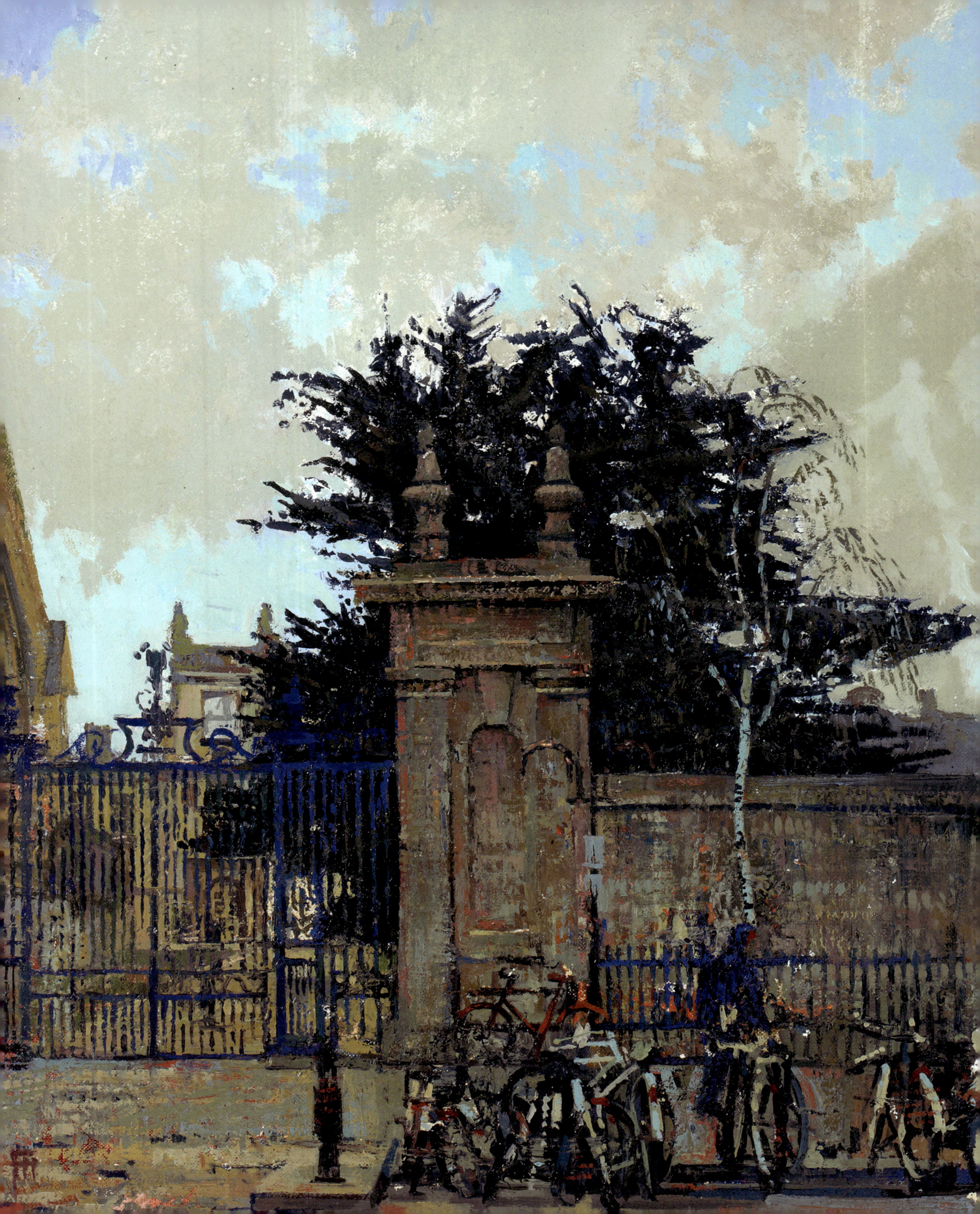

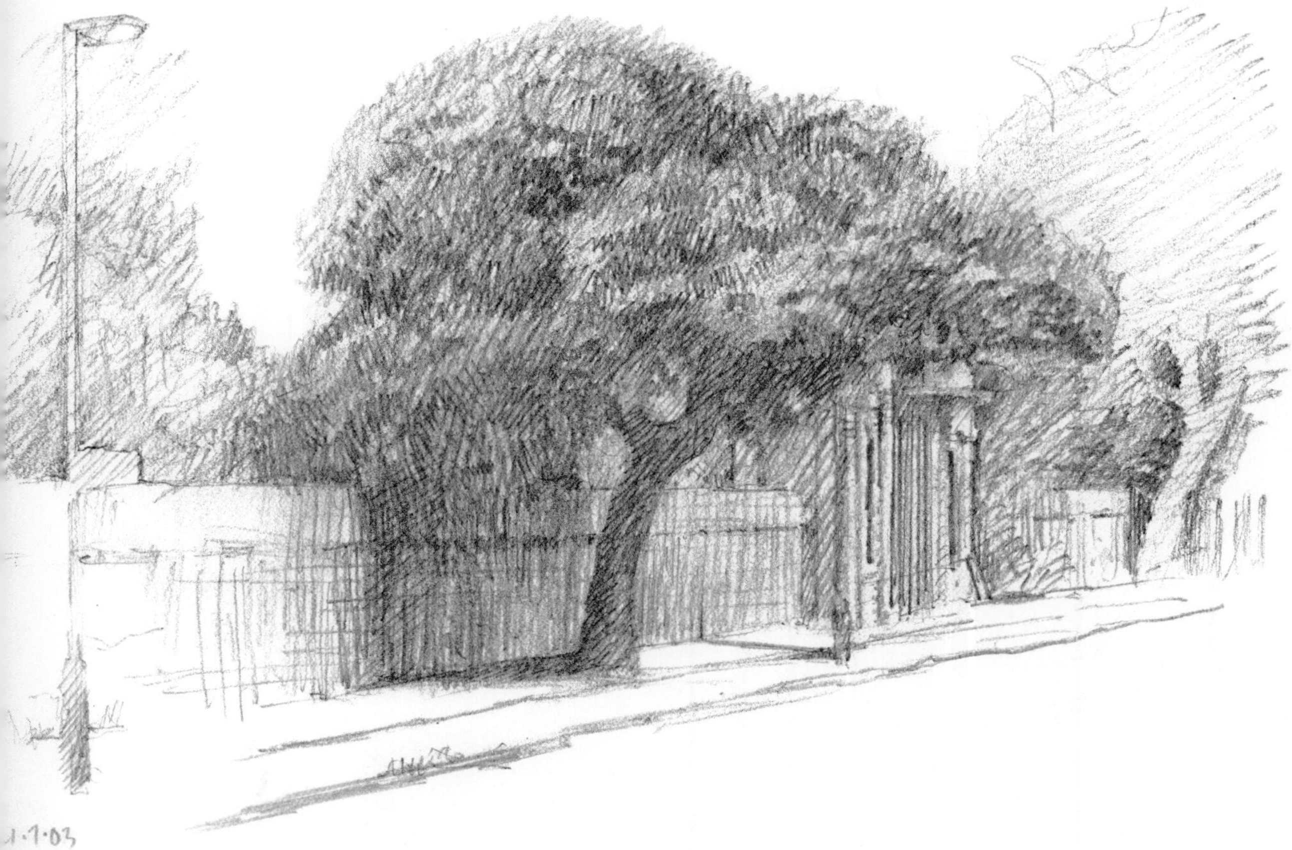

I walked down the empty Broad to breakfast, as I often did on Sundays, at a tea-shop opposite Balliol. The air was full of bells from the surrounding spires and the sun, casting long shadows across the open spaces, dispelled the fears of night. The tea-shop was hushed as a library; a few solitary men in bedroom slippers from Balliol and Trinity looked up as I entered, then turned back to their Sunday newspapers. I ate my scrambled eggs and bitter marmalade with the zest which in youth follows a restless night. I lit a cigarette and sat on, while one by one the Balliol and Trinity men paid their bills and shuffled away, slip-slop, across the street to their colleges. It was nearly eleven when I left, and during my walk I heard the change-ringing cease and, all over the town, give place to the single chime which warned the city that service was about to start.

Evelyn Waugh, *Brideshead Revisited,* 1945

Trinity
42 x 32 cm, oil on linen, 2012

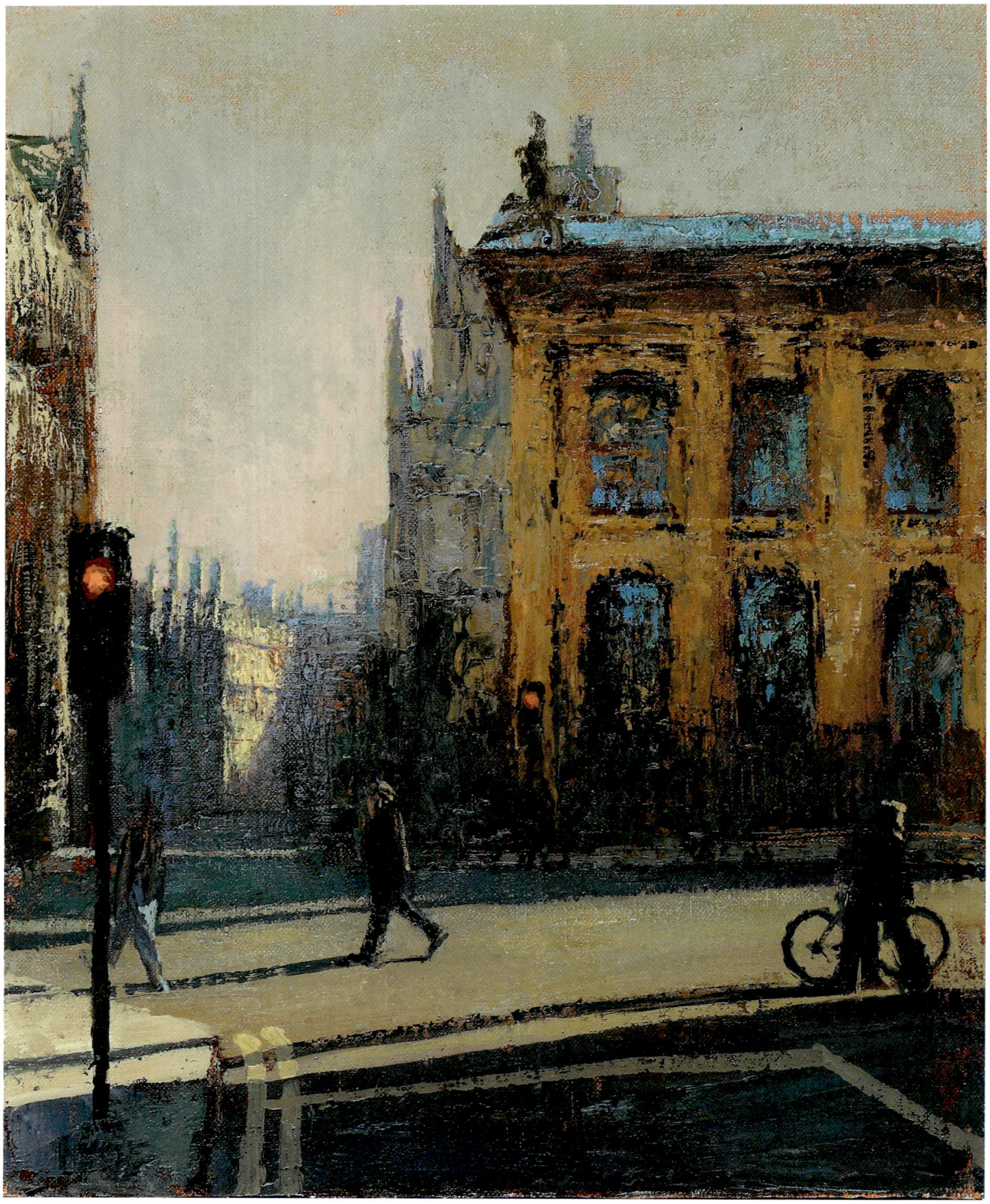

The foundation stone to an extension to the Bodleian Library was laid in 1634, not without either ceremony or incident:

"The Vice-chancellor, Doctors, Heads of Houses and Proctors, met at St. Mary's Church about 8 of the clock in the morning; from thence each having his respective formalities on, came to this place, and took their seats that were then erected on the brim of the foundation. Over against them was built a scaffold where the two Proctors with divers Masters stood. After they were all se'led, the University Musicians who stood upon the leads at the west end of the Library sounded a lesson on their wind music. Which being done the singing men of Christ Church, with others, sang a lesson, after which the Senior Proctor Mr Herbert Pelham of Magdalen College made an eloquent Oration; that being ended also the music sounded again, and continued playing till the Vicechancellor went to the bottom of the foundation to lay the first stone in one of the south angles. But no sooner he had deposited a piece of gold on the said stone, according to the usual manner in such ceremonies, but the earth fell in from one side of the foundation, and the scaffold that was thereon broke and fell with it, so that all those that were thereon to the number of an hundred at least, namely the Proctors, Principals of Halls, Masters, and some Bachelaurs fell down all together one upon another into the foundation, among whom the under Butler of Exeter College had his shoulder broken or put out of joint, and a Scholar's arm bruised, as I have been informed.

The solemnity being thus concluded, with such a sad catastrophe, the breach was soon after made up, and the work going chearfully forward, was in four years space finished."

Anthony Wood, *History and Antiquities of the University of Oxford*, 1674

Outside the King's Arms
33 x 25.5 cm, oil on panel, 2002

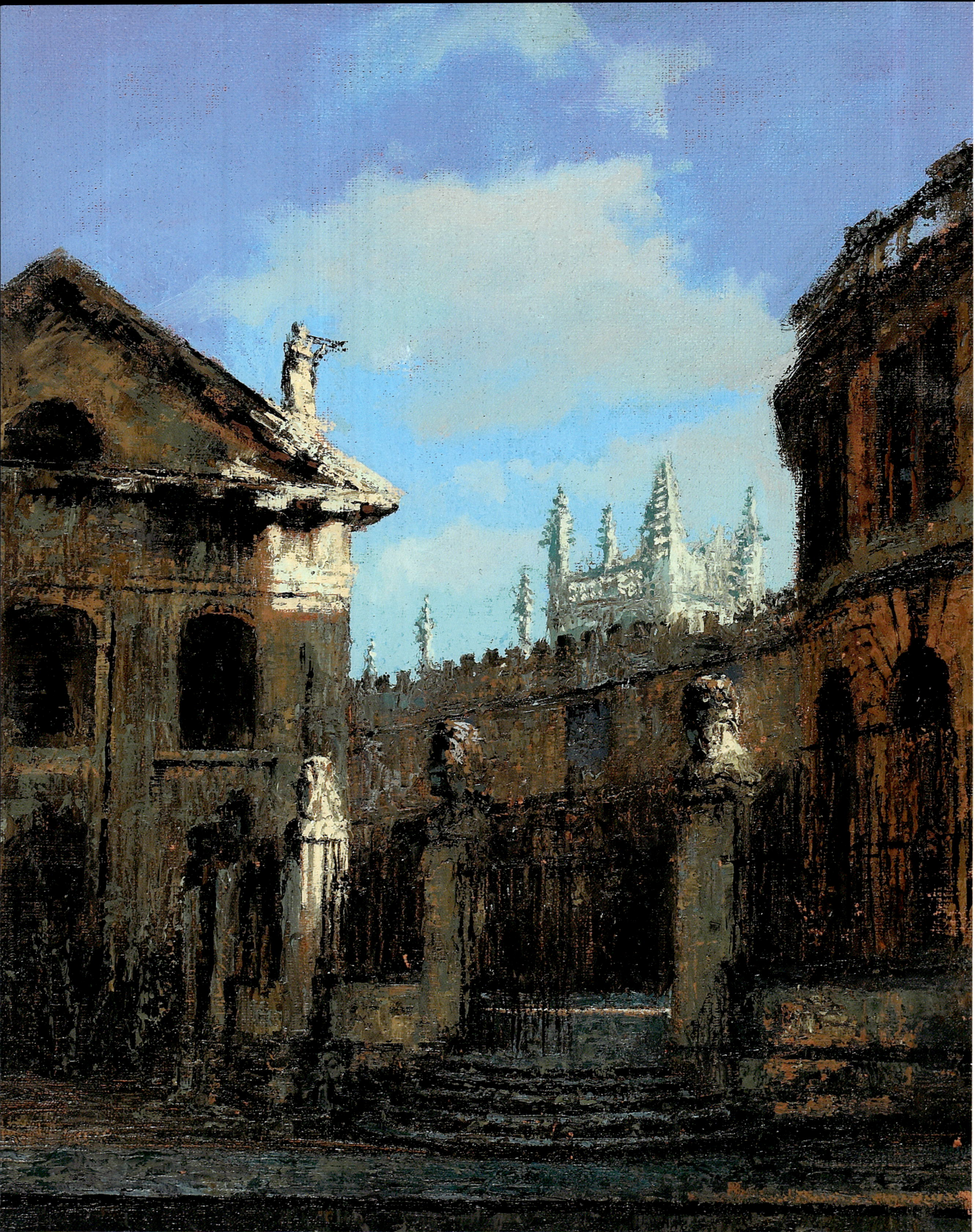

King James, 1605, when he came to our University of Oxford, and, amongst other edifices, now went to view that famous Library, renewed by Sir Thomas Bodley, in imitation of Alexander, at his departure brake out into that noble speech, If I were not a King, I would be an University man; and if it were so that I must be a prisoner, if I might have my wish, I would desire to have no other prison than that Library, and to be chained together with so many good Authors et *mortuis magistris*. So sweet is the delight of study, the more learning they have (as he that hath a Dropsy, the more he drinks the thirstier he is), the more they covet to learn, and the last day is prioris discipulus, harsh at first learning is, *radices amara*, but *fructus dulces*, according to that of Isocrates, pleasant at last; the longer they live, the more they are enamoured of the Muses. Heinsius, the keeper of the Library at Leyden in Holland, was mewed up in it all the year long; and that which to my thinking should have bred a loathing caused in him a greater liking. I no sooner (saith he) come into the Library, but I bolt the door to me, excluding lust, ambition, avarice, and all such vices, whose nurse is idleness, the mother of ignorance, and Melancholy herself; in the very lap of eternity, amongst so many divine souls, I take my seat, with so lofty a spirit and sweet content, that I pity all our great ones, and rich men that know not this happiness.

Robert Burton, *The Anatomy of Melancholy*, 1621

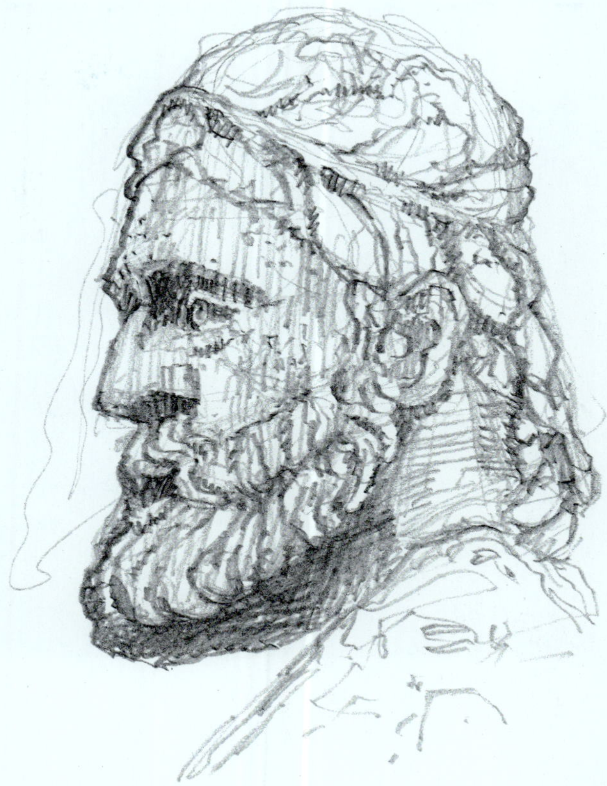

Robert Burton (1577–1640) was a fellow and librarian at Christ Church. His most notable work was *The Anatomy of Melancholy* a vast, labyrinthine and highly allusive work on depression, a surprise bestseller. Nicholas Jenkins, the narrator of Anthony Powell's *Dance to the Music of Time,* is an expert on the work. Burton was less successful as a playwright. One of his plays was presented to James I on his 1605 visit to the University and James had to be persuaded by the Chancellors of both Oxford and Cambridge Universities to stay for the play as he disliked it so much.

The Sheldonian Theatre and the Bodleian
31 x 26 cm, oil on panel, 2002

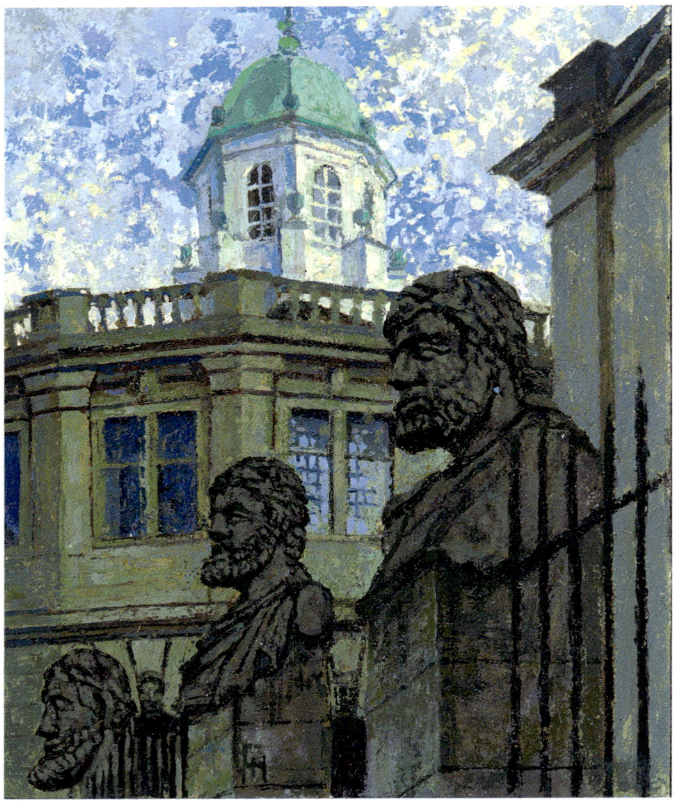

The Sheldonian Theatre
25 x 20 cm, oil on linen, 2024

Broad Street in Autumn
45 x 35 cm, oil on linen, 2024

Within the Sheldonian, rows of eager childish faces looked down, awed and marvelling, upon the complicated ceremony in the arena below; the excited atmosphere was tense with the consciousness of a dream fulfilled which had first been dreamt, years before these feminine Masters and Bachelors were born, by women long dead – women who did not care whether they saw the end so long as they had contributed to the means. Everyone pretended to ignore this atmosphere – the men assumed an attitude of determined conviction that nothing special was happening, the women wore an expression of demure severity, as though Degrees were commonplace to them – but there was no gainsaying the nervous tension of the hour, and after much robing and unrobing and clicking of Press cameras, the harassed Vice-Chancellor, in dignified confusion, tapped one candidate on the head with his mortar-board instead of with the Testament.

...When the men, in turn, had received their Degrees, renewed cheers echoed wildly to the vaulted roof as the first women stood before the Vice-Chancellor; among them were Dr. Ivy Williams, Dorothy L. Sayers, and D. K. Broster, once at St. Hilda's. Even the unchanging passivity of Oxford beneath the hand of the centuries must surely, I thought, be a little stirred by the sight of the women's gowns and caps – those soft, black pseudo-mortar-boards with their deplorable habit of slipping over one eye – which were nevertheless the visible signs of a profound revolution.

Vera Brittain, *Testament of Youth,* 1933

Vera Brittain (1893–1970) writer, pacifist, feminist and socialist. Her studies at Somerville College, were disrupted by the First World War, she volunteered as a nurse, returning to Oxford after the war. The loss of her brother, her fiancé, other friends and her own experiences nursing injured soldiers strongly marked her. *Testament of Youth* was a best-seller and remains a powerful force in setting the narrative of World War I in the popular imagination reinforced by TV and film adaptations. She was included in "The Black Book" – a list prepared by the SS in 1940 of the 3,000 Britons who were to be "arrested" after the invasion of the UK – a mark of some honour.

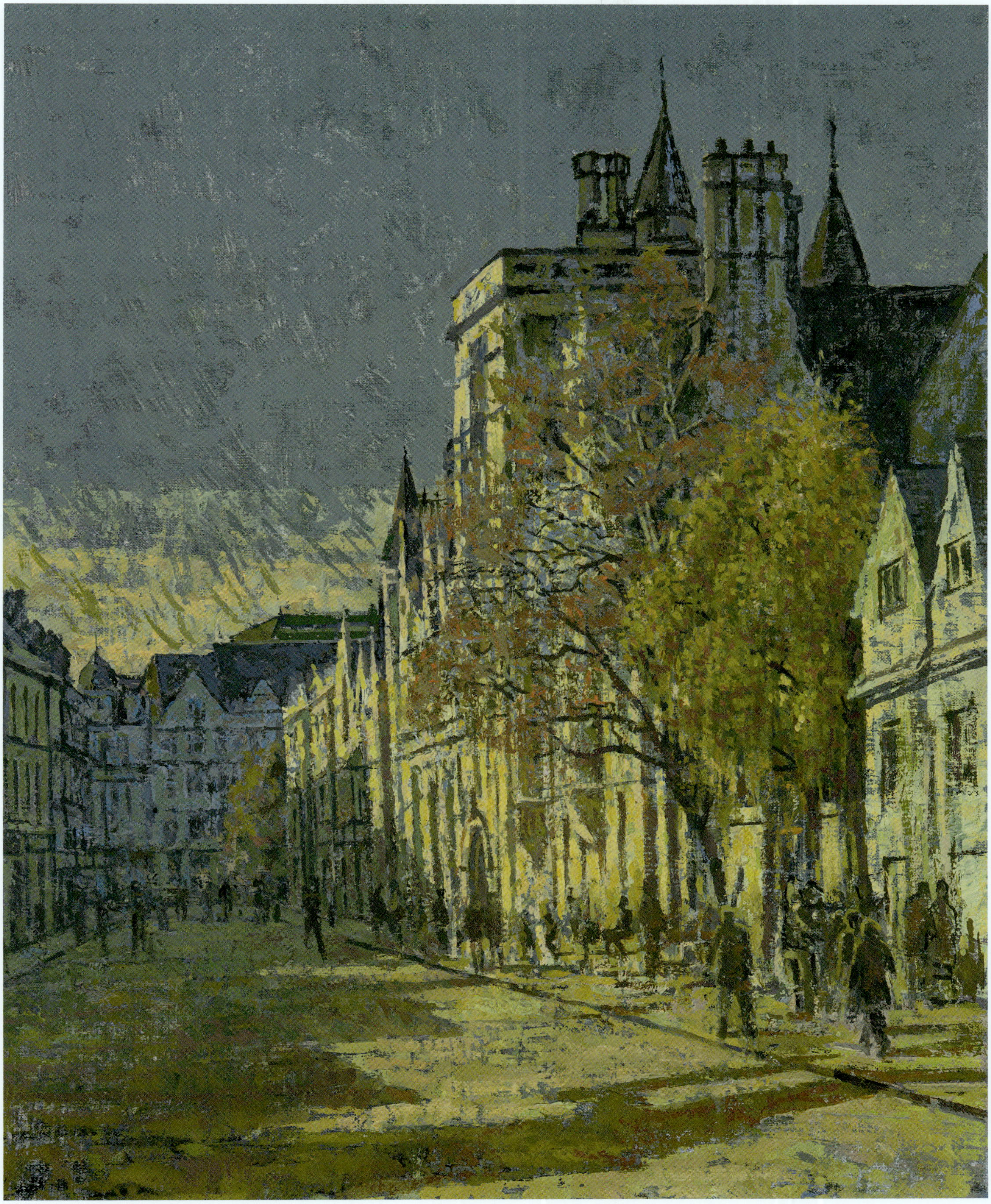

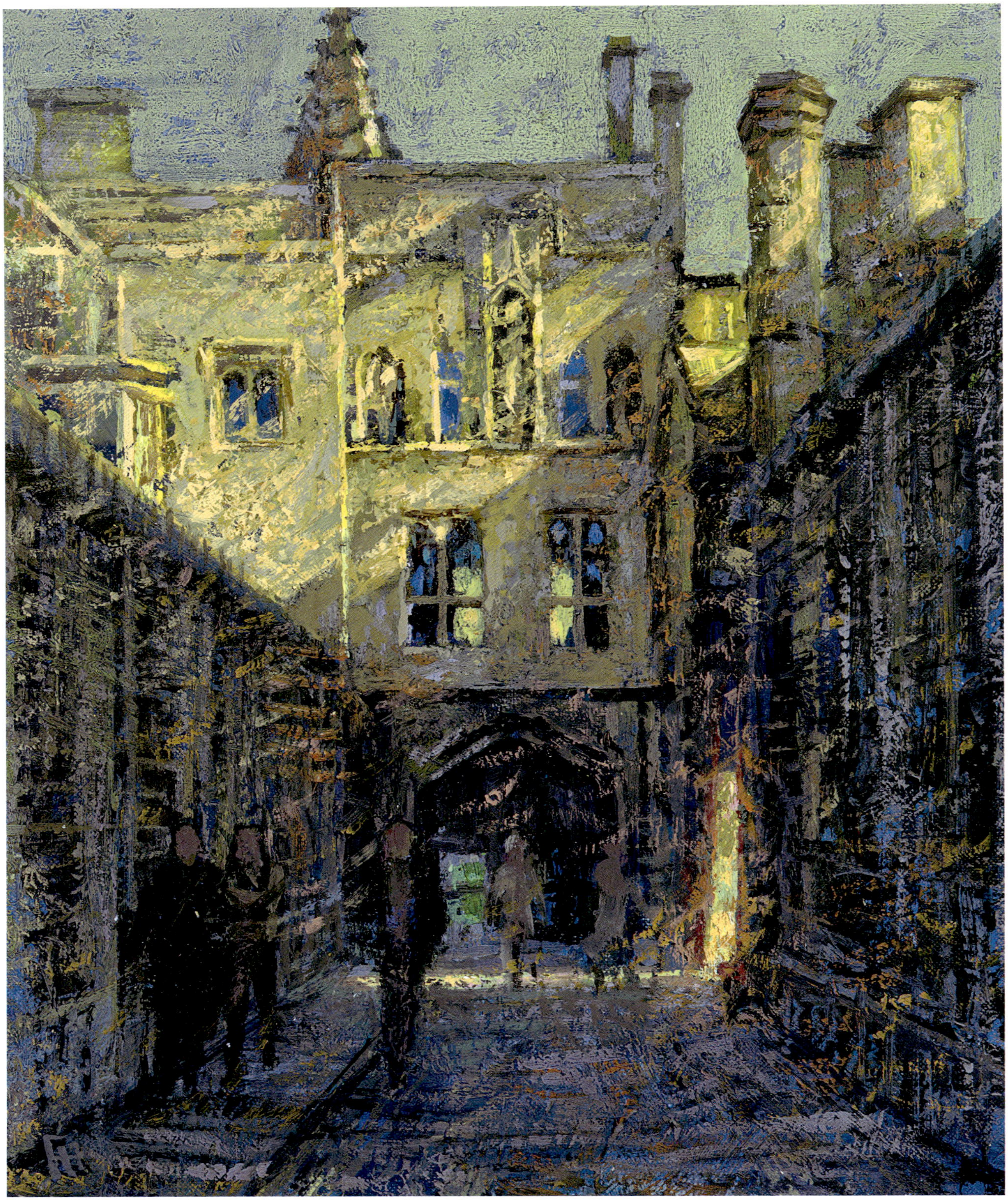

I know not whether to thank, for the beauty of the place, its genius or perhaps the divinest series of accidents that have ever agreed to foster the forward-looking designs of men. In the days when what is admirable in Oxford was built, the builder made no pretence to please his neighbour. He made what he loved. In many cases probably indifferent to everything else. But the genius of the place took care... There is a gentle and puissant harmonising influence in Oxford which nothing can escape. I am no lover of Georgian architecture and am often blind to the power of Wren; but in Oxford I have no such incapacities; and I believe that here architecture should be judged, not as Norman or classical, as the work of Wolsey or Aldrich, but as Oxford architecture.

Edward Thomas, *Oxford*, 1903

New College from New College Lane
25 x 20 cm, oil on linen, 2024

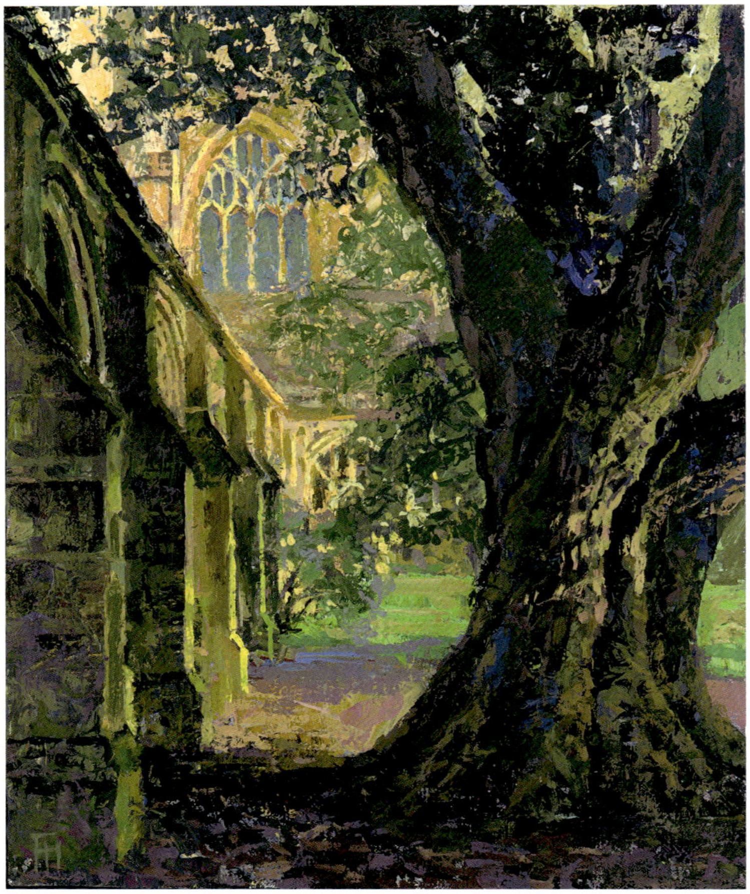

On this old lawn, where lost hours pass
Across the shadows dark with dew,
Where autumn on the thick sweet grass
Has laid a weary leaf or two,
When the young morning, keenly sweet,
Breathes secrets to the silent air,
Happy is he whose lingering feet
May wander lonely there.

The enchantment of the dreaming limes,
The magic of the quiet hours,
Breathe unheard tales of other times
And other destinies than ours;

The feet that long ago walked here
Still, noiseless, walk beside our feet,
Poor ghosts, who found this garden dear,
And found the morning sweet!

Age weeps that it no more may hold
The heart-ache that youth clasps so close,
Pain finely shaped in pleasure's mould,
A thorn deep hidden in a rose.
Here is the immortal thorny rose
That may in no new garden grow –
Its root is in the hearts of those
Who walked here long ago.

E. Nesbit, *New College Gardens*, Oxford

New College Cloisters
25 x 20 cm, oil on linen, 2024

The Evergreen Oak in New College Cloisters
46 x 36 cm, oil on linen, 2024

Edith Nesbit (1858–1924), novelist, poet and socialist, has no obvious Oxford connection. Author of over 60 books of which only her books for children, *The Railway Children, Five Children and It* and others, remain in the canon. She was an early Fabian and flirted with the more Marxist-oriented Social Democratic Federation but found it too radical. She disapproved of female suffrage, believing too many women would vote Conservative.

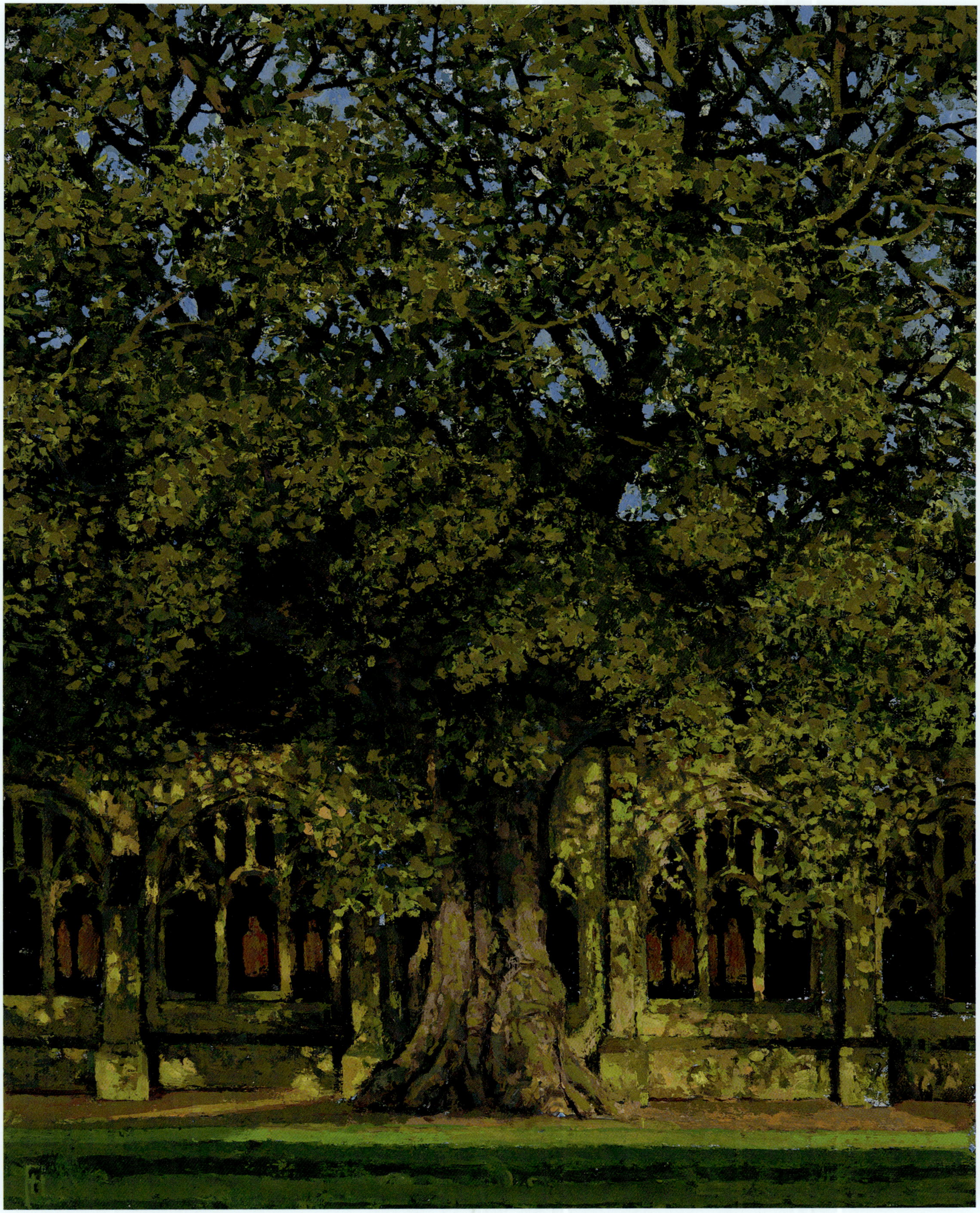

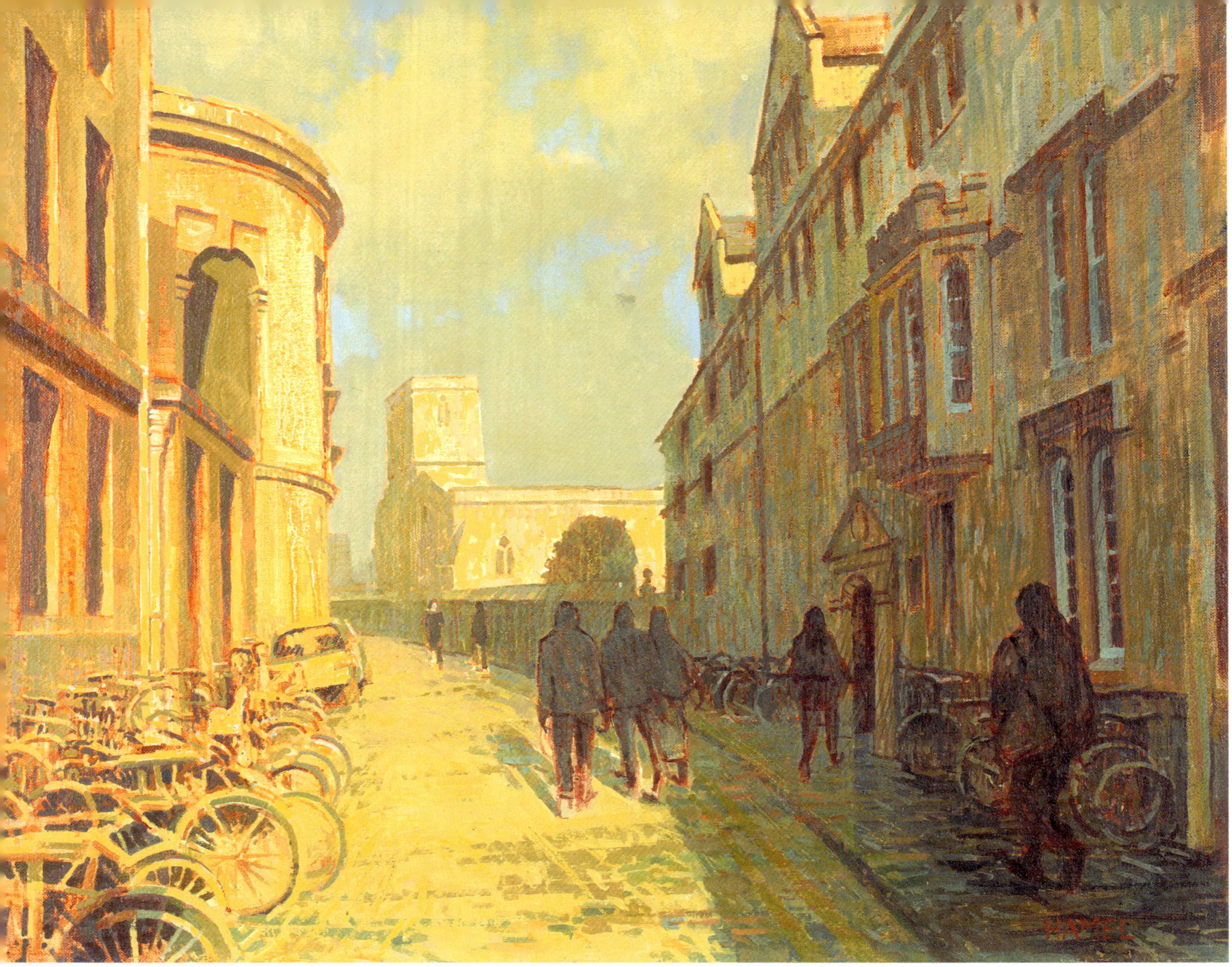

I soon discovered that unless an undergraduate came to Oxford with outstanding academic recommendations the authorities paid not the slightest attention to him. They did not care a hoot whether he sank or swam. He would have no encouragement, no help. Tuition was minimal. His tutors were either too busy or too lazy to be bothered. So long as he attended the prescribed number of lectures he would not be penalized in any way. And who the hell can learn from lectures? To pass three hours a week feverishly trying to take down notes, or memorize a string of platitudes or paradoxes usually the latter since most lecturers tend to show off is utterly useless. A student does far better to read the stuff quietly in his room. It will take him a quarter of the time, and he will thus be able to concentrate without distractions. But he does need personal guidance as well.

One would suppose the purpose of a university to be to teach the unqualified who are anxious to be taught. I went to Oxford with few academic attainments. I left with no more. My three years at the University were a complete waste of time, a blank in my life over which I do not now care to linger. As it was, the term time only covered half the year. Six months out of every twelve one was down from Oxford, idling. What was the point of the whole institution? To make us men of the world? Eton had already started that process which the world itself, the world outside Oxford, was soon to complete. Few of my Eton friends went to Oxford, where I did not make many more. True, my extreme poverty was partially responsible. Although my father was committed to paying for my board and education, if such it was, he gave me no allowance. For pocket money I was once

Queen's Lane in Sunshine
28 x 36 cm, oil on panel, 2012

Turl Street, Lincoln College
26 x 20 cm, oil on panel, 2012

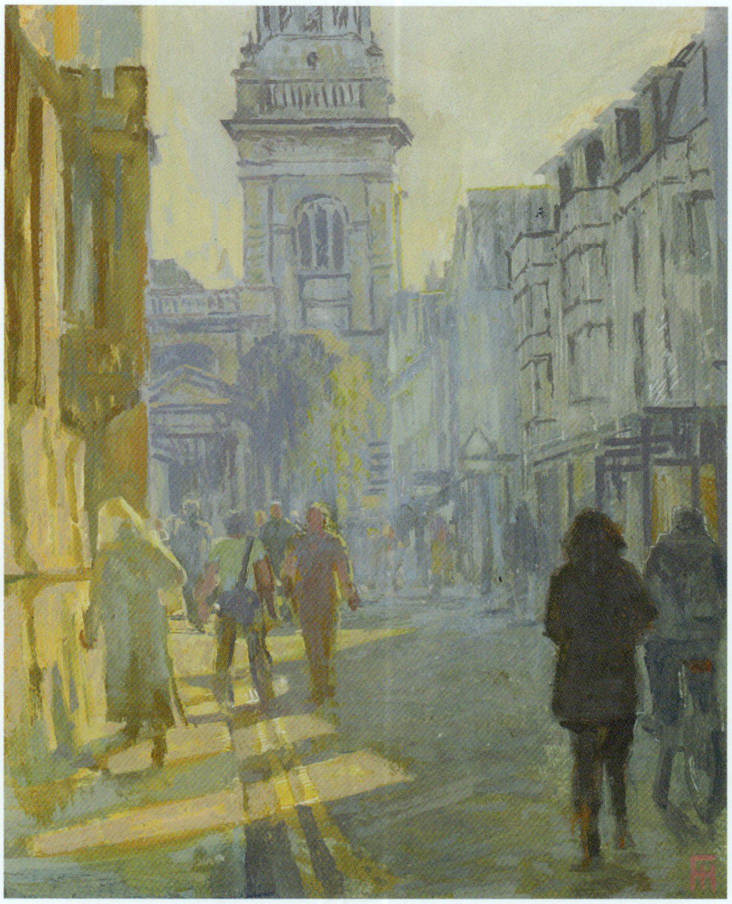

more dependent upon my mother's generosity and whim. Whereas poverty at school does not isolate a boy from his fellows, at Oxford and Cambridge in the Twenties and Thirties it ruled out most forms of social intercourse. I learned that the difference between having no private means and £200 a year of one's own was far greater than that between having £200 and £2,000.

The exclusiveness of the rich undergraduates and the cynicism of the dons were remarkable. Among the preceptors those who toadied to the *jeunesse dorée* to the neglect of the struggling scholars (among whom I cannot claim to be numbered) were probably the most intellectual in the University. The fact that the hungry sheep looked up and were not fed did not bother these tuft-hunting pedagogues. And needless to say, retribution from that two-handed engine at the door in the shape of a strong conscience was meaningless to men who propagated disbelief in all ethical values.

James Lees-Milne, *Another Self*, 1970

George James Lees-Milne (1908–1997) read Modern History at Magdalen College and worked for the National Trust, negotiating the transfer of a good slug of the Trust's Country House estate from their owners. He wrote books on architecture and biographies; responsible for the minor classic *Another Self*, an episodic memoir both funny and touching; and for his 12 volume diaries. Some claim that the diaries are great because Lees-Milne has no side and is prepared to reveal himself. I disagree, it is the fact that the author has no compunction about being unpleasant about his oldest and dearest friends or indeed anyone else which is their particular charm.

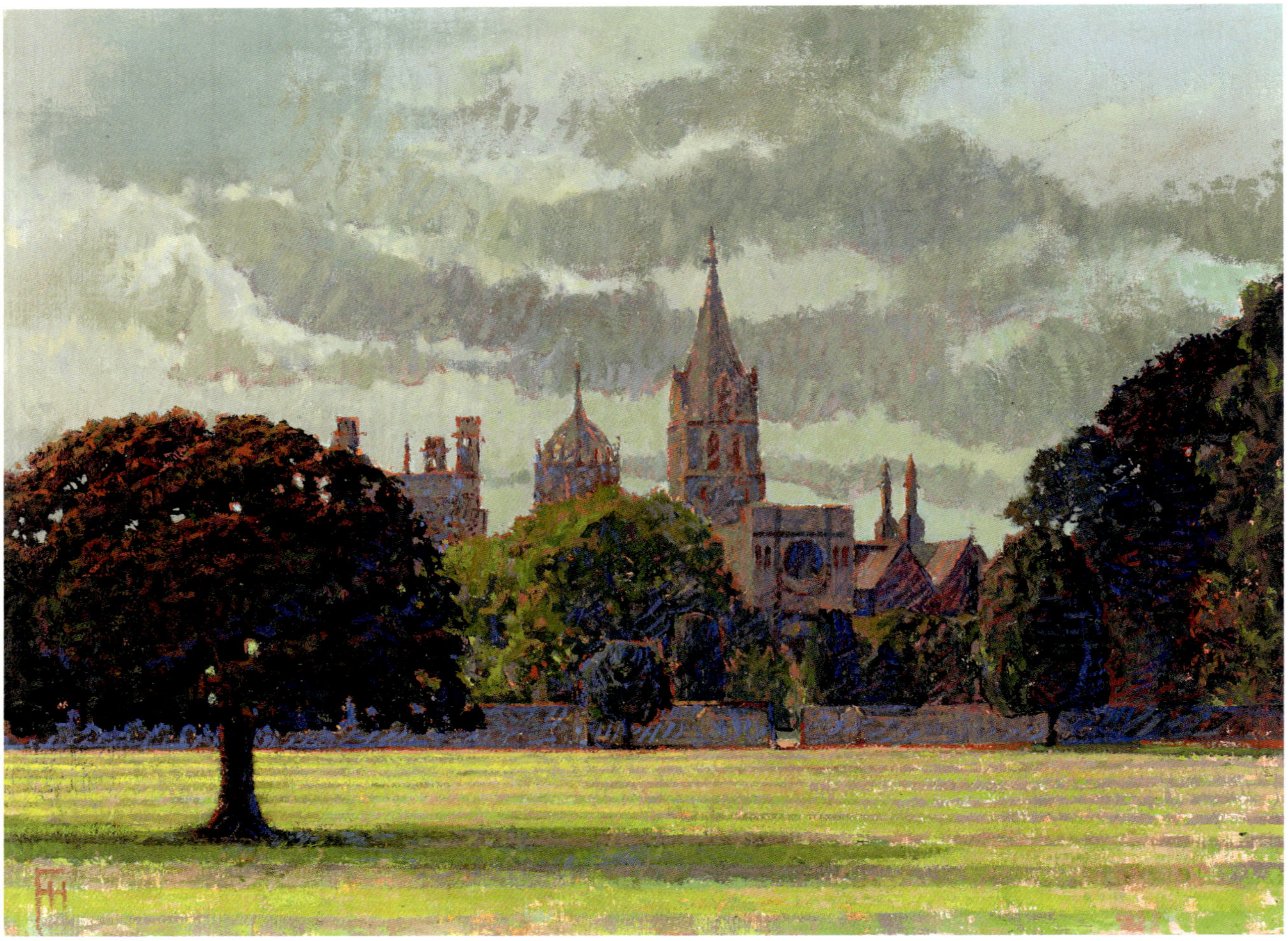

The University and City of Oxford are seated on fine rising ground, in the midst of a pleasant and fruitful valley of a large extent.... with a ridge of hills at a mile's distance.... so that the whole lies in the form of a theatre. In the area stands the city mounted on a small hill, and adorned with so many towers, spires and pinnacles; and the sides of the neighbouring hills so sprinkled with trees and villas, that scarce any place equals the prospect, and the Kings of England ever since the great and judicious King Alfred have (especially when at any time forced from London by war, plague, or other inconveniences) been wont to remove hither, not only their Royal Courts, but the Houses of Parliament and the Courts of Judicature.

John Ayliffe, *The Antient and Present State of the University of Oxford*, 1714

John Ayliffe (1676–1732), English Jurist educated at New College, practised as a Proctor in the Chancellor's Court until his inconvenient Whig views served to stall his progress. His *magnum opus* on the history of Oxford University got him into even hotter water as he was accused of libel, inappropriate language and was swiftly cancelled, being expelled from the University.

Oxford is – Oxford. Perhaps it wants its inmates to love it rather than to love one another.

E. M. Forster, *Howards End*, 1910

Edward Morgan Forster (1879–1970) was an English novelist and Bloomsburyite, whose novels have been filmed extensively. He was nominated over twenty times for the Nobel Prize for Literature but without result.

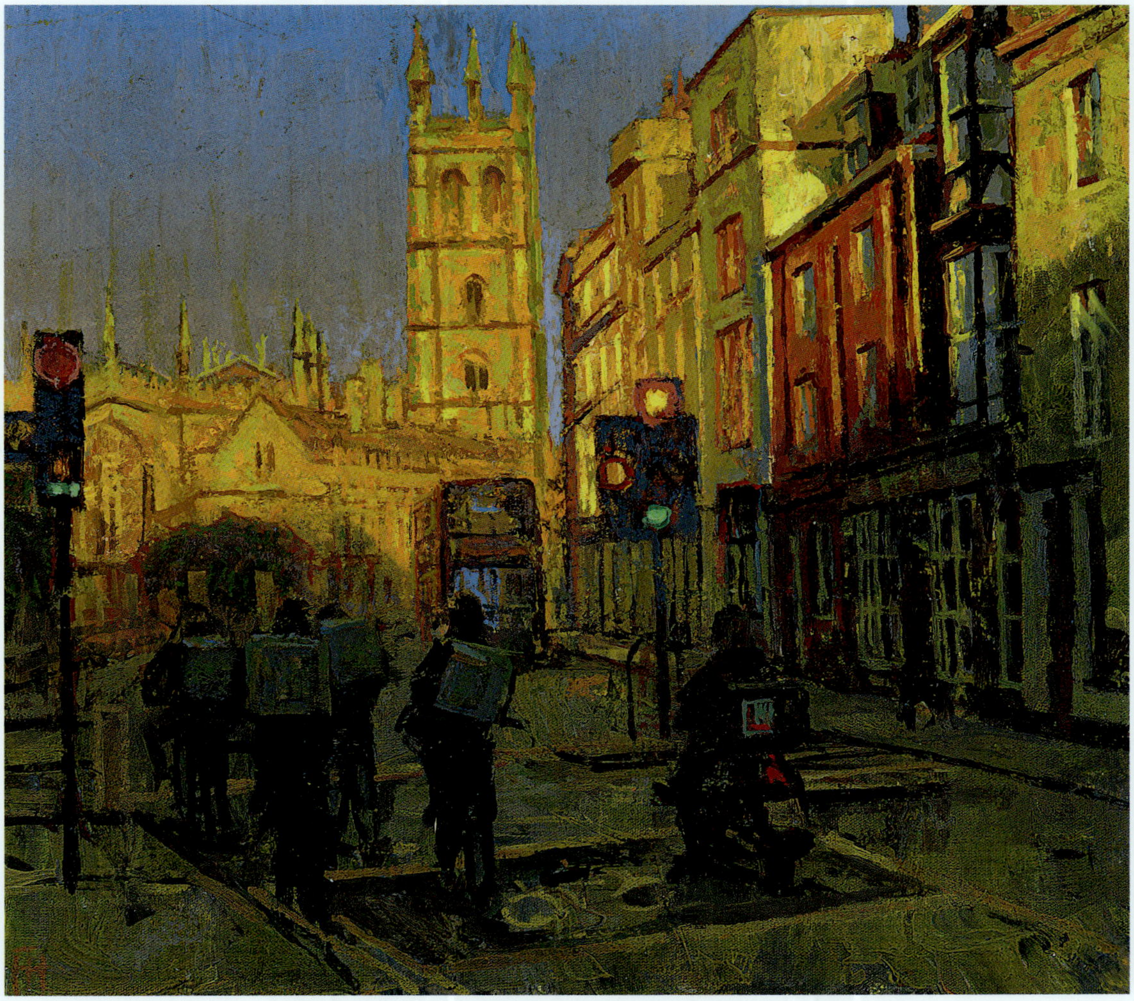

Christ Church Meadow
38 x 51 cm, oil on linen, 2012

High Street Deliveries in the Early Evening
27 x 30 cm, oil on linen, 2024

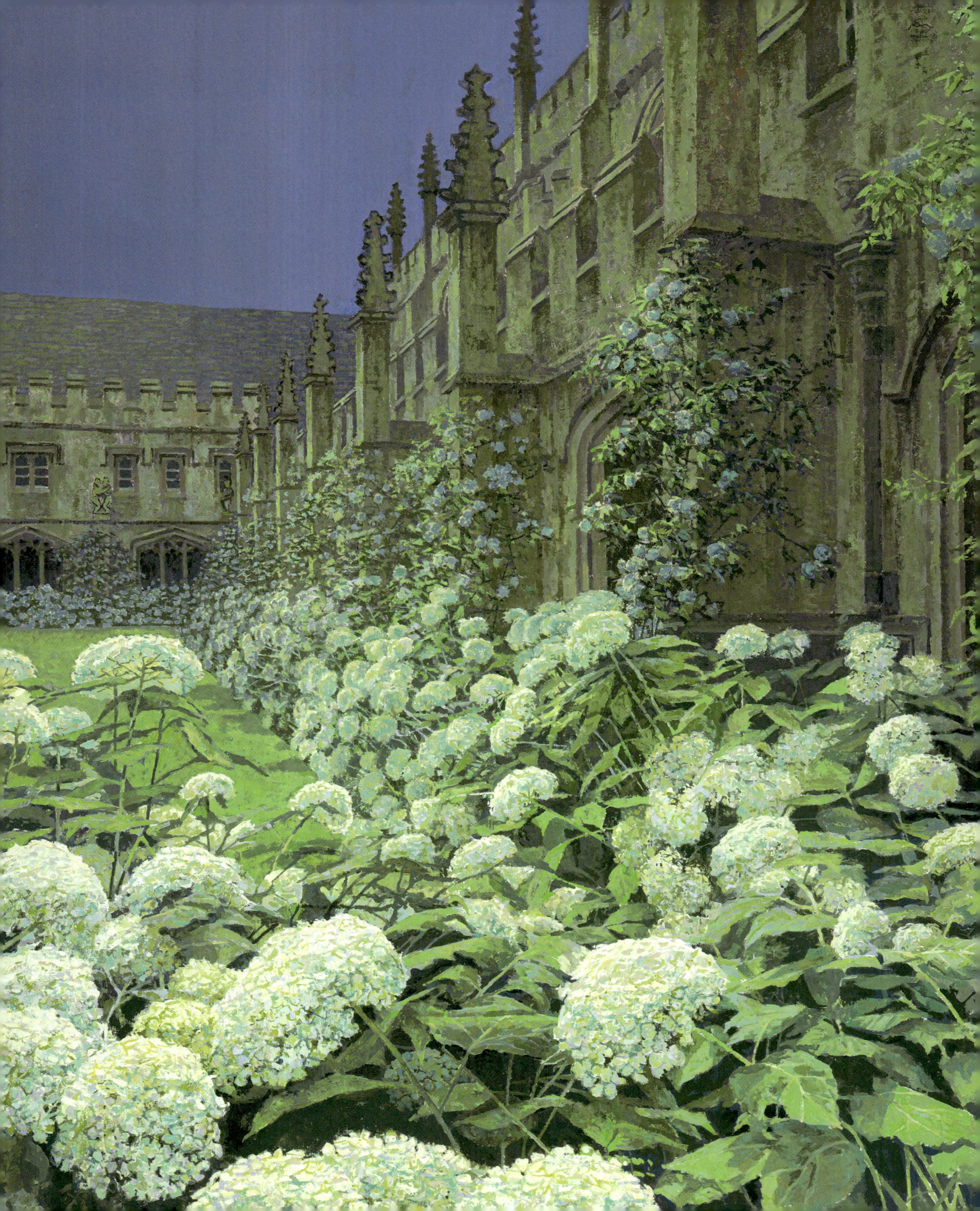

LADY BRACKNELL: Never speak disrespectfully of Society, Algernon. Only people who can't get into it do that. (*To Cecily.*) Dear child, of course you know that Algernon has nothing but his debts to depend upon. But I do not approve of mercenary marriages. When I married Lord Bracknell I had no fortune of any kind. But I never dreamed for a moment of allowing that to stand in my way. Well, I suppose I must give my consent.

ALGERNON: Thank you, Aunt Augusta.

LADY BRACKNELL: Cecily, you may kiss me!

CECILY: (Kisses her.) Thank you, Lady Bracknell.

LADY BRACKNELL: You may also address me as Aunt Augusta for the future.

CECILY: Thank you, Aunt Augusta.

LADY BRACKNELL: The marriage, I think, had better take place quite soon.

ALGERNON: Thank you, Aunt Augusta.

CECILY: Thank you, Aunt Augusta.

LADY BRACKNELL: To speak frankly, I am not in favour of long engagements. They give people the opportunity of finding out each other's character before marriage, which I think is never advisable.

JACK: I beg your pardon for interrupting you, Lady Bracknell, but this engagement is quite out of the question. I am Miss Cardew's guardian, and she cannot marry without my consent until she comes of age. That consent I absolutely decline to give.

LADY BRACKNELL: Upon what grounds may I ask? Algernon is an extremely, I may almost say an ostentatiously, eligible young man. He has nothing, but he looks everything. What more can one desire?

JACK: It pains me very much to have to speak frankly to you, Lady Bracknell, about your nephew, but the fact is that I do not approve at all of his moral character. I suspect him of being untruthful.
(*Algernon and Cecily look at him in indignant amazement.*)

LADY BRACKNELL: Untruthful! My nephew Algernon? Impossible! He is an Oxonian.

Oscar Wilde, *The Importance of Being Earnest,* 1895

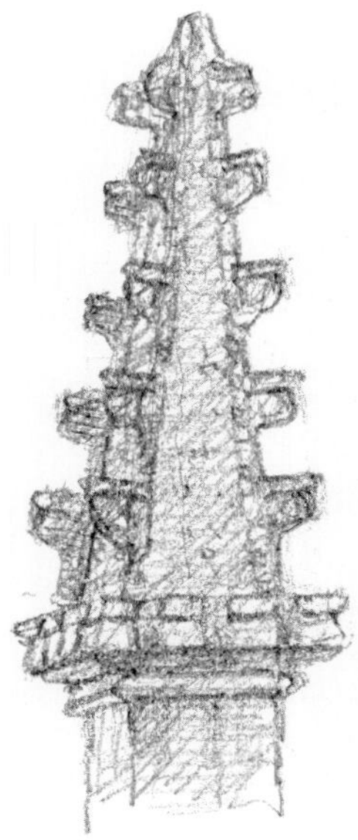

Magdalen Cloisters in the Summer
122 x 92 cm, oil on linen, 2024

All in the golden afternoon,
Full leisurely we glide;
For both our oars, with little skill,
By little arms are plied.
While little hands make vain pretence
Our wanderings to guide.

Ah, cruel Three!
In such an hour,
Beneath such dreamy weather,
To beg a tale of breath too weak
To stir the tiniest feather?
Yet what can one poor voice avail
Against three tongues together?

Thus grew the tale of Wonderland:
Thus slowly, one by one,
Its quaint events were hammered out–
And now the tale is done,
And home we steer, a merry crew,
Beneath the setting sun.

Lewis Carroll, *Alice in Wonderland*, 1865

Charles Lutwidge Dodgson (1832–1898), pen name Lewis Carroll, was a writer, poet, mathematician, photographer and Anglican Clergyman. Both an undergraduate and then a fellow of Christ Church, his academic work has been overshadowed by his creation of Alice.

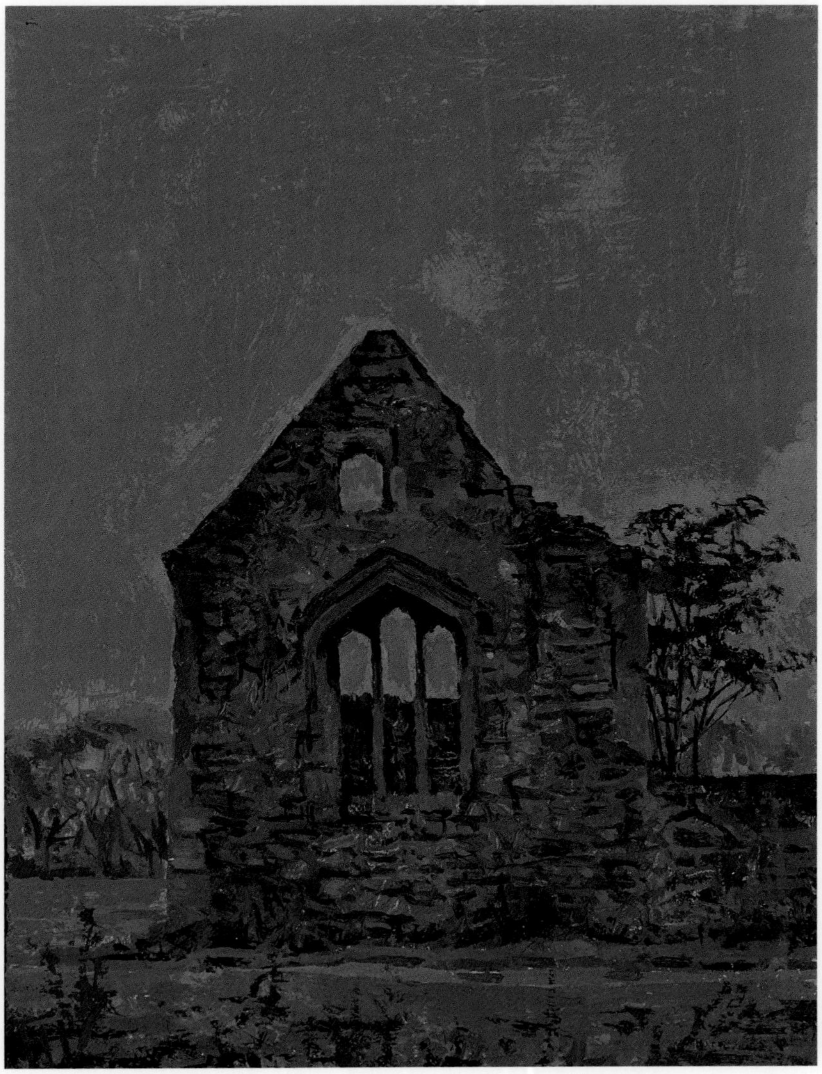

Godstow
22 x 16 cm, oil on linen, 2024

List of work

Francis Hamel is represented by the John Martin Gallery in Albemarle Street, London W1 **www.jmlondon.com**

All work is oil on linen, unless stated otherwise.

COVER: Brasenose Lane 122 x 91 cm (2024)

TITLE PAGE: New College from Holywell Street 23 x 16 cm (2024)

Hawthorn on Port Meadow from the Trap Grounds
23 x 27 cm, oil on linen, 2024

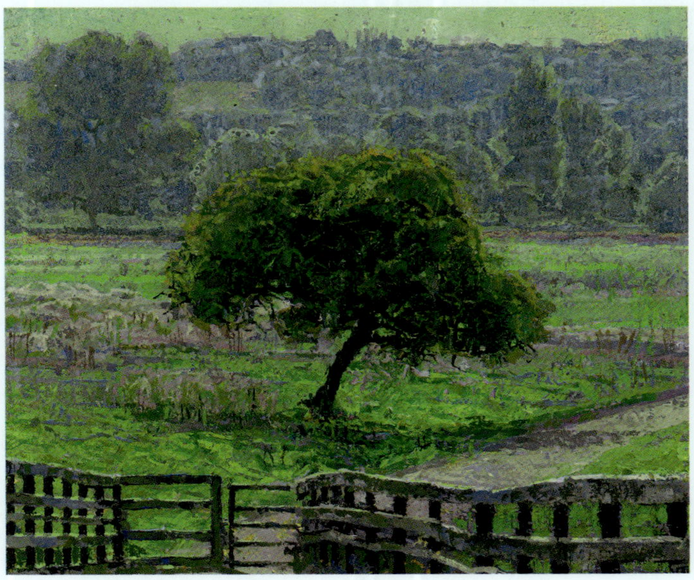

Acknowledgements

Thanks to Dinah Rose KC, the President and Fellows of Magdalen College for giving me a base from which to work.

My brother Richard has allowed me also to use The Queen's College barge on Port Meadow as another marvellous base on the west side of the city, Fiona Reid likewise has also provided generous hospitality.

Immense thanks to Ron Caffrey for finding a superb collection of written material to accompany the paintings and for his excellent captions. Catherine Snow and Clearview books have shown consistent and generous enthusiasm and support. The Rev Richard Smail has kindly and assiduously proof read the text.

Thanks to Nancy Campbell, Sunetra Gupta, Joanna Kavenna, Juliet Nicolson, Arabella Warner and A. N. Wilson for their generous contributions.

Kath Fotheringham has turned a vast, chaotic heap of material into a beautiful book with characteristic skill and sensitivity.

None of this would be possible without the energy, support and enthusiasm of John Martin, Tara Whelan and Laura Campbell at The John Martin Gallery.

Jane Dowling taught me as a student at the Ruskin and then continued to teach and guide me until she died in her nineties last year. Her understanding and her insights are never far away.

For the patience, the humour and the calm unerring eye of my darling wife Rachel, thank you.

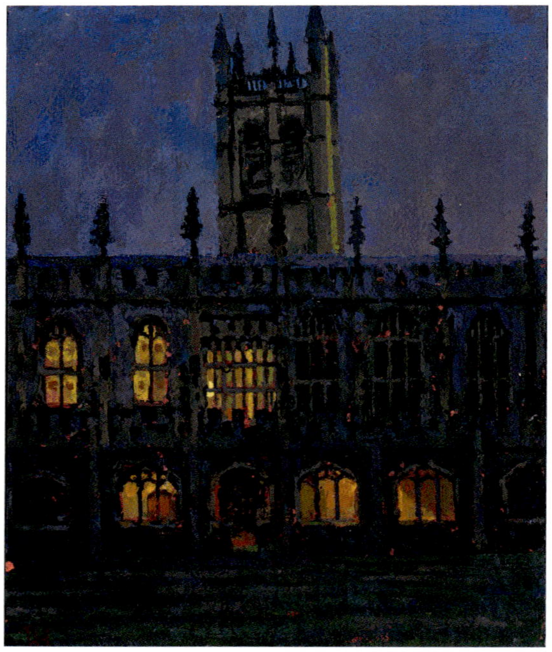

The Cloisters at Dusk
25 x 20 cm, oil on linen, 2024